Better to See You With

Perspectives on Flannery O'Connor,

Selected and New

MERCER UNIVERSITY PRESS

Endowed by

TOM WATSON BROWN
and
THE WATSON-BROWN FOUNDATION, INC.

BETTER TO SEE YOU WITH

Perspectives on
Flannery O'Connor,
Selected and New

Marshall Bruce Gentry

MERCER UNIVERSITY PRESS
Macon, Georgia

MUP/ H1020

© 2022 by Mercer University Press
Published by Mercer University Press
1501 Mercer University Drive
Macon, Georgia 31207
All rights reserved

25 24 23 22 21   5 4 3 2 1

Books published by Mercer University Press are printed on acid-free paper that meets the requirements of the American National Standard for Information Sciences—Permanence of Paper for Printed Library Materials.

Printed and bound in Canada.

This book is set in Adobe Caslon Pro.

Cover/jacket design by Burt&Burt.

ISBN   978-0-88146-825-0
Cataloging-in-Publication Data is available from the Library of Congress

for Alice Friman

Contents

Acknowledgments	ix
List of Abbreviations	xii
Looking Back, Looking Ahead: Introductions	1

Part One: Facing Cruelties

How Sacred Is the Violence in "A View of the Woods"?	13
Criminal Neglect in Flannery O'Connor's Fiction	23
Reconsidering Astor and Sulk in Flannery O'Connor's "The Displaced Person" *with Michael Faulknor*	51
O'Connor as Miscegenationist	61

Part Two: O'Connor and Gender

Flannery O'Connor's Attacks on Omniscience	75
Gender Dialogue in O'Connor	83
Wise Women, Wise Blood	99

Part Three: Religious Contexts

Flannery O'Connor's Child Bishops *with Elaine E. Whitaker*	117
The Hand of the Writer in "The Comforts of Home"	129

Part Four: O'Connor and Others

Becoming a Middle Georgia Writer: Rethinking the Influence of Carson McCullers and Erskine Caldwell on Flannery O'Connor	143
An Interview with Ashley Brown	163

"Our Conversations Were in Script": Miller Williams on
Visiting Flannery O'Connor at Andalusia
with Alice Friman 169
Prodigal Daughters: Flannery O'Connor and Alice Walker 181
He Would Have Been a Good Man: Compassion and
Meanness in Truman Capote and Flannery O'Connor 193
O'Connor's Legacy in Stories by Joyce Carol Oates and
Paula Sharp 211

Part Five: Local Connections

In Search of Vera—as Charlotte Hock and as Joy/Hulga
Hopewell *with Charles Puckett* 227
A Source for E. A. T. in "A Good Man Is Hard to Find"
with Robert J. Wilson III 235

Part Six: Conclusions

What Kind of Novel Can Be Made of Flannery O'Connor's
Heathen Manuscripts? 237
Flannery O'Connor's Letters and the Editing of
Authorial Intent 249
The History, and the Future, of Flannery O'Connor Studies 257

Biographies of Some Contributors 263
Index of Works by Flannery O'Connor 265
Index of Names 267

Acknowledgments

"Flannery O'Connor's Letters and the Editing of Authorial Intent." Essay-review on *Good Things out of Nazareth: The Uncollected Letters of Flannery O'Connor and Friends*, edited by Benjamin B. Alexander. *Resources for American Literary Study*, vol. 42, no. 1, 2020, pp. 127–34. ©2020. Reprinted with permission from *Resources for American Literary Study*. This article is used by permission of The Pennsylvania State University Press.

"The History, and the Future, of Flannery O'Connor Studies." Essay-review on *The Critical Reception of Flannery O'Connor, 1952–2017: "Searchers and Discoverers,"* by Robert C. Evans. *Resources for American Literary Study*, vol. 41, no. 2, 2019, pp. 399–404. © 2019. Reprinted with permission from *Resources for American Literary Study*. This article is used by permission of The Pennsylvania State University Press.

"Becoming a Middle Georgia Writer: Rethinking the Influence of Carson McCullers and Erskine Caldwell on Flannery O'Connor." *Middle Georgia and the Approach of Modernity: Essays on Race, Culture and Daily Life, 1885–1945*, edited by Fred R. van Hartesveldt, Jefferson, NC, McFarland, 2018, pp. 105–20. Reprinted from *Middle Georgia and the Approach of Modernity: Essays on Race, Culture and Daily Life, 1885–1945* © 2018 Edited by Fred R. van Hartesveldt by permission of McFarland and Company, Inc., Box 611, Jefferson, NC 28640. www.mcfarlandbooks.com.

"Criminal Neglect in Flannery O'Connor's Fiction." *The Centrality of Crime Fiction in American Literary Culture*, edited by Alfred Bendixen and Olivia Carr Edenfield, New York, Routledge, 2017, pp. 185–206. Routledge Interdisciplinary Perspectives on Literature. Reprinted with permission from Copyright Clearance Center for Taylor and Francis Group LLC–Books and Routledge.

"In Search of Vera—as Charlotte Hock and as Joy/Hulga Hopewell." With Charles Puckett. *Flannery O'Connor Review* vol. 15, 2017, pp. 80–85. Reprinted with permission from *Flannery O'Connor Review*, Georgia College.

"Ashley Brown." *At Home with Flannery O'Connor: An Oral History*, edited by Craig Amason and Marshall Bruce Gentry. Milledgeville: Flannery O'Connor-Andalusia Foundation, 2012, pp. 111–15. Reprinted with permission from Andalusia, Georgia College.

"Wise Women, Wise Blood." *Wise Blood: A Re-Consideration*, edited by John J. Han, Amsterdam, Neth., Rodopi, 2011, 309–31. Dialogue 13. Reprinted with permission from Brill and permission from John J. Han.

"A Source for E. A. T. in 'A Good Man Is Hard to Find.'" With Robert J. Wilson III. *Flannery O'Connor Review*, vol. 9, 2011, pp. 36–38. Reprinted with permission from *Flannery O'Connor Review*, Georgia College.

"O'Connor as Miscegenationist." *Flannery O'Connor in the Age of Terrorism: Essays on Violence and Grace*, edited by Avis Hewitt and Robert Donahoo, Knoxville, University of Tennessee Press, 2010, pp. 189–200. Reprinted with permission from University of Tennessee Press.

"'Our conversations were in script': Miller Williams on Visiting Flannery O'Connor at Andalusia." Interview with Miller Williams. Conducted with Alice Friman. *Flannery O'Connor Review*, vol. 7, 2009, pp. 10–17. Revised as "Miller Williams" for *At Home with Flannery O'Connor: An Oral History*, edited by Craig Amason and Marshall Bruce Gentry. Milledgeville, Flannery O'Connor-Andalusia Foundation, 2012, pp. 31–41. Reprinted with permission from *Flannery O'Connor Review*, Georgia College, and from Andalusia, Georgia College.

"He Would Have Been a Good Man: Compassion and Meanness in Truman Capote and Flannery O'Connor." *Flannery O'Connor's Radical Reality*, edited by Jan Nordby Gretlund and Karl-Heinz Westarp, Columbia, University of South Carolina Press, 2006, pp. 42–55. Reprinted with permission from The University of South Carolina Press.

"Prodigal Daughters." *Aspects of the Transatlantic Exchange: The American South in Europe—Europe in the American South*, edited by Waldemar Zacharasiewicz, Vienna, Aus., Wiener Universitätsverlag, 2006, pp. 67–75. Reprinted with permission from Facultas und Maudrich and with permission from Waldemar Zacharasiewicz.

"How Sacred Is the Violence in 'A View of the Woods'?" *"On the Subject of the Feminist Business": Re-Reading Flannery O'Connor*, edited by Teresa

Caruso, New York, Peter Lang, 2004, pp. 64–73. Reprinted with permission from Copyright Clearance Center for Peter Lang Copyright AG.

"Gender Dialogue in O'Connor." *Flannery O'Connor: New Perspectives*, edited by Sura P. Rath and Mary Neff Shaw, Athens, University of Georgia Press, 1996, 57–72. Reprinted with permission from The University of Georgia Press.

"O'Connor's Legacy in Stories by Joyce Carol Oates and Paula Sharp." *The Flannery O'Connor Bulletin*, vol. 23, 1994–95, pp. 44–60. Reprinted with permission from *Flannery O'Connor Review*, Georgia College.

"The Hand of the Writer in 'The Comforts of Home.'" *The Flannery O'Connor Bulletin*, vol. 20, 1991, pp. 61–72. Reprinted with permission from *Flannery O'Connor Review*, Georgia College.

"Flannery O'Connor's Attacks on Omniscience." *The Southern Quarterly*, vol. 29, no. 3, 1991, pp. 53–61. Reprinted with permission from *The Southern Quarterly*, The University of Southern Mississippi.

Abbreviations for Texts by Flannery O'Connor

CS	*The Complete Stories*
CW	*Flannery O'Connor: Collected Works*
GT	*Good Things out of Nazareth: The Uncollected Letters of Flannery O'Connor and Friends*
HB	*The Habit of Being: Letters*
Letters FO/CG	*The Letters of Flannery O'Connor and Caroline Gordon*
MM	*Mystery and Manners: Occasional Prose*

Looking Back, Looking Ahead: Introductions

I

The greatest benefit from reading criticism about the works of Flannery O'Connor may be that it shakes up any reader who is serious about figuring out how reading O'Connor is valuable, useful, pleasurable, even therapeutic. O'Connor challenges us with satirical plots that look simple enough, but her novels and stories are also delightfully complex, always promising and delivering additional provocations. As we feel and think our way through repeated readings, we may be tempted to settle in with some of our conclusions, to get comfortable, but O'Connor always offers fresh questions about things that matter to us, and good criticism can help the fiction do its work. While the contents of this volume were composed with great commitment, and while I hope that my claims are well supported, my goal is not to create converts to my way of thinking through the spelling out of a grand overview of exactly what O'Connor's works should mean to us all. Rather, I hope that portions of what is presented here will be helpful to any reader who is intent upon figuring out how to create the most valuable version of O'Connor.

Individual pieces in the collection, pieces written over approximately thirty years, may contradict each other, but I hope that those contradictions might open up the space so that an attentive reader can return once again to O'Connor's fiction with fresh strategies for arriving at personal conclusions. For years I have required that if students in my O'Connor course read any of my writing about O'Connor, they must disagree with me when they write their research papers. Few of my students have had any trouble with that requirement, and I find it generally fascinating to learn how my students go beyond and against my claims. I continue to create my version of O'Connor, and she continues to elude me. The whimsical title of this collection—based on the words of the Big Bad

Wolf—is intended to suggest that I do *not* think my ways of looking at O'Connor are authoritative.

It has been a great pleasure to work with others on some of the pieces (and not just the interviews) in this collection. Michael Faulknor, as he was earning his MA in English at Georgia College, started a conversation with me over his research paper on "The Displaced Person," and that discussion has continued long after Faulknor graduated. Alice Friman did a much better job than I could have done of interviewing Miller Williams about his poetry. Charles Puckett provided introductions and research that supplied most of what he and I talk about in our article about his relative Vera Puckett. Elaine E. Whitaker, once my department chair, sat in on my O'Connor course, twice, then published an article on "Parker's Back" and taught me about medievalism. Robert J. Wilson III, long the official University Historian at Georgia College, provided key insights into the man whose initials, E. A. T., O'Connor famously carved into a watermelon. Although I made final decisions about each piece published here, and although I say things with which some of these people may still want to reason with me, these people are my co-authors.

II

Reviewing my writings during a time in which there are renewed calls for racial justice, and a time in which O'Connor's racial attitudes are being freshly scrutinized, I find my attitudes undergoing some adjustment. I had never thought all that much about my own White privilege, even though going to the Little Rock Central High School building for kindergarten during the desegregation crisis of the late 1950s should have made me more thoughtful. Tuition at the University of Arkansas and at the University of Texas was close to free in my time, so I had the ability to complain that I had to pay over three thousand dollars for a year of graduate school at the University of Chicago. It's amazing what one can believe in order to boost one's self-esteem.

I used to say that my job is a matter of working for Flannery O'Connor, of doing whatever I think she would want. My respect for O'Connor remains immense, and I thank her for a career filled with learning about literary pleasure, but my attitude toward O'Connor has undergone an adjustment. Here's a thought experiment: What if we turn

Introduction

back on O'Connor one of her famous criticisms of James Baldwin? What if someone were to say the following?

> About the Whites, the kind I don't like is the philosophizing prophesying pontificating kind, the Flannery O'Connor kind. Very ignorant but never silent. O'Connor can tell us what it feels like to be a Catholic White woman who did not often leave her Middle Georgia farm, but she tries to tell us about everything else too.

Here I have applied to O'Connor her words against Baldwin in a 21 May 1964 letter to Maryat Lee (*HB* 580, *CW* 1208). Is such a critique of O'Connor justified? O'Connor could be very modest about her intellect and her philosophizing and her prophesying; it's O'Connor's critics—fans like me, I'm afraid—who have insisted on promoting her opinions on "everything" as universally valuable and even prophetic. Still, O'Connor could be heard by powerful people and be taken quite seriously, despite her outspoken modesty, in part because she *was* White, and it is because of White privilege that she could afford to be so modest. I am not trying to demote O'Connor's status as a writer. O'Connor's voice may ultimately be more powerful, in the long run, as we pay more attention to her race, class, gender, and disability—even as we note her errors about race. But my self-imposed job description now is to try to provide what O'Connor the writer needs, not so much what O'Connor the human being might want.

III

Rethinking my essays on O'Connor of course involves remembering my monograph. In 1986, my book *Flannery O'Connor's Religion of the Grotesque*, based on my 1984 dissertation at the University of Texas, was published by the University Press of Mississippi. The book applied several of the ideas of Mikhail Bakhtin to the study of O'Connor. In contrast to a traditional notion that the grotesque is entirely horrible, and that grotesque images in literature signal that we are to be disgusted, Bakhtin taught us that the grotesque can be positive rather than merely negative, life-affirming rather than just life-negating. A grotesque image is a degradation of an ideal, and the degradation can lead to the renewal of that ideal. Another of Bakhtin's notions is that grotesquerie can relate to *how* fiction is presented—that narration in fiction, at its most fascinating, can stage battles among an author and a narrator and a character, and that characters might well manage to establish authority over a narrator or an author. In my reading of O'Connor, her religious redemptions are largely a matter of characters' unconsciously using the grotesque to achieve religious redemptions that the authoritarian O'Connor narrator wants to deny them.

A few years ago, I heard from a friend, Margaret Earley Whitt, about a devilishly clever classroom exercise that illustrates and extends the idea of O'Connor's fiction as subversive in its grotesquerie. Teaching the story "Revelation," Whitt says, she invites students to rank the characters in terms of their grotesque horribleness. The students typically join in eagerly, condemning characters to different extents for having bad taste, eating bad food, making racist and classist comments, being fat, being ugly, etc. And before you know it, Whitt would point out, her class has created just the sort of ranking of people that the protagonist, Mrs. Turpin, mistakenly creates *within the story* (*CW* 636). Why did the students so eagerly fall into Mrs. Turpin's flaw? Well, the teacher told them to, and the voice that tells the story also encourages the reader to overestimate one's ability to judge. Authority in O'Connor is almost always asking to be overturned. We are always being tricked. We are all tempted to assume authority, and we all overdo it.

Not that long ago, a graduate student visiting my campus asked me if I still believe what I said in my 1986 book. So I rethought what, if anything, I would change if I were writing it now. While I told the visiting student that I still believe everything I said, and while I *do* indeed basically agree with everything I said almost forty years ago, I opened my book again and tried to take stock. Revisiting my book also involved reviewing the reactions the book provoked. I believe my study started a significant, if minor, trend in O'Connor studies. Emphasizing the grotesque these days in O'Connor studies, like emphasizing Catholicism or emphasizing southern history in O'Connor studies, is sometimes considered a bit passé, but I want to make the case that applying Bakhtin's notions is still quite valuable.

Back to reviewing reactions: Robert H. Brinkmeyer, Jr., published *The Art and Vision of Flannery O'Connor*, a book that expands on my application to O'Connor of Bakhtin's ideas about narration. Brinkmeyer calls the typical O'Connor narrator a fundamentalist, a designation that still seems a little odd to me, but he agrees with me that O'Connor's works are battles between narrator and character. I especially admire his insight that sometimes O'Connor creates a character to be the image of

Introduction

O'Connor's narratorial stance. His best example is Julian from "Everything That Rises Must Converge," a character who judges everyone else from within a false personal bubble of supposed superiority. Julian is the O'Connor narrator whose monological authority is overthrown (Brinkmeyer 69–71). In 1993, Anthony Di Renzo published *American Gargoyles*, in which he develops Bakhtin's ideas about the positive effects of the grotesque as they apply to O'Connor's works. Di Renzo's book is more optimistic than mine on the subject of how well O'Connor's explosion of grotesque imagery can lead toward carnivalesque renewal and redemption. And as the decades have passed, I feel myself moving in Di Renzo's direction to some extent. My sense of my book's primary originality is that I take Bakhtin to be consistent and coherent in his theorizing. Narrative subversiveness and grotesque imagery work together. In 1996, Mary Neff Shaw published "'The Artificial Nigger': A Dialogical Narrative," the best article I've seen in terms of pushing and challenging my approach to come up with a fresh Bakhtinian reading of a story.

However, for the most part, O'Connor scholars have avoided a Bakhtinian approach. Sarah Gordon, my predecessor at Georgia College—who even wrote a blurb for my book—dismisses the Bakhtinian approach as insufficiently Catholic. In *Flannery O'Connor: The Obedient Imagination*, Gordon says she is sure that O'Connor was entirely devoted and obedient to church authority, to the Patriarchy, and therefore no sort of revolt against that authority can succeed. For Gordon, O'Connor is "monologic" (44), not dialogic. But at least Gordon pays attention, for which I am grateful. A Bakhtinian approach of any sort is so rarely discussed that I find myself pleased to be attacked in Michael Mears Bruner's *A Subversive Gospel*. According to Bruner, I make the mistake of too easily seeing redemption at the ends of O'Connor's ambiguous works (196), but then I also make the mistake of denying characters "any *truly* redemptive end" (197, emphasis mine) because if characters are battling their narrators, then I'm mistakenly claiming that characters "must *control*" redemption (197, emphasis in original). My response to Bruner is that I'm thankful for the close attention; I think he understands my claims, although he then rejects them as insufficiently religious.

Looking back on my book now, I think my major blind spot was gender. (I was not yet married when I wrote my book.) I think that if I had the book to do over again, I would treat such characters as Sarah Ruth Cates in "Parker's Back" and Miss Willerton in "The Crop" as characters with hidden female power, able to take over and rule a story's meaning in opposition to the bossiness of a narrator. I have also written an article that is much more upbeat than my book is about a female character in *Wise Blood*, Sabbath Lily Hawks. And then there's the question of what gender the O'Connor narrator is. Is the O'Connor narrator male, as I think I once assumed? O'Connor herself would admit that she was trying to follow advice to make her narrator sound not like herself but like Samuel Johnson. (O'Connor wrote in a letter, by the way, that "…it is a great strain for me to speak like Dr. Johnson" [3 Mar. 1954, *HB* 69].) I think it also makes sense to think that if O'Connor's narrator was the voice of religious authority, she might have been giving voice to the Patriarchy, making her narrators masculine. But it also makes sense to think that O'Connor's narrator was sometimes somewhat female. I believe that many of the down-home details that O'Connor worked into her fiction were filtered through the perspective of her mother. Meals with Regina Cline O'Connor, during which the mother lectured her daughter about all the happenings on their farm, surely had an effect on how the stories were told. And as we are learning more about how influential O'Connor's mentor Caroline Gordon was, we may well decide that O'Connor allowed her teacher to influence how her narrators sound. It was Caroline Gordon, after all, who commanded that O'Connor sound like the authoritative Dr. Johnson.

If I had it to do over again, I would probably find even more of O'Connor's characters—even her men—to be on their way to what O'Connor defines as the redemptive moment. A good example would be Gen. George Poker Sash in "A Late Encounter with the Enemy," who I have come to think is approaching redemption as he invites his own death. Mr. Paradise of "The River," a pig-like pedophile who loves to mock religion because of his cancer, may have a change of attitude when he sees little Harry/Bevel in the process of committing suicide. And even several male inhabitants of O'Connor's wasteland city in *Wise Blood*, characters whose lives I once considered totally empty and hopeless—Asa Hawks, Solace Layfield, and even Hoover Shoats, aka Onnie Jay Holy—now seem to me to be on their way to a better place. It's now easier for me to list the few remaining unredeemable characters in O'Connor, and I can do it on one hand: the adult men of "A View of the Woods," Sheppard in "The Lame Shall Enter First," and the rapist in *The Violent Bear It Away*.

IV

Robert C. Evans, in his book *The Critical Reception of Flannery O'Connor, 1952–2017: "Searchers and Discoverers,"* concludes with several suggestions about where O'Connor studies should go. I agree with Evans that studying O'Connor in relation to religion or in relation to southern history is not as productive as it used to be. While race and gender are likely to remain hot topics, Evans recommends that we study O'Connor as an artist, and that we emphasize her themes of family relations and of death. I would add that talking about O'Connor in relation to disability, to technology, and to ecology is quite worthwhile. On all these topics, I'm tempted to say, conflicts between what narrators seem to think and what characters seem to desire are more complicated, and more interesting, than we have appreciated, and for that reason, I think Bakhtin's approach to literature is still quite relevant to the future of O'Connor studies.

How might a Bakhtinian critic of the future approach these subtopics? Here are some thoughts:

On the subject of race, a Bakhtinian attention to the grotesque promises to complicate further an already very complex topic. Grotesque art appears to produce revolution, but one can reasonably wonder whether the revolution is long-term or short-term, permanent...or not really revolutionary at all. Does symbolically giving power to or siding with African Americans, and/or does temporarily overthrowing White power in O'Connor's works, result in significant change? When we get to the end of "The Artificial Nigger," has racism been reduced because Mr. Head and Nelson felt that in Atlanta they experienced one day's worth of the humiliation constantly experienced by Blacks? If Sarah Ham in "The Comforts of Home" is symbolically Black, as John N. Duvall has recently argued (85–86), does that really change any characters' racial attitudes? When we get to the end of "Revelation" and imagine what will happen the next day, after Ruby has experienced her redemptive vision, do we think that Mrs. Turpin will be nicer to her African-American employees?

Family relations: If you have forgotten how distressingly grotesque O'Connor can be on the topic of family, reread "A View of the Woods," in which a grandfather's apparent favoritism toward his granddaughter slides toward sexual abuse and ends in murder. Or consider the suicides of O'Connor children, in "The River" or in "The Lame Shall Enter First." The urge on the part of O'Connor characters to overthrow authority, whether that authority takes the form of a mother or a father, often results in the death of a child, and one wonders how far one can go in applying to O'Connor stories Bakhtin's emphasis on the rebirth that often can follow death.

While we are on the topic of death, I think it is fair to add that the typical O'Connor narrator enjoys the idea of condemning the characters to death, especially a grotesque death, and O'Connor characters are always maneuvering to make death more of a victory than the narrators realize.

Disability: The 2020 volume of the *Flannery O'Connor Review* includes a special feature of three articles on O'Connor and disability studies. It's clear from the work of the contributors to this special feature (guest edited by Bruce Henderson) that O'Connor characters have very different ideas about disability than their narrators do, and O'Connor's stories sometimes seem to work against some of what O'Connor said about her own disability. O'Connor is famous for seeing a silver lining around the cloud of her grotesque experience of lupus, but she is complicated, and, it seems to me, often in denial, when it comes to believing that her disease did not affect her writing. O'Connor characters often disagree with their author about the grotesquerie of disease, and there's plenty for future critics to debate.

Technology studies and ecocriticism: These are both approaches to the study of literature on which I admit to being a beginner. If some of the voices of authority in the back of O'Connor's head were those of the Southern Agrarians—with their tendency to say tech is all bad and that nature, and farming, are all good—then I can see how the study of grotesquerie can lead to more insights about how O'Connor was revolutionary. I recently published an article by Mark A. Noon that makes a persuasive case that when Mrs. Turpin sees people going to heaven at the end of "Revelation," we should see their ascent as a version of a technological blast-off brought to us by the US space program. O'Connor characters are sometimes satirized for their faith in technology, but what about Mr. Guizac, often considered a Christ symbol in "The Displaced Person," who also seems totally at home with letting new technology rule? I recall an experience when I first started teaching my O'Connor course in Milledgeville at O'Connor's alma mater. I had a graduate student who announced on the first night of class that he was a contemporary Agrarian, taking the class to find an ally in O'Connor. When he read such stories as "A Circle in the Fire" and "Greenleaf," however, his faith that O'Connor loves farms was severely tested. Does O'Connor want more technology or less, and are her characters as right as O'Connor and her narrators when there is a difference of opinion?

What else is going to happen in the future of O'Connor studies? The O'Connor Estate seems increasingly generous when it comes to giving permissions for people to publish previously unpublished works by O'Connor. There's even talk of an edition of O'Connor's third novel, *Why Do the Heathen Rage?*, which I believe should be published but as a novella. (O'Connor, I suspect, would object, but she's just the author, right?) There is new material for O'Connor scholars to peruse in the O'Connor collection at Emory, including a mountain of letters from Flannery to her mother and several unpublished stories O'Connor wrote while she was working toward her MFA at Iowa. There's juvenilia, some of which may soon be under contract for publication. There are O'Connor's paintings, which I understand have been thoroughly restored but which are mostly currently hidden from the eyes of scholars. Most of these paintings are copyrighted, but someday the visual aspects of O'Connor will be all the rage. You may have seen O'Connor's rather grotesque self-portrait, and if you have visited Milledgeville you may have seen O'Connor's headless member of a church choir. That's in the one painting Georgia College owns. There's more where that came from. The thorough work of restoration going on at Andalusia now that Georgia College owns the O'Connor farm should help to make O'Connor more widely known to the public and should open up new areas of research.

V

As I mentioned earlier, this volume collects various pieces written over the last thirty years or so. Along with three essays previously unpublished, there are seventeen reprinted essays and interviews, mostly featuring modest revisions and updates of the versions originally published. In addition to my gratefulness to my co-authors, I want to close this intro by expressing my gratitude to a few of the many people who have helped me with this collection and throughout my career. I'll start with all the editors and publishers who provided permission to reprint—after having helped me get the essays into shape for their original publication. I am grateful to the National Endowment for the Humanities for grants to conduct NEH Summer Institutes on O'Connor; to my able and enthusiastic co-directors for those Summer Institutes, John D. Cox (in 2007) and Robert Donahoo (in 2014); and to all the college teachers who participated in those Summer Institutes. I thank Georgia Humanities for more than one grant in support of O'Connor events. I thank Sarah Gordon for her criticism on O'Connor and for being the perfect former Editor of the *Flannery O'Connor Review*. I thank Nancy Davis Bray and the staff of Special Collections at the Georgia College Library for constant assistance with O'Connor projects. I honor everyone involved in the work of preserving Andalusia. I thank the University of Indianapolis for its support of my scholarship in the early years of my career, and I thank Georgia College, especially for the year of Professional Leave that allowed me to compile and complete this collection. For sharing their ideas with me, I thank all the students in my O'Connor classes at Georgia College and all the participants in our local O'Connor Book Club. I thank Mary Barbara Tate for inviting me to get involved in Book Club meetings years ago, I thank the Georgia Writers Museum in Eatonton for giving the Book Club a home when we needed one, and I thank Irene Burgess, the Executive Director of Georgia College's Andalusia Institute, for promoting the latest version of the O'Connor Book Club through Zoom meetings that have come to reach all over the world. I thank Elizabeth Coffman and Mark Bosco, S.J., for including me in their documentary film *Flannery*. Special thanks for patience and hard work go to my former student Kristy Maier, who worked with me on the *Flannery O'Connor Review* for three years and then provided hours of work to update, retype, and polish the contents of this collection.

WORKS CITED AND CONSULTED

Bakhtin, M[ikhail] M[ikhailovich]. "Discourse in the Novel." *The Dialogical Imagination: Four Essays*, edited by Michael Holquist, and translated by Caryl Emerson and Michael Holquist. Austin, University of Texas Press, 1981, pp. 259–422.

———. *Problems of Dostoevsky's Poetics*, edited and translated by Caryl Emerson. Minneapolis, University of Minnesota Press, 1984.

———. *Rabelais and His World*, translated by Hélène Iswolsky. Cambridge, MA, MIT Press, 1968.

Brinkmeyer, Robert H., Jr. *The Art and Vision of Flannery O'Connor*. Baton Rouge, Louisiana State University Press, 1989.

Bruner, Michael Mears. *A Subversive Gospel: Flannery O'Connor and the Reimagining of Beauty, Goodness, and Truth*. Downers Grove, IL, IVP Academic-Intervarsity, 2017.

Di Renzo, Anthony. *American Gargoyles: Flannery O'Connor and the Medieval Grotesque*. Carbondale, Southern Illinois University Press, 1993.

Introduction

Duvall, John N. "O'Connor and Whiteness Studies." *Approaches to Teaching the Works of Flannery O'Connor*, edited by Robert Donahoo and Marshall Bruce Gentry. New York, Modern Language Association, 2019, pp. 81–87.

Evans, Robert C. *"The Critical Reception of Flannery O'Connor, 1952–2017: "Searchers and Discoverers."* Rochester, NY, Camden House, 2018.

Gentry, Marshall Bruce. *Flannery O'Connor's Religion of the Grotesque.* Jackson, University Press of Mississippi, 1986.

Gordon, Sarah. *Flannery O'Connor: The Obedient Imagination.* Athens, University of Georgia Press, 2000.

Henderson, Bruce, guest editor. "Flannery O'Connor and Disability Studies." *Flannery O'Connor Review*, vol. 18, 2020, pp. 92–144. The special feature contains articles by Sonya Freeman Loftis, Connie Chen, and Henderson.

Noon, Mark A. "Pigs in Space: Notes on Flannery O'Connor's Pig Astronaut in 'Revelation.'" *Flannery O'Connor Review*, vol. 18, 2020, pp. 1–19.

O'Connor, Flannery. *Flannery O'Connor: Collected Works*, edited by Sally Fitzgerald. New York, Library of America, 1988.

———. *The Habit of Being: Letters*, edited by Sally Fitzgerald. New York, Farrar, 1979.

Shaw, Mary Neff. "'The Artificial Nigger': A Dialogical Narrative." *Flannery O'Connor: New Perspectives*, edited by Sura P. Rath and Mary Neff Shaw. Athens, University of Georgia Press, 1996, pp. 139–51.

How Sacred Is the Violence in "A View of the Woods"?

Although Flannery O'Connor's "A View of the Woods" was selected for both *The Best American Short Stories of 1958* and *Prize Stories 1959: The O. Henry Awards* after originally being published in *Partisan Review*, many readers have been troubled by this story, in part perhaps because it has seemed to be reducible to an Agrarian lecture insisting on the value of southern provincialism, in part because it allows a father who abuses his child to triumph, and in part because the story seemed to be telling us things we do not want to hear about, such as the value of a child's cooperating with her father's beatings so that she could be made a martyr for Agrarianism of a particularly Catholic sort. I once accepted the common reading that the story's violence is linked to the sacred in that the grandfather, Mr. Fortune—as he watches his son-in-law Mr. Pitts beat Mary Fortune Pitts and then later as he is finally attacked by this granddaughter—has a chance to discover the mysterious power of the woods, which have a value more religious than capitalistic.

My desire in reconsidering this story has been to find a way to like the story better. I used to think that O'Connor was intentionally putting into this story some of her less pleasant beliefs about the need to spank children regularly. I have since begun to wonder how much O'Connor approved of the extreme obedience required of her when she attended her first elementary Catholic school in Savannah (Cash 13–14). I have also wondered how O'Connor would react to charges that the Church has ignored priests' acts of child sexual abuse. I have now, I hope, reached what I consider a more satisfying point in my ongoing attempts to understand "A View of the Woods," because I see O'Connor herself standing in questioning awe about the point to which some of her principles lead her. It is as if O'Connor is asking herself whether revelations about the sacred ever come at too high a price.

While I am pleased to see Jon Lance Bacon say that O'Connor considered the cultural battle to save an Agrarian way of life to be over and lost when she wrote this story in the middle 1950s (128–29), the book most responsible for giving me a new way to consider "A View of the Woods" is a 1980 study of German child-rearing, which was a best-seller in Germany for almost two years, translated as *For Your Own Good: Hidden Cruelty in Child-Rearing and the Roots of Violence*, by the German psychologist Alice Miller. The most memorable line from Miller's book is the statement that "60 percent of German terrorists in recent years have been the children of Protestant ministers" (65). Miller explains this shocking statistic by analyzing traditional German child-rearing theories, which generally insist that a child must respect the parent to the point of voicing no real objection to any parental demand. We do not want to get carried away here with all of the details of Miller's argument about the childhoods of a female teenage drug addict, of Adolf Hitler, and of a man who murders young boys, but I do want to say that I think O'Connor, at least in "A View of the Woods," intuited much of what Miller later attempted to demonstrate. O'Connor, who was deeply aware of the Holocaust and who worked it into the background of many of her stories, would probably agree with Miller's idea that the abused child may well be worse off psychologically than an adult inmate of a concentration camp:

> The abused inmates of a concentration camp…are inwardly free to hate their persecutors. [Children, however,] *must not* hate their father…[and] they *cannot* hate him either, if they must fear losing his love as a result; finally, they do not even *want* to hate him, because they love him. (118)

Rereading "A View of the Woods" with what I imagine to be Alice Miller's perspective, I see a child caught in a double whammy that is worse than anything else faced by a child in O'Connor's works. On the one hand, Mary Fortune Pitts must idealize her father, absurdly forcing herself to believe that he is a good father because he has land and a way to see the woods, even denying that he beats her—a denial she expresses by repeating her terrifying refrain, "nobody beat me" (*CW* 530). The story presents no clear evidence, by the way, that Mr. Pitts shares his daughter's fondness for a view of the woods; despite an apparent claim to the contrary by O'Connor herself, in a letter of 28 Dec. 1956 to "A"/Betty Hester (*HB* 189–90), all Mr. Pitts clearly demonstrates is that he values pasture. While Mary Fortune's inclination to deny the beatings by her father is for many readers the most puzzling part of the story, Miller presents an interesting explanation. Miller discusses the absurd lengths to which abused children will often go to believe that they are loved by abusive parents (120), and she points out that Adolf Hitler, like many others, was able to claim that his abusive father did not beat him (259).

The other half of the double whammy is that things are no better with Mary Fortune's relationship with her grandfather. She probably realizes that he, too, wants to be told that nobody beats her. That it is totally absurd for her to deny the beatings—absurd because she knows that Mr. Fortune has watched her while she was being beaten—does not matter; the abused child knows that she must always give the parent what is desired, no matter how high the absurdities may mount. If Mr. Fortune looked at his own behavior with any care for its effects on the child whom he says he loves, he would see that for some time, he has regularly beaten his granddaughter, at least in the sense that he brings about the confrontations with Mr. Pitts that will cause the father to beat the child. At one point Mr. Fortune claims that Mr. Pitts beats the child "for no reason" (*CW* 530), but on the next page it is clear that Mr. Fortune knows Mr. Pitts beats the child to revenge himself in response to Mr. Fortune's actions (531). Mr. Fortune can say to himself, "It was as if it were *he* that Pitts was driving down the road to beat and it was as if *he* were the one submitting to it" (531, my emphasis). However accurately this line describes the relationship between Mr. Fortune and Mr. Pitts, it also indicates how thoroughly Mr. Fortune ignores the harm done to his granddaughter. What Mr. Fortune wants from his granddaughter is a sense of his own control, and he is happy to trick her in order to bring about his awareness of his power. In a line that could have come from one of the German child-rearing books that practice what is sometimes called "poisonous pedagogy" (Miller 10), Mr. Fortune thinks, "With grown people, a road led either to heaven or hell, but with children there were always stops along the way where their attention could be turned with a trifle" (*CW* 538).

Mary Fortune Pitts responds to her grandfather in ways that Alice Miller would predict. She gives him everything he wants, she makes a show of acting just the way he wants her to, and all the while she is silent about her feelings. The story regularly shows the reader that the child neglects to express agreement with Mr. Fortune's statements about progress, statements that are likely to bring the child into the middle of a conflict between the father and the grandfather. Although Mr. Fortune blindly assumes that she likes the earthmover she intently watches at the beginning of the story, it makes sense to believe that she actually hates the earthmover, but that she feels forced to allow her grandfather to maintain his illusions. While the grandfather thinks he is her ally, and while she probably has to try to force herself to believe that her father and grandfather are both lovable, the child has no allies in this story. Even her mother accuses her of causing Mr. Fortune to do things that hurt the Pitts family (*CW* 534), and there is no sign that Mary Fortune's siblings are any comfort. When Mr. Fortune is trying to make up with his granddaughter at one point and we are told that she looked at the woods "as if it were a person that she preferred to him" (537), it is reasonable to see her as frightened and without alternatives; her desire for someone to talk to similarly leads her to talk silently to her own feet, the part of her that her father beats, which are "encased in heavy brown school shoes" (540). While one might agree with John Roos that Mary Fortune Pitts shows "trust" in and "hope" for her grandfather whenever she puts her wounded feet on his shoulders (168, 174), one might also take this gesture as a sign of the extent of the child's desperation.

Although O'Connor would agree, in her 28 Dec. 1956 letter to Hester, that if there is a "Christ Symbol" in this story, the woods play "that role" (*HB* 190), I believe that the child's assertion of her fondness for the woods has little to do with Agrarian values or the various readings that emphasize the significance of the woods as a Christ symbol. Mary Fortune's assertions about the woods have more to do with the required allegiance to her father and her constantly failing quest for someone with whom she could be her true self. Perhaps she treats her feet and her woods as if they were people because on a couple of occasions in the story, she does at least achieve a bit of relief by allowing her feet to carry her out into the landscape.

Mr. Fortune tells himself, of course, that his granddaughter is totally independent and strong, with only one tiny bit of her that is fouled with the genes of Mr. Pitts. The truth is that she has formed her character while she is around her grandfather—not with the goal of expressing her own needs and desires, but rather with the goal of mirroring him in precisely the ways he demands. Even Mr. Fortune is able to say (without realizing what he is admitting) that when he is supposedly having a battle with his granddaughter and complimenting himself for making her independent, he is really only demonstrating the extent of the control he has over her: "He had frequent little verbal tilts with her but this was a sport like putting a mirror up in front of a rooster and watching him fight his reflection" (*CW* 531). When Mr. Fortune tells her that he "refuse[s] to ride a Jezebel" in his car, he is pleased that the child's answer is "And I refuse to ride with the Whore of Babylon" (533). When he tries to continue his toying with Mary Fortune Pitts by pointing out that "A whore is a woman!" and adding "That's how much you know!" (533), it does not occur to him that her ignorance about the meaning of her own words calls into question her supposed independence. Mr. Fortune refuses to admit that Mary Fortune Pitts gives her grandfather the kind of speech he demands without an adult level of thought behind it. I agree with Margaret Early Whitt that the child "is a pawn in a role that is larger than her comprehension" (129). Mr. Fortune and Mr. Pitts are killing the child's soul, without paying attention enough to realize that they are doing it, and this breaking of the spirit occurs long before the child is killed physically at the end of the story.

Katherine Hemple Prown makes the fascinating argument that Flannery O'Connor, early in her career, wrote to express feminist complaints against patriarchy, but that she then learned to quiet those female voices. "A View of the Woods" is an unusual story, according to Prown, because in it "O'Connor never entirely suppressed the female-sexed voice" (113). For Prown, Mary Fortune Pitts is powerful: "…the narrator never subjects her to the ironic observation that she is not really the person she believes herself to be. *Her* pride, in other words, remains justified" (155). As much as I admire this approach to O'Connor, on this story I think Prown understates O'Connor's critique of patriarchy. I prefer to see O'Connor as more feminist than Prown does, to regard O'Connor's goal to be to show us how the patriarchy enjoys playing with its female puppets. Her father and grandfather reduce Mary Fortune Pitts into an abject child, without pride, probably without a sense of believing herself to have a self. Although I question Richard Giannone's labeling of Mary Fortune as "irksome," he is correct to emphasize "Mary Fortune's loss of…her will to paternal cruelty" (*Flannery* 209, 208).

While it may seem that Mary Fortune's acts of violence near the end of the story prove that her will has not been broken, Alice Miller suggests the opposite: "[P]eople who must always be on their guard to keep the dam that restrains their feelings from breaking," Miller claims, may "experience occasional outbursts of inexplicable rage directed against substitute objects or will resort repeatedly to violent behavior such as murder or acts of terrorism" (65). Mary Fortune's bottle-throwing episode at Tilman's store (*CW* 542–43) may have less to do with her thinking that

Tilman looks like a devilish snake, or with her objecting to Tilman's buying land from Mr. Fortune, than with the fact that she can substitute him for the father and grandfather toward whom she feels such strong and taboo rage. Her subsequent and climactic attack on her grandfather may also be read as an expression of forbidden rage against her father.

If we want to, of course, we may still choose to read the story as being essentially about Mr. Fortune, and certainly O'Connor's careful reworking of Mr. Fortune's final vision suggests that she may have thought of Mary Fortune Pitts at times as a prop for analyzing Mr. Fortune. I am generally inclined to interpret O'Connor's protagonists as unconsciously setting traps for themselves to reconnect with ideals they reject on the conscious level, and one can construct such a reading of Mr. Fortune. To some extent, Mr. Fortune wants to become one of the Pittses. In this reading, he identifies with Mary Fortune not merely because she is a Fortune, but more importantly because she is a Pitts and because Mr. Fortune views her as his connection to the Pitts family. Also to some extent, he values the Pittses' closeness to the land, what he perceives as their closeness to each other, their fertility (since pits are seeds, after all), and the strategy for defeating death that the Pittses' fertility implies. While consciously rejecting the Pittses, Mr. Fortune even constructs ironic tributes to them by digging literal pits all over the landscape. One could also argue that Mr. Fortune longs to be beaten by Mr. Pitts and thus to be forced to submit to Mr. Pitts's values. When Mr. Fortune unconsciously plots to trick Mary Fortune Pitts into preferring her father over him, Mr. Fortune in effect admits that it is inherently more valuable to be a Pitts than to be a Fortune.

Mr. Fortune's desire for union with the Pittses comes out even in his insistence on his own purity. As soon as Mr. Fortune says he is "PURE Fortune," he sees in the child's face "the Pitts look, pure and simple," and as a result of his imagined similarity to the child, he is able, however illogically, to feel "personally stained by it, as if it had been found on his own face" (*CW* 541). Mr. Fortune is perfectly capable of interpreting the child's "Pitts look" as evidence of his own contrasting purity as a Fortune; that he chooses to imagine within himself the stain of Pitts indicates a deeper, countering desire. Mr. Fortune forces himself toward Mr. Pitts finally by deciding to whip Mary Fortune in the manner used by Mr. Pitts. Mr. Fortune tells himself that by whipping Mary Fortune Pitts he will be able to improve his relationship with her, but he surely senses on some level that to attempt to whip a Pitts will bring matters to a head. When the child attacks her grandfather, it is surely significant that Mr. Fortune "seemed to see his own face coming to bite him from several sides at once" (545). When he is almost beaten, Mr. Fortune looks up "into his own image" and hears the potentially profound words, "I'm PURE Pitts" (545). I think this would be the moment when Mr. Fortune has the chance to change his life, and his actions do deliver the land to Mr. Pitts, perhaps as Mr. Fortune desired all along. Perhaps Mr. Fortune could also become another in a series of O'Connor's males for whom redemption is experienced as transformation into a female who is being raped. Is this not the experience of Tarwater, raped at the end of *The Violent Bear It Away*, and of Asbury Fox, transformed in "The Enduring Chill" into a Yeatsian Leda about to be raped by a god in the form of a bird-shaped waterstain? If one focuses one's attention on Mr. Fortune, it may be possible to accept the almost absurd interpretation that his granddaughter becomes the rapist finally delivering the seed that the name Pitts implies.

But Mr. Fortune rejects the transformation he has prepared for himself, the rejection occurring not so much when he kills his granddaughter as when he ultimately pronounces, "There's not an ounce of Pitts in me" (*CW* 545). I think Margaret Earley Whitt and Richard Giannone are absolutely correct in pointing out that when Mr. Fortune finally sees a "huge yellow monster which sat to the side, as stationary as he was, gorging itself on clay" (546), he is actually looking at his dead granddaughter in her yellow dress (Whitt 131; Giannone, *Flannery* 213). Presumably Mary Fortune's position in death is not sitting, but lying with her face in the dirt, her mouth open. Not only has Mr. Fortune made sure that his granddaughter will always be a Pitts (for she will never grow up to marry and change her name), but he has also stopped seeing her as human. Flannery O'Connor is perfectly capable of writing works in which a murder helps to bring about a murderer's redemption—one thinks of Hazel Motes's killing Solace Layfield in *Wise Blood*, or of Tarwater's killing Bishop in *The Violent Bear It Away*. But I think there is no other work by O'Connor in which the murder victim is so thoroughly robbed of a soul.

In the letter to Hester of 28 Dec. 1956, O'Connor says Mary Fortune "is saved and [Mr. Fortune] is dammed [sic] and there is no way out of it, it must be pointed out and underlined" (*HB* 190). I fear that this answer to a correspondent's question has been taken as an insistence by O'Connor that suspense about Mr. Fortune's spiritual outcome should be the reader's major concern. Whether O'Connor intended to or not, she wrote a story here in which the plight of the abused child is more emotionally affecting than the issue of whether Mr. Fortune can find a strategy for saving his own soul. I have not yet mentioned that there is talk in the story of how Mr. Fortune is accustomed to finding his granddaughter in his bed most mornings, and the removing of Mr. Pitts's belt as preparation for beating a child implies what Richard Giannone has called the father's "phallic power" ("Displacing" 83)—so we can say that at least the threat of sexual abuse also hovers over the story. I can accept Katherine Hemple Prown's bold assertion that at the story's end, the reader may even be tricked into enjoying a display of incest: "…the reader is permitted the voyeuristic pleasure of watching as the death/rape scene unfolds and the old man literally mounts Mary Fortune" (52–53).

I have reviewed a lot of very good O'Connor criticism in preparing this essay, and I am struck by the variety of ingenious strategies we critics are able to construct for downplaying the horror of what is done to Mary Fortune Pitts. There is plenty of evidence that in her own life, O'Connor worked to find value in "'mysterious' suffering" (Edmondson 140), and sometimes we look for ways in which the suffering of Mary Fortune might be good for her. Sometimes we call her death an accident caused by her grandfather's love for her (Kazin 61). Sometimes we say that the beatings and the child's reactions to them are more "symbolic" than real (Wyatt 75). They are seen as fitting into Mary Fortune's plan to exercise power over her father and grandfather (Giannone, *Flannery* 209). They are seen as portions of a philosophical stance the nine-year-old child has worked out, like a belief in "the sanctity of the pastoral landscape" (Westling 170) or "a vision of family, life and nature that is beyond that of the pursuit of Lockean self-interest" (Roos 165). They are seen as part of the child's development, "in a warped way," into "a Christ figure" (Burkle 67). While I understand and appreciate such readings, I also want us to remind ourselves of the story's horrors for the "frightened child" who gets up from the dinner table to be beaten by her father (*CW* 534). I want to say, as Flannery O'Connor herself taught me to, that if it's all just a symbol, then to hell with it.

I am grateful that O'Connor abandoned her original ending for the story, an ending that might be taken to be saying that Mary Fortune Pitts had to go through all of her suffering so that her father could have a climactic recognition scene. Sally Fitzgerald, as editor of *The Habit of Being*, provides the abandoned ending in a footnote:

Pitts, by accident, found them that evening. He was walking home through the woods about sunset. The rain had stopped but the polished trees were hung with clear drops of water that turned red where the sun touched them; the air was saturated with dampness. He came on them suddenly and shied backward, his foot not a yard from where they lay. For almost a minute he stood still and then, his knees buckling, he squatted down by their sides and stared into their eyes, into the pale blue pools of rainwater that the sky had filled. (190n)

Joanne Halleran McMullen detects patterns of circularity in this story (125–26), and it is easy for me to see why they belong. I probably would not believe it if the story attempted to suggest that Mr. Pitts would learn his lesson on the basis of finding the bodies. He could probably find vindication in the scene. Before we shut down the story by deciding on its meaning, before we make all the violence a pathway to the sacred or the philosophical, let us remember that Mr. Pitts, triumphant, with a wife and six kids left, shows no sign of breaking out of the circular patterns of abuse. The story's final version asks us to wonder how Mr. Pitts will pick the next family member to suffer his fury.

WORKS CITED

Bacon, Jon Lance. *Flannery O'Connor and Cold War Culture.* New York, Cambridge University Press, 1993. Cambridge Studies in American Literature and Culture 72.

Burkle, Howard. "The Child in Flannery O'Connor." *The Flannery O'Connor Bulletin*, vol. 18, 1989, pp. 59–69.

Cash, Jean W. *Flannery O'Connor: A Life.* Knoxville, University of Tennessee Press, 2002.

Edmondson, Henry T., III. *Return to Good and Evil: Flannery O'Connor's Response to Nihilism.* Lanham, MD, Lexington, 2002.

Giannone, Richard. "Displacing Gender: Flannery O'Connor's View from the Woods." *Flannery O'Connor: New Perspectives*, edited by Sura P. Rath and Mary Neff Shaw, Athens, University of Georgia Press, 1996, pp. 73–95.

———. *Flannery O'Connor, Hermit Novelist.* Urbana, University of Illinois Press, 2000.

Kazin, Alfred. Review of *The Complete Stories*, by Flannery O'Connor. *New York Times Book Review*, 28 Nov. 1971, pp. 1, 22. Reprinted as "Flannery O'Connor: *The Complete Stories*." *Critical Essays on Flannery O'Connor*, edited by Melvin J. Friedman and Beverly Lyon Clark, Boston, G. K. Hall, 1985, pp. 60–62. Critical Essays on American Literature.

McMullen, Joanne Halleran. *Writing against God: Language as Message in the Literature of Flannery O'Connor.* Macon, Mercer University Press, 1996.

Miller, Alice. *For Your Own Good: Hidden Cruelty in Child-Rearing and the Roots of Violence*, translated by Hildegarde Hannum and Hunter Hannum. New York, Farrar, 1983.

O'Connor, Flannery. *Flannery O'Connor: Collected Works.* Edited by Sally Fitzgerald. New York, Library of America, 1988.

———. *The Habit of Being: Letters.* Edited by Sally Fitzgerald. New York, Farrar, 1979.

Prown, Katherine Hemple. *Revising Flannery O'Connor: Southern Literary Culture and the Problem of Female Authorship.* Charlottesville, University Press of Virginia, 2001.

Roos, John. "The Political in Flannery O'Connor: A Reading of 'A View of the Woods.'" *Studies in Short Fiction,* vol. 29, 1992, pp. 161–79.

Westling, Louise. *Sacred Groves and Ravaged Gardens: The Fiction of Eudora Welty, Carson McCullers, and Flannery O'Connor.* Athens, University of Georgia Press, 1985.

Whitt, Margaret Earley. *Understanding Flannery O'Connor.* Columbia, University of South Carolina Press, 1995. Understanding Contemporary American Literature.

Wyatt, Bryan T. "The Domestic Dynamics of Flannery O'Connor: *Everything That Rises Must Converge.*" *Twentieth Century Literature,* vol. 38, 1992, pp. 66–88.

Criminal Neglect in Flannery O'Connor's Fiction

Wherever one looks in the works of Flannery O'Connor is crime—theft, arson, rape, assault, provocation to suicide, abandonment, and of course, murder. O'Connor is often credited with understanding the criminal mind[1] and with—as she investigates the moral, philosophical, and religious causes and effects of criminal acts—making crime deeply meaningful. She explained the violence in her fiction by asserting that "...violence is strangely capable of returning my characters to reality and preparing them to accept their moment of grace" (*MM* 112). O'Connor's Catholicism thus seems to provide an explanation for everything violent in her fiction, including her motivation to create works that seem violently to attack her readers. Everyone needs to wake up to sinfulness, the argument goes. O'Connor refers to the "violent means" necessary to deal with a "hostile audience," famously adding that "...to the hard of hearing you shout, and for the almost-blind you draw large and startling figures" (*MM* 34). In an effort to move beyond readings of O'Connor in which violence seems straightforwardly and easily to lead to redemption, my purpose here is to investigate how subtly and how thoroughly O'Connor dramatizes the criminality of neglect, often in the form of failing to care for family members, especially children. After reviewing examples of O'Connor's early interest in crime fiction, I will examine a number of works in which neglect takes the form of a parent's choice of what I call a substitute child. I will conclude with an extended argument that O'Connor could convict of criminal neglect even a character almost always treated as a moral exemplar: the priest, Father Flynn, in "The Displaced Person."

---

[1] Certainly Truman Capote believed that O'Connor had a useful understanding of criminals. In "He Would Have Been a Good Man," I argue that O'Connor's works profoundly influenced Capote's nonfiction novel *In Cold Blood*.

O'Connor wrote about crime enthusiastically even as an undergraduate at Georgia State College for Women (now Georgia College). The files in her alma mater's O'Connor Collection include "A Place of Action," which describes a mysterious murder that occurs among a group of Blacks (file 4i). An untitled piece describes the fear of a character named Myrtice that people suspect her of garroting her mother (file 4h). And "Elegance Is Its Own Reward," published in a GSCW publication, is a Poe-influenced piece in which a man succeeds in his determination to murder his second wife in a manner more elegant than the one employed when he killed his first wife. Although there is little criminality in O'Connor's MFA thesis at Iowa,[2] O'Connor did treat crime—and familial neglect—in a serious manner in her graduate school years, in "The Coat," which Virginia Wray calls "a late apprentice piece" that shows O'Connor steadily preparing to write *Wise Blood* (149).[3] Rosa, a Black woman who does others' laundry for a living, discovers the coat-less corpse of a recently killed White man and concludes wrongly that her husband Abram was guilty of the murder. She endeavors to help her husband Abram as he tries to bury the body at night, but White hunters (probably attracted by Rosa's shouts at her husband) happen upon him

---

[2] Exceptions in *The Geranium: A Collection of Short Stories* are on the level of fantasy: the writer Miss Willerton in "The Crop" fantasizes about Lot Motun, the sharecropper character she has created, and then she somehow does away with Lot's wife in order to become Lot's new wife. In "The Turkey," young Ruller fantasizes about becoming a bad boy within a plot from a western. See Susan F. Presley for an argument that several of O'Connor's fictional young men are developing normally according to the standards taught in O'Connor's classes at GSCW. Later in this essay I will discuss "Judgment Day," a revision of the title story from the thesis.

[3] Katherine Hemple Prown has argued that the Iowa Writers' Workshop taught O'Connor that she should write like a man (38–40), and perhaps O'Connor's decision to write about crime in "The Coat" was part of such a strategy. When O'Connor submitted "The Coat" to *The Southwest Review*, she received a rejection letter from Allen Maxwell addressed to "Mr. Flannery O'Connor," even though she submitted the story after Maxwell had rejected O'Connor's "Wildcat" and asked "Mr. Flannery O'Connor" to send more work. O'Connor did find a publisher for "The Coat," but Sally Fitzgerald reports in her *Collected Works* Chronology that O'Connor in 1946 "refuses to let it be published without payment" (*CW* 1241).

and kill him as he tries to escape. The surprise ending reveals that Abram was not the killer, a discovery that transforms the story into an inquiry into the relationship between Rosa and Abram. Beneath the sketchy plot of the never-solved murder lies a more complex investigation: Why does Rosa lack faith in her husband when he claims simply to have found the coat and money that Rosa assumes prove his criminality? Even in this early story, O'Connor's writing about crime focuses on neglect within a supposedly loving family. That Rosa considers her strong husband to be also "her chile,...the onliest one she'd got" (40) adds another layer to her betrayal.

Both of O'Connor's novels have been read as demonstrating the religious value of violent crime. *Wise Blood* climaxes with Hazel Motes's killing of his double, Solace Layfield, and this act of murder, as a rejection of his own falsity, may well be necessary for Hazel's redemption. The title of her second novel, *The Violent Bear It Away*, seems to be an endorsement of violence. Old Mason Tarwater shoots his nephew Rayber, and Young Tarwater climactically kills Bishop, turning himself into a prophet. The murder of Bishop can make Tarwater a prophet even if, or especially if, as Louise Y. Gossett suggests, Young Tarwater symbolically kills Old Tarwater as he literally kills Bishop (91). The possibility that crime leads to salvation is even more complicated than it looks, an idea I shall return to later.[4]

Here I want to emphasize a pattern that lies beneath the "large and startling figures" and the shouting in O'Connor's fiction—a pattern of familial neglect that affects more people than major crimes do. Although love within a family is generally hard to find in O'Connor's works, and failures of a subtle sort within a family lead toward O'Connor's criminal fireworks, particularly interesting is the substitute-child theme. In its simplest form, by making a show of kindness to a substitute child, a parent tortures his or her own child. The father or mother often tries to

---

[4] Gary M. Ciuba provides a spirited argument that *The Violent Bear It Away* opposes the use of violence. See his chapter "'Like a Boulder Blocking Your Path': O'Connor's Skandalon in *The Violent Bear It Away*" (115–64). For a positive interpretation of O'Connor's violence, in relation primarily to stories not treated here, see Fowler. Also important to consider are two essay collections, one edited by Avis Hewitt and Robert Donahoo, the other by Susan Srigley, that address violence in the novels from a variety of interpretive angles.

prove to the child that the parent acts like a good caretaker toward an often more deserving substitute. O'Connor's variations on this theme are many and mysterious. To study this pattern at length makes much of O'Connor's project an examination of insidious crimes against children.

O'Connor's stories (about half of the mature stories, by my estimate) are filled with examples of crimes clearly caused by or influenced by neglect based on the substitute-child pattern. When it is a father who finds a substitute child, the results may be especially painful for the characters and for the reader. In "The Lame Shall Enter First," the story about which O'Connor admitted to novelist John Hawkes that "…the devil's voice is my own" (5 Feb. 1962, *HB* 464), Sheppard displays great kindness to the delinquent Rufus Johnson, in part as a way to torture his son, Norton, in whom Sheppard is very disappointed and to whom he constantly expresses that disappointment. Certainly Norton is aware that Rufus receives preferential treatment despite his bad behavior. When Norton complains that Rufus "went in [Norton's dead mother's] room and used her comb!" and "put on her corset" as well, Sheppard merely replies by complaining that Norton is capable of nothing more than "tattling" (*CW* 608). Even Rufus points out to Norton how badly the real son is treated: "'God, kid,' Johnson said in a cracked voice, 'how do you stand it?'" (609). Sheppard then ups the ante: he "whipped" Norton "in anger" when Norton objects to Rufus's sleeping in the dead mother's bed (610). Sheppard's generosity toward the substitute child extends to the purchase of a telescope that intrigues Rufus—as well as, eventually, Norton. Sheppard torments his son for his initial lack of interest: "Don't you want to get up and look through the telescope, Norton?…Rufus is going to be way ahead of you" (610). Sheppard shames Norton instead of encouraging him. Norton's feeling unloved by his father leads him toward suicide even before Rufus begins to manipulate him in that direction. When O'Connor felt that one of her correspondents was missing the full significance of the telescope, she wrote that Sheppard "wasn't interested in training his own child to reach the stars. Rufus was the incentive" (27 Jan. 1963, *HB* 507). Sheppard's betrayal clearly hits home for Norton when his father pointedly ignores his son's beckoning to him after an emotional conversation in which Sheppard calls the visitor "son" (*CW* 619). It is no wonder that, when Sheppard experiences a too-late recognition scene, the crucial lines he repeats to himself are "I have nothing to reproach myself with" and "I did more for him than I did for my own son" (631). Here in a few words we have the tragedy of the parent who chooses a substitute child.[5]

In "A View of the Woods," perhaps the O'Connor story in which criminal neglect is most horrific, Mr. Fortune and his granddaughter Mary Fortune Pitts end up murdering each other, and the grandfather's supposed expressions of love for his granddaughter are part of the cause. Mr. Fortune is determined to torture his daughter, Mrs. Pitts (a character critics generally ignore), by preferring his granddaughter. My reading of this story underlines the extent to which O'Connor damns Mr. Fortune (cf. letter to Betty Hester, 28 Dec. 1956, *HB* 190) and the patriarchy for which he stands.

Mr. Fortune is determined to torture his daughter Mrs. Pitts, whom I think it is fair to say he hates: "He didn't have any use for [Mary Fortune's] mother, his third or fourth daughter (he could never remember which), though she considered that she took care of him" (*CW* 526). Mr. Fortune thinks most often about his dispute with her husband, Mr. Pitts, but it is likely that the real dispute, made worse by his general inclination to dismiss or ignore her, is with the daughter: "The daughter had been born and raised on [the family farm] but the old man considered that when she married Pitts she showed that she preferred Pitts to home; and when she came back, she came back like any other tenant..." (526).[6] A similar negative comment about his daughter is Mr. Fortune's claim that she needs to learn that she is no better than Mr. Tilman (539). Mr. Fortune has apparently made up a story for himself about his daughter's snobbery, but this is a very flimsy construction. His sense of her pride seems to be based on the fact that she cares for her father (527), that she "airily" refers to the field in front of her house as "the lawn" (532), and that she thinks that she and her husband will be able to buy Mr. Fortune's land when he dies. This is the supposed snobbery of a woman with seven children (526). Mr. Fortune obsesses over his granddaughter's allegiance to Pitts, but surely what Mr. Fortune really cares about is the

---

[5] A comparable pattern might be found in Rayber's treatment of his son Bishop and the substitute child Young Tarwater in *The Violent Bear It Away*. Later in this essay I will apply the substitute-child theme to this novel in a different manner.

[6] Here and in a number of other instances, O'Connor is probably revising and using the parable of the prodigal son.

daughter's marriage. When Mr. Fortune complains about how Mary Fortune Pitts "had never left him...for Pitts" (536), surely a large portion of what Mr. Fortune is *really* mad about is that his daughter left him for Pitts. He and his granddaughter engage in a painfully comic dispute about whether she is a "Jezebel" and whether he is the "Whore of Babylon," but one clear lesson here, one clear assumption, is that evil can be located in an adult woman (533)—such as Mrs. Pitts. Mr. Fortune tells himself that he has kept it a secret that Mrs. Pitts will never get his land, because he has secretly made his lawyer his executor and left everything to Mary Fortune Pitts. He hopes that Mary Fortune will "make the rest of them jump" (527), which is code for his hope that Mary Fortune will figuratively whip her family. (Mr. Fortune uses the word "jump" when he describes how his granddaughter receives beatings [530].)

It would be one thing if Mr. Fortune were able to keep a secret of his hatred for his daughter. But he has made his hatred clear to her, even about his refusal to let his daughter inherit anything, through praise for his granddaughter as a substitute child: Mr. Fortune considers Mary Fortune Pitts "the smartest and the prettiest child he had ever seen"—smarter and prettier than his daughter, of course—"and he let the rest of them know that if, IF that was, he left anything to anybody, it would be Mary Fortune he left it to" (*CW* 526). So in writing the will to leave the land to Mary Fortune, he has only done what he has told his daughter he probably would do. And since the Pittses could well end up with the land at the end of the story, the land is clearly *not* the real issue for Mr. Fortune.

Has Mr. Fortune beaten his daughter? Probably. After Mary Fortune Pitts explodes at Tilman's store, Mr. Fortune's thoughts suggest a back-story about his daughter Mrs. Pitts:

> He had never seen a child behave in such a way in his life. Neither his own children or anyone else's had ever displayed such temper in his presence, and he had never for an instant imagined that the child he had trained himself, the child who had been his constant companion for nine years, would embarrass him like this. The child he had never lifted a hand to! (*CW* 543)

Surely this passage suggests that he has whipped his own daughter in the past, and that she has accepted her whippings. Earlier in the story, Mr. Fortune has said that the other Pitts children "should be whipped once a week on principle," and he also recalls that "he had never allowed [Mrs.

Pitts] or [Mary Fortune's] brothers or sisters so much as to slap [Mary Fortune]" (529). It is very unusual not to whip a child, and Mr. Fortune has found a way to punish his daughter with whipping as well as with non-whipping. The story's crisis comes as Mr. Fortune decides to sell what his daughter—and therefore his granddaughter—call "the lawn" (532). His announcement of the upcoming sale causes his daughter to "let out a moan as if a dull knife were being turned slowly in her chest" (533). When the mother claims that Mary Fortune "puts you up to everything," Mr. Fortune gives his daughter a grand dose of verbal abuse he has probably been saving for some time: "You're no kind of a mother! You're a disgrace! That child is an angel! A saint!" (534). It is clear that Mr. Fortune attempts to turn his daughter and the substitute child against each other, and he has succeeded. Mrs. Pitts has fallen into a cycle of blaming her child in a manner similar to the way her father has blamed her. It is worth noting here that much of my thinking for this reading is inspired by an excellent book by Claire Raymond about sadism and those who witness it. Raymond concludes about this story that Mrs. Pitts "take[s] pleasure in...knowing of the violation of a young girl" (160), thus making Mrs. Pitts very similar to Mr. Fortune. I am less inclined to blame Mrs. Pitts quite so much, because she is such a victim of the patriarchy.

Near the end of the story, Mr. Fortune tells himself that he is trying to figure out what all the fuss is about with saving the landscape. He has a momentary vision in which "someone...were wounded behind the woods and the trees were bathed in blood" (*CW* 538). We have thought about the trees as a Christ symbol in this story so much that we have missed a more literal explanation for this passage—that perhaps Mr. Fortune is on the verge of noticing how badly he has wounded his daughter.

Mary Fortune's position as a substitute child does not work to her advantage. She has to sense that her grandfather does not recognize her as anything more than a prop. Perhaps she realizes at the end of the story that when her grandfather tries to beat her, he is starting to treat her the way he has treated Mrs. Pitts. When Mary Fortune says she is "PURE Pitts" (*CW* 545), she is saying what her mother said as she married. Still, her mother is unable to make an ally of her daughter. Mary Fortune's tragedy is that being a substitute child makes her nobody's child. Neglected by all, she explodes into violence.

A less horrific situation in which a father chooses a substitute child is in O'Connor's final story, "Judgment Day," even though one could say

O'Connor created this story by adding a murder to her first published story, "The Geranium." The protagonist of "Judgment Day," T. C. Tanner, has been brought from Georgia to the North to live with his daughter because of her sense of duty and her modicum of respect for him. Tanner had made clear his reluctance to live with her: "I wouldn't come with you for no million dollars or no sack of salt" (*CW* 680). He lets her know he would rather live with his Black friend and substitute child, Coleman Parrum, and as Tanner's health worsens, he also lets his daughter know that he wants to go back to Coleman (691), if only to be buried. Tanner tries (and fails) to make his new Black neighbor in the North into another version of Coleman. The neighbor, deeply offended by Tanner's racism, eventually kills the old man, perhaps with O'Connor's consent. In spite of all Tanner's offenses against his daughter, their last conversation is one that she can accept as a reconciliation. The only thing that saves her sanity is her father's shift into uncommunicative fantasy. A related story in which a father chooses a substitute child is "Why Do the Heathen Rage?" When the father, Tilman, returns home to recover from a stroke, "the only gesture of affection he had given" to anyone in the house is directed toward his Black worker Roosevelt (798). As O'Connor worked to develop "Heathen" into her third novel, she had Tilman demonstrate his preference for Roosevelt over his son, Walter (the protagonist of the planned novel), and Walter amazingly takes a photograph of Roosevelt, sends it to Oona Gibbs, a woman Walter is falling in love with, and tells Oona that the photo is one of Walter. O'Connor never decided how this strategy of turning himself into the substitute child would work out for Walter.

    Mothers in O'Connor are even more likely than fathers to choose a substitute child, and the results are generally bad. In "Greenleaf," it may seem that Mrs. May ends up being gored by a bull because her sons neglect her, but she neglects them as well, and her neglect is so great that it causes them to ignore any threats she faces. She drives Wesley and Scofield, her sons, to distraction by treating as substitute children the mysterious but successful O. T. and E. T. Greenleaf. She has been excessively nice to these twins for years: "They swam in my pond and shot my birds and fished in my stream and I never forgot their birthday and Christmas seemed to roll around very often if I remember it right" (*CW* 518). Although O. T. and E. T. give Mrs. May plenty to complain about—including the fact that they own the bull that runs loose until Mrs. May is gored by it—she is also willing to praise the Greenleaf boys in order to torment Wesley and even to give her sons over to the scandalously mud-wallowing Mrs. Greenleaf: "'O. T. and E. T. are fine boys,' she said. 'They ought to have been my sons.' The thought of this was so horrible that her vision of Wesley was blurred at once by a wall of tears. All she saw was his dark shape, rising quickly from the table. 'And you two,' she cried, 'you two should have belonged to that woman!'" (511). When Wesley soon thereafter starts a fight with his brother, he does so—significantly, as Doreen Fowler points out, in "Greenleaf English" (139)—by recalling his mother's slight: "...neither you nor me is her boy" (*CW* 517). The battle between brothers (easy to imagine taking place in the dining room of the main house at Andalusia) leaves Wesley in a Kafkaesque position, looking like the victim of a parent: "lying like a large bug on his back with the edge of the over-turned table cutting him across the middle and broken dishes scattered on top of him" (517).

In "A Circle in the Fire," Mrs. Cope is only slightly, but still overly, generous to the delinquents who take advantage of her farm and then set fire to it. The real harm is that Mrs. Cope's politeness, however shallow, toward the boys (and her refusal to take real action to remove them) is in such pointed contrast to her treatment of her daughter, Sally Virginia, who expresses her own attitude toward the boys, "as if she were going to vomit," by saying loudly, "Ugggghhrhh" (*CW* 242). Sally Virginia clearly would not tolerate the boys' presence. When Mrs. Cope concludes incorrectly that the boys have left the farm, she calls them "poor things" and starts repeating one of her standard speeches, about "how much" she and Sally Virginia

> had to be thankful for, for she said they might have had to live in a development themselves or they might have been Negroes or they might have been in iron lungs or they might have been Europeans ridden in boxcars like cattle, and she began a litany of her blessings, in a stricken voice, that the child, straining her attention for a sudden shriek in the dark, didn't listen to. (247)

Another reason the daughter tries not to listen to this speech is that nowhere does Mrs. Cope say she is thankful to have Sally Virginia as a daughter. The next morning, in fact, Mrs. Cope complains to her daughter, "Why do you have to look like an idiot?" (*CW* 247). She adds another insult that disowns her daughter: "I look at you and I want to cry! Sometimes you look like you belong to [their employee] Mrs. Pritchard!" (248). When in the final lines of the story we read a description of the boys as "prophets…dancing in the fiery furnace, in the circle the angel had cleared for them" (251), we should keep in mind that these lines reflect the point of view of Sally Virginia, who is all too aware of how her mother has too generously cleared a space for the boys' crimes. I can agree with much of Lisa Babinec's argument that Mrs. Cope makes a "surrogate daughter" of her farmland (22), but I also see Mrs. Cope sacrificing the farm to the boys.

"I don't think it makes a bit of difference what size you are. You just can't beat a good disposition" (*CW* 634). This is one of the comments used by Mary Grace's mother in "Revelation" to show her daughter that she is a good parent, if only toward a substitute child, in this case the young-looking Mrs. Ruby Turpin. Mary Grace's mother and Mrs. Turpin agree with each other on all sorts of topics—including race—about which one imagines disagreements between the college student and her mother. To some extent, though Mrs. Turpin claims there is no similarity between herself and Mary Grace, she responds to the mother's reference to the girl's "bad disposition" as if she and Mary Grace are indeed worthy of comparison. Mrs. Turpin is quick to claim "a good one" (643). That Mary Grace's mother intends to torment her daughter is clearest when she talks about her as if she were merely an acquaintance: "'I know a girl,' she said, 'who has parents who would give her anything,…but who can never say a kind word…'" (644). The daughter's violent response—she throws at Mrs. Turpin her book, *Human Development*,[7] tries to strangle her, and curses her as an "old wart hog" (646)—is motivated by a feeling that Mrs. Turpin is an alternative version of her mother, a mother figure she can allow herself to attack.[8] Mrs. Turpin surely acquired some sense of the motherly role into which Mary Grace casts her;

---

[7] Such a weapon-like book exists, with 400 pages and a blue cloth cover. A study of socialization and of child and adolescent psychology with the title mentioned in "Revelation" was produced by Ira J. Gordon in time for Flannery O'Connor perhaps to see it before writing the story. I thank Irwin H. Streight for donating a copy of *Human Development* to the O'Connor Collection at Georgia College.

[8] While Mary Grace is "eighteen or nineteen" (*CW* 635), her mother is "grey-haired" (*CW* 633), so it is possible for them to interpret Ruby Turpin, aged 47 but with "not a wrinkle in her face" (635), as simultaneously a mother figure and a substitute child. See Babinec for a compatible reading of Mary Grace and her mother (18–21).

although Ruby is childless, she ends the story by playing mother. Asking "How am I a hog?" (652), she has a revelation as she imagines herself into her farm's pig parlor containing "an old sow" with "seven long-snouted bristly shoats" that are "like idiot children" (651).

Like Mary Grace's mother, Julian's mother in "Everything That Rises Must Converge" uses talk about race to irritate her child. She brings up the topic so often that Julian "knew every stop, every junction, every swamp along the way" (*CW* 487). In spite of all the many things that Julian's mother continues to do for him, when he takes off his tie, his mother says "You look like a—thug" (459), so we know she has negative feelings toward his looks as well. She tries to take as her substitute child, ironically, a Black boy, Carver, "who might have been four," who takes a seat on the bus beside Julian's mother. Julian knows that his mother thinks "...little Negroes were on the whole cuter than little white children" (495), and this knowledge can hurt Julian, who is quick to note that his mother and the boy's mother have "swapped sons." Julian's mother smiles at Carver even as Carver's mother calls him away, and when Julian's mother says "I think he likes me," her condescending motherliness causes Julian to see "everything lost" (497). Julian's mother keeps up her irritation of Julian and Carver's mother by continuing to play peek-a-boo with the boy. And when Julian's mother tries to give a coin to Carver as the two mother-son couples depart the bus, both Julian and Carver's mother are enraged: he lectures his mother sternly, and Carver's mother (perhaps expressing some of what Julian feels along with her own anger) uses her pocketbook as a weapon. Julian may learn a valuable lesson, but he will probably continue to be manipulated by his mother's power to place her love elsewhere, as Bettina L. Knapp has suggested (101). The story concludes with a chilling detail, that Julian's mother's eye "raked his face again, found nothing and closed" (*CW* 500).

Unlike Sally Fitzgerald, who sees the mother in "Good Country People" as "well-meaning" ("Penetration" 10), I see "Good Country People" beginning with the mother, Mrs. Hopewell, subjecting her daughter, Hulga/Joy Hopewell, to subtle cruelty that opens the way for the more perverse, horrific cruelty of the Bible salesman Manley Pointer toward Hulga at the story's end.[9] Hulga's mother "had no bad qualities of her

---

[9] Fitzgerald insists that O'Connor sees children and parents as always equally at fault ("Penetration" 7-8). For an extended study of "Good Country

own but she was able to use other people's in such a constructive way that she never felt the lack" (*CW* 264). She invites the obnoxious Mrs. Freeman into the house each morning and encourages her conversation, and they regularly discuss before Hulga the daughters of Mrs. Freeman, Glynese and Carramae. Cindy Beringer considers Mrs. Hopewell to be starved for "companionship" (132), but I think that the mother's motives are less justifiable than that. Mrs. Hopewell knows that Hulga dislikes the girls (whom she refers to as Glycerin and Caramel), but Mrs. Hopewell "liked to tell people"—surely including Hulga—"that Glynese and Carramae were two of the finest girls she knew and that Mrs. Freeman was a *lady* and that she was never ashamed to take her anywhere or introduce her to anybody they might meet" (*CW* 264). Clearly Mrs. Hopewell is attacking Hulga here, as she is doing whenever "Mrs. Hopewell said that people who looked on the bright side of things would be beautiful even if they were not" (267) and when she says "...there were not many girls with Glynese's common sense" (274). I agree with Lisa Babinec that the comparison of Hulga to the Freeman girls is deeply unfair (14). When Manley Pointer arrives, Mrs. Hopewell again turns on the inviting tolerance that irritates Hulga, even though Mrs. Hopewell can hear "a groan" from Hulga as Mrs. Hopewell acts on her belief that "*I* can't be rude to anybody" (*CW* 271). When Mrs. Hopewell "overflow[s] with hospitality to make up for Joy's lack of courtesy" (272) toward the young man, she is once again twisting the knife in her daughter. Hulga's desperation to prove she can in some way be loved makes possible Manley Pointer's success as a sadist.

In "The River," Harry/Bevel Ashfield seems so eager to have someone select him as a substitute child that readers are likely to see it as valuable for his babysitter, Mrs. Connin, to take on the role of his mother and for the Rev. Bevel Summers to adopt, however briefly, the role of father. Almost all readings of this story are critical of Harry's real parents, the Ashfields, but I believe Harry/Bevel's drowning can be considered a result of several forms of neglect. The story seems more masterful when one begins to question how well Harry is treated by Mrs. Connin and the preacher. While I believe that Rev. Summers means well—and that he

---

People" as an illustration of D. W. Winnicott's views on the psychology of children's development, see Lebeck, who treats Hulga/Joy as somewhat less injured by bad mothering than is Asbury Fox of "The Enduring Chill."

simply needs to spend more time with the child—Mrs. Connin's behavior is more questionable, especially when one considers her family. When Mrs. Connin's four children first meet Harry/Bevel, he is introduced as special because his name is that of the preacher Mrs. Connin likes. The Connin children immediately shift into attack mode, as if they have already formed an expectation from experience that the children Mrs. Connin babysits for will receive preferential treatment. "She'd kill us," one Connin child says, attempting to talk the group out of the mistreatment they plan for Harry—an attack by a pig (*CW* 158). The Connin kids are relieved to think they will bring Bevel/Harry down to their level: "Maw ain't going to like him lettin out thet hawg" (159). But they are mistaken. When Harry receives his scare, he is treated especially well by Mrs. Connin, who works to calm him, provides breakfast "and let him sit on her lap while he ate it" (159), and reads a book to him (160). When they all head to the river to see Rev. Summers, it is Harry's hand Mrs. Connin holds, and upon arriving at the river, she "pushed" her boys "so that they wouldn't linger by the food" (161) and proceeds to make Harry the center of attention. Harry realizes that it is not much fun to be her real child. When he returns to the river, he goes on a day when he knows none of the Connins will be home.

"A Good Man Is Hard to Find" may be O'Connor's most famous story because of the shock effect of its crimes: six characters are shot to death by The Misfit—who may be based on one or more real criminals O'Connor read about in the newspaper (Tate 98-101)—and his henchmen beside a little-used road in middle Georgia. The story's reputation may have grown because the crime is so meaningful: decades of critical analysis have insisted that the grandmother is saved by the experience of facing death and that The Misfit's act of murder is indirectly good for his soul. The grandmother's reaction to him, O'Connor herself notoriously suggested, "will grow to be a great crow-filled tree in the Misfit's heart, and will be enough of a pain to him there to turn him into the prophet he was meant to become" (*MM* 113). O'Connor felt such instruction was necessary because some people react to the crimes in her story quite differently. She once heard from a teacher who wanted her opinion about the possibility that everything in the story after the wreck of the car driven by Bailey, and perhaps the accident as well, is "Bailey's dream" and that "Bailey...identifies himself with the Misfit..." (*HB* 436). Replying in a letter that this reading is "about as far from my intentions as it could get to be," O'Connor closed by saying that she was "in a state of shock" (28 Mar.

1961, *HB* 437). Dawn Keetley argues that it does makes sense to see The Misfit as expressing the anger of another, but Keetley nominates the grandmother as the one whose anger at her family unleashes The Misfit and his murderous violence (76). I find both of these rather fanciful readings intriguing, and if one asks the broader question of who has criminal thoughts in this story, it is plausible to conclude that The Misfit embodies anger felt not only by Bailey and the grandmother, but also by the unloved children June Star and John Wesley, as well as their generally disrespected mother. That vacation car is a powder keg.

Bailey has plenty to be upset about. The grandmother apparently identifies Bailey as "the son she lived with, her only boy" (*CW* 137). The story begins with the grandmother's wish "to visit some of her connections" (137). Are there other children of hers, daughters she prefers? Unable to change Bailey's mind about the trip, she sneaks into the car a substitute "child" that she knows Bailey dislikes—in the form of the male cat, Pitty Sing (138). Ironically, the grandmother tells herself she is taking the cat on the trip because he might have an accident if left at home. Her nostalgia about good children must sound like an insult to Bailey also: "In my time...children were more respectful of their native state and their parents and everything else" (139). Her story about missing out on rich Mr. Teagarden as a husband could easily be taken by Bailey as a sign of his mother's regret over the family life she has had (140). She tells Red Sammy Butts, proprietor of a barbecue joint called The Tower, that he is "a good man!" (142), a bit of praise her son never hears directed his way. When the family leaves The Tower, Bailey has a car accident as his mother's beloved substitute springs onto his shoulder and clings to his neck (144). The grandmother then tells The Misfit that he too is "a good man," just after Bailey "said something to his mother that shocked even the children" (147). When the grandmother repeats again that The Misfit is "a good man," Bailey yells "Hush!" (148). Then Bailey goes to the woods to be shot, without much of a fight, claiming "I'll be back in a minute, Mamma, wait on me!" (148).[10]

Part of the power of "A Good Man" is that O'Connor takes the substi-

---

[10] In a reading of O'Connor's treatment of families that is otherwise often similar to mine, Helen S. Garson blames Bailey for his "inability to assert himself against his mother's pressures" so that he is guilty of leading "the family to the fatal area in which they are all murdered by The Misfit..." (120).

tute-child theme in an unusual direction, having the parent finally express some love for her real child after mixing up the child and the substitute. The grandmother starts to regard The Misfit as her child as soon as she "noticed how thin his shoulder blades were just behind his hat because she was standing up looking down on him" (*CW* 149). When The Misfit puts on the distinctive "yellow shirt with bright blue parrots" that has been taken from the murdered Bailey, "The grandmother couldn't name what the shirt reminded her of," (150) a confusion that suggests she is starting to lose the distinction between Bailey and The Misfit. The grandmother calls to "Bailey Boy!" near the story's end, still, close to the passage in which she looks at the yellow-and-blue-shirted male before her and says "You're one of my own children!" She reaches toward him with love for both her dead child and the substitute child, and she "touched him on the shoulder" that she had just recently seen as thin, as that of a child (152). Of course this breakthrough toward love was never heard by her real boy. It was so very hard for her to find a good man in Bailey. The paradox is that as Bailey Boy misses out on the moment, both the grandmother and The Misfit—who shoots her when she touches him—may experience a moment of grace. The grandmother's neglect against her child benefits both her and her murderer, even if, as O'Connor herself said, "...the grandmother is not in the least concerned with God..." (5 Mar. 1960, *HB* 379).

To say that O'Connor can find some good in a pattern of criminal neglect against children should not be that surprising, since O'Connor always finds the evil in good and the good in evil. In most of the stories I have been reviewing here, for that matter, there is evidence to suggest that religious benefit is achieved through criminal neglect. Tanner's fantasy of fondness for his imagined substitute child, Coleman, may be his redemption. Mrs. May might be redeemed because she neglects her sons and thus makes possible her divine goring. Mrs. Cope may be redeemed by bringing about the boys' purifying fire. Mrs. Turpin benefits spiritually, even if temporarily, from her peculiar role in Mary Grace's family drama, and Julian's plunging into a "world of guilt and sorrow" (*CW* 500) involves spiritual insight as well. I balk at saying that Hulga/Joy Hopewell benefits at the end of her story, although some readers are eager to see Hulga enlightened. After the story ends, I imagine, she will be tortured forever by the questions Mrs. Hopewell will allow the substitute child, Mrs. Freeman, to ask Hulga. Harry/Bevel Ashfield may be happily on his way with "the waiting current" that "caught him like a long gentle hand and pulled him swiftly forward and down" in the river (171). Or will he think it is a parental hand that drowns him?

There is at least one crime story in which O'Connor treats the parent's substitute-child behavior as an almost total good, even as it leads to murder: "The Comforts of Home," a story complete with references to crime movies (*CW* 579) and a sheriff who tries to explain the story's murder (594). Thomas's mother chooses a substitute child in Sarah Ham, aka Star Drake, lavishing charitable comforts on the troubled girl and constantly infuriating her adult son with the idea that he and the girl are comparable. The story opens with a situation that could be tragic in a slightly different context: Thomas insists that his mother choose between him and the substitute, and the mother chooses the substitute. Thomas ends up shooting his mother. As Helen S. Garson points out, the directness of this violence by an adult child toward a parent is unique in O'Connor (121). The tragic potential is shifted somewhat toward a comedic sort of resolution by the fact that Thomas needs to be deprived of all the comforts to which he has grown excessively, even ridiculously accustomed.[11] It is reasonable to speculate that part of the reason O'Connor wrote "The Comforts of Home," which she composed shortly after writing the horrific story "A View of the Woods," was to try to balance things out a bit.

In both of O'Connor's novels, the substitute-child theme takes a more clearly religious form than it has in most of the stories. When Hazel Motes's mother and grandfather torment him with their devotion to a substitute, or when Tarwater's great-uncle, Old Mason Tarwater, neglects him for another, the preferred substitute is Jesus. Hazel's mother greets him, when he returns from a carnival, by beating him with a stick and saying "Jesus died to redeem you" (*CW* 36), even though she has no clear idea what the child has been doing. Hazel's grandfather would preach by saying, in the child's presence, that "...even for that boy there, for that mean sinful unthinking boy standing there with his dirty hands clenching and unclenching at his sides, Jesus would die ten million deaths before he would let him lose his soul" (11). In O'Connor's second

---

[11] I analyze elsewhere ("Hand") the beneficial lessons—religious and sexual—in the realizations Thomas consciously resists. Thomas, perhaps a male version of Hulga/Joy Hopewell, needs lessons more than she does. For a quite different reading of the relationship between Thomas and his mother, see Westling, who concludes that O'Connor's fiction is an example of the "disastrous consequences" of "finding her allegiance in the father's power" (121).

novel, Old Tarwater, who describes himself as a "prophet" (332), bosses his great nephew Young Tarwater to prepare to bury Old Tarwater, saying "Burying the dead right may be the only honor you ever do yourself" (338). Young Tarwater may also be tortured by the knowledge that he is a substitute for Rayber, the nephew that Old Tarwater shot twice after the two of them had a falling out (333). Hazel and Tarwater are tormented by their ancestors' implications that they must be good at parenting because they are totally devoted to religion. Hazel's and Tarwater's struggles with religion have much to do with the strange mix of religiosity and their family members' refusal to show love. The protagonists of both novels are nearly destroyed by that substitution: love of Jesus for love of children. While I do not believe O'Connor ever questioned her Catholic principles, I do believe she was capable of questioning a religious character who substitutes religiosity for taking care of those who need help.

"The Displaced Person" persuades me that O'Connor could also fault a deeply religious Catholic character as guilty of criminal neglect. It is tempting, of course, to assume that the priest, Father Flynn, who arranges for the coming of the Displaced Person to the middle Georgia farm, must be endorsed by O'Connor because he is Catholic and because he brought the story's apparent Christ-symbol to the farm. The problem is that Flynn, who ought to act like a father toward everyone, chooses the Displaced Person as his substitute child and encourages Mrs. McIntyre to make the same mistake.

The tendency among critics is to consider the priest insignificant or purely virtuous or both. In contrast to the many critics who say next to nothing about Father Flynn, Richard Giannone calls him courageous, praises him as a figure "in whom prayer becomes action" (143), and says that when Flynn appears in one of Mrs. McIntyre's dreams, referring to her "tender heart" (*CW* 322), he demonstrates that he has "cultivated [his own] heart that discerns undercurrents of the inner world" (Giannone 142). Jon Lance Bacon praises Flynn on a more practical level: O'Connor's strategy is to embody an anti-Catholic stereotype—of the invasive priest scheming to indoctrinate—and then to show how the invasiveness can be "fortunate" (81), so that Flynn deserves praise as "an agent of change, not an apologist for the status quo" (78). My view of Father Flynn is less positive. We consistently hear Flynn repeating the speech tag "Arrrrrrr," figuratively "grating to a halt" (*CW* 316). This voice is hardly the sound of progress.

Almost never has anyone (other than characters within the story) suggested there is anything wrong with the priest. At most, readers may agree that Flynn "inadvertently sets in motion a train of events that leads to the Pole's 'accidental' death" (Schneiderman 95). Sarah Gordon comes close to criticizing Flynn, but she is more inclined to fault O'Connor herself for failing to show "any connection between the individual's experience of God's grace and the necessity for that individual to assume political responsibility" (187). Gordon equates Father Flynn and the Church (190–91), so when Gordon faults O'Connor for failing to realize "the logical outcome of her own argument—that even the Church is capable of refusing to see the *whole* of humanity" (187)—there is at least an implied critique of Father Flynn.

Examining the priest's relationship with the Displaced Person and his family, his attitude toward the other farm workers, and his relationship to Mrs. McIntyre and her birds leads me to conclude that he is guilty of criminal neglect, that he is significantly responsible for the death of the Displaced Person (hereafter, D. P.), his substitute child. I believe that, however much Flannery O'Connor was "a dutiful daughter of the traditional Church" (Gordon 192), as a *writer*, she could and did criticize those within the Church. In Father Flynn she even suggests a critique of the paralysis of the Church during WWII, its "near silence during the Holocaust" (Gordon 192). The priest's work to bring the displaced Polish family to Mrs. McIntyre's farm is not itself a crime, by any means. It is an act of generosity and religious duty performed in difficult circumstances, perhaps without time to be picky about details. The more one examines the atrocities of WWII, the less one will question any effort to save people from its horrors. And certainly one is grateful that the priest appears immediately when Mr. Guizac is killed (*CW* 326). However, as the family of Displaced Persons arrives on the farm of Mrs. McIntyre in O'Connor's story, the priest begins to earn his name: Flynn. Here it is worthwhile to examine O'Connor's reading of James Joyce, which is probably the most specific source for O'Connor's use of the common Irish name Flynn. O'Connor studied carefully Joyce's story "Araby" in the anthology she recommended regularly to others who wanted to be good readers or writers: *Understanding Fiction*, edited by Brooks and Warren.[12] Reading "Araby"

---

[12] The commentary to "Araby" in the Brooks and Warren anthology claims that the story discusses the priest at length in order to emphasize a "growing

surely contributed to O'Connor's desire to get her own copy of Joyce's story collection *Dubliners*, and she seems to have paid significant attention to its opening story, "The Sisters." Here we find a priest named "Father Flynn" who lingers significantly in the mind of the other characters after his death. Joyce's Flynn is described as suffering paralysis, and the word "paralysis" sticks in the protagonist's mind alongside the word "simony," as if the priest's paralysis had something to do with a moral flaw.

In O'Connor's own copy of *Dubliners*, she marked several passages in the story, and in fact "The Sisters" is the most heavily annotated story in the collection. (It is likely that O'Connor read this book before she wrote "The Displaced Person" because she composed in the back some lines for *Wise Blood*, including some dialogue for Mrs. Watts.) Among the marks in the story "The Sisters" is her underlining of the words "simony" and "paralysis" in the opening paragraph (7), the latter word clearly referring to the condition of the priest. Three pages later, as the protagonist falls toward sleep, he imagines the dead priest trying to confess to him "in a murmuring voice and I wondered why [his face] smiled continually and why the lips were so moist with spittle. But then I remembered that [the priest] had died of paralysis and I felt that I too was smiling feebly as if to absolve the simoniac of his sin" (10). O'Connor's marginal comment here is "the mysterious strong words" (see Kinney 157); she is referring back to the words "paralysis" and "simony" in the opening paragraph. Her markings suggest that as O'Connor borrows the name Flynn for her priest, she also borrows the question of whether there is moral culpability attached to the priest's paralysis.[13] (I find this response to the name Flynn more interesting and persuasive than another possibility: that it plays on the phrase "in like Flynn"—meaning as easily successful as actor Errol Flynn was in his romances.)

While O'Connor's Father Flynn certainly performs a good act in bringing the Guizacs to the farm, *after* that point, he slides toward a bad

---

sense of isolation," the loneliness, of the story's young protagonist (420). I think this commentary connects with O'Connor's story insofar as Mrs. McIntyre's relationship to Father Flynn and the Guizacs creates more distance between her and the farm's long-term workers.

[13] See Robinson for a comparison of Joyce and O'Connor on the subject of "paralysis" (93), among other topics, based primarily on a comparison of "Araby" to O'Connor's "A Temple of the Holy Ghost."

case of paralysis. The priest takes little responsibility for making their stay beneficial to all concerned. While he does drop by to make sure that his substitute child, the D. P., keeps his job (*CW* 300), he does not push for details about Mr. Guizac's behavior. When Mrs. McIntyre criticizes the D. P., the priest, rather than asking for details, merely changes the subject. When the priest talks about Mrs. McIntyre's Christlike peacocks, he is basically dodging topics that he ought to pursue. "Where is that beautiful birrrrd of yours?" Father Flynn asks to avoid talking about problems between Guizac and the other workers (316). Even the sincere-sounding exclamation "Christ will come like that!" (317) is part of this strategy. He characterizes all practical problems on the farm as "a trifle" (317) and chooses the not-at-all-helpful strategy of staying away from the farm "as if he had been frightened" (320). He remains blissfully ignorant of the issues that drive the story toward its climax. He does not care that Mrs. Shortley is given a stroke due to her hatred of the D. P.—not that I justify that hatred, but the priest might be held responsible for not trying to improve that situation. He never attempts to interact with the Shortleys. Claire Kahane has identified the Judge, dead husband of Mrs. McIntyre, as the story's father figure (452), but it makes more sense to assign to Father Flynn the fatherly responsibility to care for everyone on the farm.

One significant problem to which the priest chooses to be blind is that the marriage deal between Mr. Guizac and Sulk is morally questionable at least and possibly criminal. Richard Giannone scolds Mrs. McIntyre for feeling so little sympathy for the Polish woman who wants to marry for "basic freedom" (140), but I doubt that the theoretical bride has been consulted about Mr. Guizac's plan. Something is fishy here, as Astor seems to think when he tells Mrs. Shortley about the deal (*CW* 299). Mr. Guizac has seen Sulk stealing food, and his response was to try to have Sulk punished (293). When Guizac then tells Sulk to give him $3 per week,[14] what is Sulk to believe? That he is going to get a wife from Poland? Sulk tries to believe it, or pretends that he tries, but he soon becomes skeptical (311). When he goes along with Guizac's pressure, paying half the $6 per week

---

[14] According to Samuel H. Williamson's website MeasuringWorth, $3 in 1954 or 1955 could be worth anything from $22.40 to $158.00 in 2018 dollars, depending on how one looks at it. Regardless of the difficulty of translating the value of money from one era to another, I think it is safe to say that Sulk is being asked to contribute substantially to Mr. Guizac.

supposedly devoted to bringing the woman to America for an illegal marriage, the most reasonable conclusion is that Guizac is bossing, perhaps even bullying Sulk.[15] Notice that Mr. Guizac, who makes $70 per month, is extracting $12 per month from a man who presumably earns under $70. And the priest knows less than anyone else about how Mr. Guizac is learning to fit in with how people use each other on this farm. As Michael Faulknor has pointed out to me, Guizac surely would have already told Father Flynn about the desperate situation of his cousin. Not only has Flynn failed to find a solution, but he acts innocent of the crisis (Faulknor). I would not agree with Mrs. Shortley's speculation that Flynn "is putting [Guizac] up to" trying to get money from Sulk (*CW* 300), but Flynn has apparently done nothing to give Guizac an alternative. Faulknor suggests that insofar as we take "The Displaced Person" to be an allegory, we might interpret Flynn as a representative of the US government and its failure to deal fully with the Holocaust.

As for my sense that Flynn might talk to the Shortleys, I should concede that the Shortleys would not welcome the priest's attention if it were offered. Mr. Shortley says, "I aint going to have no Pope of Rome tell me how to run no dairy" (*CW* 292). While that may seem a mere joke, the

---

[15] The real-life troubles at Andalusia between Mr. Matysiak (the basis for Mr. Guizac) and Shot (the basis for Sulk) are revealed in letters O'Connor wrote to Caroline Gordon. In a letter Christine Flanagan dates as 15 Dec. 1953 (but that Benjamin B. Alexander dates as 18 Dec. 1953; see *GT* 81), O'Connor writes, "The D.P. is currently telling Shot that he can get him a wife from Germany but that he'll have to pay five hundred dollars for her." Then O'Connor reports that Regina O'Connor, who has discouraged this offer, "has had a lot of trouble anyway with Shot's matrimonial complications. He is estranged from his first wife who used to have him put in jail every month because he wouldn't support his child. My mother finally...had it arranged so that she sends the check for the child every month—twelve dollars" (*Letters FO/CG* 92). Note that Shot's child support is coincidentally the same amount that Sulk is giving Mr. Guizac in the story for Guizac's cousin. Relations between Shot and Mr. Matysiak seem to have worsened by 8 Feb. 1954, when O'Connor wrote to Gordon, "The D.P. and Shot nearly choked each other in the wagon the other day and now my mother is almost afraid to send them to the field together for fear one won't come back" (*Letters FO/CG* 100). After Regina lectured Mr. Matysiak and then Shot, O'Connor reports, Shot "agreed with every word, but said Mr. Matysiak had hit him first" (101).

priest needs to be more concerned, not less, with how a farm community interacts. Robert Coles devotes a number of pages to spelling out, basically in a sympathetic fashion, the viewpoints of the Shortleys and of the farm's Black workers (14–32), making clear that these workers deserve attention. There is a relevant line from the original *Sewanee Review* version of the story, the version without a peacock, which ends with Mrs. Shortley's death. Mrs. Shortley imagines the priest's face as having "the look of some secret, opened out and still hidden, as if he were saying: I can tell you something that you won't believe. That she wouldn't" (649). The final revision of this story does nothing to dispel the notion here that the priest shuts out the Shortleys, promoting the welfare of only the substitute child. The final version of the story eliminates the suggestion that Flynn and Mrs. Shortley know they cannot talk to each other.

When Mrs. McIntyre tells Flynn that she plans to fire the Shortleys, he does nothing to soften the blow that this down-on-its-luck family is likely to suffer (*CW* 302). There is little indication that he would have been more concerned if Mrs. McIntyre had announced that she were going to leave her Black workers jobless. It is reasonable to consider the priest heartless about what will happen to the non-D. P. workers on the farm. When he hears her announce that she will fire people much less able than the Guizacs "to get along" (302), we are told that "The priest scarcely seemed to hear her he was so busy wiggling his finger inside the wire..." of the turkey brooder (303). Furthermore, I see little to suggest that the priest realizes that Mrs. McIntyre is unlikely to carry through with her threats.

Of course, the story is full of examples of Mrs. McIntyre's also choosing the D. P. as her preferred substitute for her other workers. Nobody in the story is literally her child, but it is easy to see that classism and racism keep her from treating anyone on the farm properly, and she seems to enjoy tormenting Mrs. Shortley with praise for Mr. Guizac. Cindy Beringer has argued that "In O'Connor's stories the female farmer-to-worker relationship is typically one of parent to perpetual child"; Beringer sees "a direct correlation between a woman's success in business and her abysmal failure as nurturer" (126). Part of my argument is that the priest should help Mrs. McIntyre understand more of her responsibility to all her workers. Instead, the priest consistently brings up the topic of religion with Mrs. McIntyre without showing her the relevance of religion, explicating points of dogma in order to avoid the issue at hand, an issue directly relevant to his work to save Displaced Persons.

What is going on between the D. P. and Mrs. McIntyre and the rest of the workers on the farm? The priest never knows, apparently, that the D. P. wants to marry his cousin to a person he thinks should be punished for thievery. When Mrs. McIntyre complains about money, the priest lets out an "ugly bellow" of amused mockery, but he does no better than she does at facing real issues (*CW* 321). It is significant that Mrs. McIntyre "had never known a priest until she had gone to see this one on the business of getting her the Displaced Person" (316); my response to the fact that it was she, not the priest, who started the hiring process is that Mrs. McIntyre was eager to find a substitute child, while the priest may have initially been reluctant to take on the work of placing Displaced Persons.

By the end, Mrs. McIntyre lies paralyzed, unable to resist continued visits, with religious lectures, from Father Flynn. For many critics, this is the happy ending, a "new beginning" (O'Gorman 185), in that the priest is able to use "coercion" (Bacon 81) on a woman who has previously possessed "a violent warring attitude no different from Hitler's" (Lake 46) to "potentially" receive her into the Church at last (Sykes 161). I am less hopeful. Will Mrs. McIntyre undergo purgatorial purification? That is not enough, for me, to expiate Father Flynn's other errors. It makes sense that there is blood on the Priest after the D. P. dies (*CW* 326).[16]

"The Displaced Person" is a story about inaction, a story filled with the paralyzed, the lifeless, the dead—from the Judge haunting his old farm, to the story's stone angels, to the dying-off peacocks, to the bodies of Holocaust victims, to Mr. Shortley playing dead for his wife. Sometimes paralysis may be good. Surely it is good to think about death, and who more than O'Connor teaches us about the value of facing the approach of death? Perhaps we should consider Catholicism a positively paralyzed religion in this story—in that it has not changed for centuries. Mrs. McIntyre's paralysis could be considered good in that it may have been part of an unconscious plan to save herself, and her paralyzed position at the end may allow the tractor that is Father Flynn to run her down in a good sense. But when the priest—as well as the Church and the nation he represents—neglects those he should serve, it is generally, in O'Connor's eye, a crime, part of a larger pattern of parental neglect that O'Connor treated throughout her career.

To what extent did Flannery O'Connor have personal experience of

---

[16] I thank Robert Donahoo for pointing out this symbolism.

crime? She could easily make comments in letters about identifying with Rufus Johnson or with The Misfit, perhaps in reaction to her anger over her lupus, as Susanna Gilbert argues, and Josephine Hendin concludes, "Flannery O'Connor became more and more the pure poet of the Misfit, the damaged daughter, the psychic cripple—of all those who are martyred by silent fury and redeemed through violence" (155). Perhaps it is significant that O'Connor could identify with her mistreated characters; she did agree that in her famous self-portrait, she "looks like…Mary Pitts" (10 Nov. 1957, *HB* 252). However, I am inclined to believe that O'Connor's experience of crime was almost entirely imaginative. While O'Connor may have had a mother who would hold up as a role model a classmate like Mary Virginia Harrison,[17] and while one can find other women in Milledgeville whom Regina treated well, we should not reduce Flannery O'Connor to a victim of neglect as we appreciate her imaginative understanding of crimes both obvious and subtle. Sally Fitzgerald quotes from a journal that O'Connor kept when she was seventeen, about how she (at age fifteen) and her mother felt when O'Connor's father died: "The reality of death has come upon us and a consciousness of the power of God has broken our complacency like a bullet in the side" (qtd. in Fitzgerald, "Rooms" 17). Here she tries to accept her sense of herself as victim, and one should note that she also sees her mother as a victim here. Anne Reuman inclines more than I do toward the view that O'Connor constantly expressed through fiction her anger toward her mother. When it comes to O'Connor's experiencing the trauma of the neglect of children, O'Connor again used her ability to imagine herself into the lives of others. In a touching letter to Betty Hester (5 Oct. 1957, *HB* 244), O'Connor writes about her experience with neglect, and one can see her sympathetic response to orphaned children who suffer neglect in ways she never did. O'Connor talks about visiting St. Mary's Home in Savannah in order "to visit the Sisters or some orphan distant-cousins; also probably as a salutary lesson. 'See what you have to be thankful for. Suppose you were, etc.'—a lesson my imagination played on exhaustively." The orphanage was adequate in that "…there was doubtless plenty of love…"; the problem is that the love "was

---

[17] I thank Robert J. Wilson III for directing me to a research paper on Mary Virginia Harrison by Elizabeth Stephens, one of Wilson's students at Georgia College in a course on local history.

official, and you wouldn't have got yours from your own God-given source. Anyway, to me it was the ultimate horror." O'Connor concludes the paragraph by writing, "Anyway, I have been at least an Imaginary Orphan and that was probably my first view of hell. Children know by instinct that hell is an absence of love, and they can pick out theirs without missing."

WORKS CITED

Babinec, Lisa. "Cyclical Patterns of Domination and Manipulation in Flannery O'Connor's Mother-Daughter Relationships." *The Flannery O'Connor Bulletin*, vol. 19, 1990, pp. 9–29.

Bacon, Jon Lance. *Flannery O'Connor and Cold War Culture*. New York, Cambridge University Press, 1993. Cambridge Studies in American Literature and Culture 72.

Beringer, Cindy. "'I Have Not Wallowed': Flannery O'Connor's Working Mothers." *Southern Mothers: Fact and Fictions in Southern Women's Writing*, edited by Nagueyalti Warren and Sally Wolff. Baton Rouge, Louisiana State University Press, 1999, pp. 124–41.

Brooks, Cleanth, Jr., and Robert Penn Warren. "Interpretation" [on "Araby"]. *Understanding Fiction*, 1st ed., New York, Appleton-Century-Crofts, 1943, pp. 420–24.

Capote, Truman. *In Cold Blood: A True Account of a Multiple Murder and Its Consequences*. New York, Random, 1965.

Coles, Robert. *Flannery O'Connor's South*. Baton Rouge, Louisiana State University Press, 1980.

Ciuba, Gary M. *Desire, Violence, and Divinity in Modern Southern Fiction: Katherine Anne Porter, Flannery O'Connor, Cormac McCarthy, Walker Percy*. Baton Rouge, Louisiana State University Press, 2007. Southern Literary Studies.

Driggers, Stephen G., and Robert J. Dunn, with Sarah Gordon. *The Manuscripts of Flannery O'Connor at Georgia College*. Athens, University of Georgia Press, 1989.

Faulknor, Michael. Consultations with Marshall Bruce Gentry via e-mail and annotations. Apr. 2019, Nov. 2019, Dec. 2020.

Fitzgerald, Sally. "The Penetration of Experience: Permutations in the Fiction of Flannery O'Connor." Bunting Institute Colloquium, Radcliffe College, 7 May 1980. A working paper, 21 pp. of typescript, in the O'Connor Collection at Georgia College.

———. "Rooms with a View." *The Flannery O'Connor Bulletin*, vol. 10, 1980, pp. 5–28.

Fowler, Doreen. "Flannery O'Connor's Productive Violence." *Arizona Quarterly: A Journal of American Literature, Culture, and Theory*, vol. 67, no. 2, 2011, pp. 127–54.

Garson, Helen S. "Cold Comfort: Parents and Children in the Work of Flannery O'Connor." *Realist of Distances: Flannery O'Connor Revisited*, edited by Karl-Heinz Westarp and Jan Nordby Gretlund. Aarhus, Den., Aarhus University Press, 1987, pp. 113–22.

Gentry, Marshall Bruce. "The Hand of the Writer in 'The Comforts of Home.'" *The Flannery O'Connor Bulletin*, vol. 20, 1991, pp. 61–72.

———. "He Would Have Been a Good Man: Compassion and Meanness in Truman Capote and Flannery O'Connor." *Flannery O'Connor's Radical Reality*, edited by Jan Nordby Gretlund and Karl-Heinz Westarp. Columbia, University of South Carolina Press, 2006, pp. 42–55.

Giannone, Richard. *Flannery O'Connor, Hermit Novelist*. Chicago, University of Illinois Press, 2000.
Gilbert, Susanna. "'Blood Don't Lie': The Diseased Family in Flannery O'Connor's *Everything That Rises Must Converge*." *Literature and Medicine*, vol. 18, no. 1, 1999, pp. 114–31. *ProQuest Research Library*, accessed 31 July 2012.
Gordon, Ira J. *Human Development: From Birth Through Adolescence*. New York, Harper, 1962.
Gordon, Sarah. *Flannery O'Connor: The Obedient Imagination*. Athens, University of Georgia Press, 2000.
Gossett, Louise Y. *Violence in Recent Southern Fiction*. Durham, NC, Duke University Press, 1965.
Hendin, Josephine. *Vulnerable People: A View of American Fiction Since 1945*. New York, Oxford University Press, 1978.
Hewitt, Avis, and Robert Donahoo, editors. *Flannery O'Connor in the Age of Terrorism: Essays on Violence and Grace*. Knoxville, University of Tennessee Press, 2010.
Joyce, James. "The Sisters." *Dubliners*, New York, Modern Library, 1926, pp. 7–19. O'Connor's copy of *Dubliners* is at Georgia College.
Kahane, Claire. "The Re-Vision of Rage: Flannery O'Connor and Me." *The Massachusetts Review*, vol. 46, 2005, pp. 439–61.
Keetley, Dawn. "'I forget what I done': Repressed Anger and Violent Fantasy in 'A Good Man Is Hard to Find.'" *"On the subject of the feminist business": Re-Reading Flannery O'Connor*, edited by Teresa Caruso. New York, Peter Lang, 2004, pp. 74–93.
Kinney, Arthur F. *Flannery O'Connor's Library: Resources of Being*. Athens, University of Georgia Press, 1985.
Knapp, Bettina L. "Flannery O'Connor's 'Everything That Rises Must Converge': Sacrifice, a Castration." *Women in Twentieth-Century Literature: A Jungian View*. University Park, Pennsylvania State University Press, 1987, pp. 87–101.
Lake, Christina Bieber. *The Incarnational Art of Flannery O'Connor*. Macon, Mercer University Press, 2005.
Lebeck, Sherry Lynn. *Paradise Lost and Paradise Regained: An Object Relations Analysis of Two Flannery O'Connor Mother-Child Dyads*. 1999. San Francisco School of Psychology, PhD dissertation. N.p., Dissertation.com, 2000.
Maxwell, Allen. Letters to "Mr. Flannery O'Connor." 25 June 1946 and 16 July 1946. Flannery O'Connor Collection, Special Collections. Georgia College Library and Instructional Technology Center, Milledgeville.
O'Connor, Flannery. "The Coat." *DoubleTake*, vol. 2, no. 3, 1996, pp. 38–41.
———. "The Displaced Person." *Sewanee Review*, vol. 62, 1954, pp. 634–54. Original published version.
———. *Flannery O'Connor: Collected Works*, edited by Sally Fitzgerald. New York, Library of America, 1988.
———. *The Habit of Being: Letters*, edited by Sally Fitzgerald. New York. Farrar, 1979.
———. *Mystery and Manners: Occasional Prose*, edited by Sally Fitzgerald and Robert Fitzgerald. New York, Farrar, 1969.
———. Unpublished manuscripts. Flannery O'Connor Collection, Special Collections, Georgia College Library and Instructional Technology Center, Milledgeville.
O'Gorman, Farrell. *Peculiar Crossroads: Flannery O'Connor, Walker Percy, and Catholic Vision in Postwar Southern Fiction*. Baton Rouge, Louisiana State UP, 2004.

Presley, Susan F. "Through the Eyes of Boys 'Going Bad': Childhood in Flannery O'Connor's Fiction." 2008. Georgia College, MA thesis.
Prown, Katherine Hemple. *Revising Flannery O'Connor: Southern Literary Culture and the Problem of Female Authorship.* Charlottesville, University Press of Virginia, 2001.
Raymond, Claire. *Witnessing Sadism in Texts of the American South: Women, Specularity, and the Poetics of Subjectivity.* Burlington, VT, Ashgate, 2014.
Reuman, Ann E. "Revolting Fictions: Flannery O'Connor's Letter to Her Mother." *Papers on Language and Literature,* vol. 29, no. 2, 1993, pp. 197–214.
Robinson, Gabrielle Scott. "Irish Joyce and Southern O'Connor." *The Flannery O'Connor Bulletin,* vol. 5, 1976, pp. 82–97.
Schneiderman, Leo. *The Literary Mind: Portraits in Pain and Creativity.* New York, Insight, 1988.
Srigley, Susan, editor. *Dark Faith: New Essays on Flannery O'Connor's* The Violent Bear It Away. Notre Dame, IN, University of Notre Dame Press, 2012.
Stephens, Elizabeth. "Mary Virginia Harrison Russell." Research paper for History 4010, Fall 2005 course on Local History, Georgia College, taught by Robert J. Wilson III. The research paper is on file in Special Collections in the Georgia College Library.
Sykes, John D., Jr. *Flannery O'Connor, Walker Percy, and the Aesthetic of Revelation.* Columbia, University of Missouri Press, 2007.
Tate, J. O. "A Good Source Is Not So Hard to Find." *The Flannery O'Connor Bulletin,* vol. 9, 1980, pp. 98–103. The final page of this article reprints from the 25 Oct. 1952 issue of the Atlanta *Constitution* a photograph of James Francis Hill, a likely basis for The Misfit.
Westling, Louise. "Fathers and Daughters in Welty and O'Connor." *The Female Tradition in Southern Literature,* edited by Carol S. Manning. Urbana, University of Illinois Press, 1993, pp. 110–24.
Williamson, Samuel H. "Seven Ways to Compute the Relative Value of a U.S. Dollar Amount, 1790 to Present." *MeasuringWorth,* accessed Apr. 2019.
Wray, Virginia. "Flannery O'Connor's Long Apprenticeship: Honing the Habits of Irony and Satire." *Antigonish Review* New Series, no. 99, 1994, pp. 139–49.

Reconsidering Astor and Sulk in Flannery O'Connor's "The Displaced Person"

with Michael Faulknor

For a long time I've been interested in how subtly and how thoroughly O'Connor dramatizes neglect, often in the form of failing to care for family members, especially children. This essay reflects my work to revise and expand on my article "Criminal Neglect in Flannery O'Connor's Fiction," which discusses a number of O'Connor's works in which neglect takes the form of a parent's choice of what I call a substitute child. That article concludes with an argument that O'Connor could convict of neglect even a character almost always treated as a moral exemplar: the priest, Father Flynn, in "The Displaced Person." "Criminal Neglect" might make one wonder whether there are any respectable characters in "The Displaced Person." In this essay, then, with inspiration from my former graduate student Michael Faulknor, I will examine the African-American characters in the story, Astor and Sulk, arguing that they are much more admirable than most critics claim. Insofar as "The Displaced Person" calls for parental figures to treat better their figurative children, Astor and Sulk, despite their ages, are treated as the characters most deserving of better treatment by figurative parents.

Perhaps at this point it would be useful for me to summarize, briefly and sneakily, "The Displaced Person." It's a story where many plans go unfollowed. After WWII, farm owner Mrs. McIntyre brings a family of Displaced Persons from Poland to her dairy farm. The White workers on the farm, Mr. and Mrs. Shortley, soon feel threatened, because Mr. Guizac (the D. P.) is a good worker. Although Guizac catches one of the African-American workers, Sulk, stealing a turkey, Guizac comes up with a plan to bring his cousin from a D. P. camp to the US by having Sulk contribute toward the expenses. Guizac tells Sulk the cousin will marry Sulk. The problems are that interracial marriage is illegal (as it would be throughout O'Connor's life) and that Guizac is taking over a sixth of Sulk's salary. Mrs. McIntyre, ignorant of the marriage plan, decides she is going to fire Mr. Shortley so she can pay Guizac better. When Mrs. Shortley finds out her husband is to be fired, she insists her family leave the farm immediately. In the rush, Mrs. Shortley gives herself a fatal stroke. That's the end of Part One. In the rest of the story, Mrs. McIntyre realizes the marriage negotiation is going on. When Mr. Shortley returns and asks to resume his old job, she agrees, and she says that she plans to fire Guizac. Mrs. McIntyre finds she cannot take action, but one day Mr. Guizac is killed by a runaway tractor, and nobody else around, Mrs. McIntyre or Mr. Shortley or Sulk, prevents Guizac's death. The end.

My point with this summary? Notice that it is possible for me to retell this plot without mentioning two of the characters I am inclined to emphasize when I analyze the story, Father Flynn and the African-American worker Astor. The fact that one can summarize the story's main events without mentioning these characters is significant.

The answer to the question of whom I might respect or admire in this story does not seem to have that much to do with religion, because, while I think that Father Flynn and Mr. Guizac and Mrs. McIntyre and Mrs. Shortley may well all be on their way to salvation, I do not think the story insists that we approve of their behavior. My strongest inclination is to defend Astor, a character who is usually dismissed or criticized, but whom I consider a serious candidate for the role of the story's main hero. While his name may seem a laughably ironic reference to the powerful and wealthy Astor family of long ago and far away, I take the name Astor to be a hint that the O'Connor character is, at least potentially, more powerful than he seems.

Sometimes O'Connor critics have treated Astor as part of the problem on Mrs. McIntyre's farm. Astor is often simply dismissed as insignificant. Suzanne Morrow Paulson says that Astor is merely a sort of stand-in for Mrs. Shortley after Mrs. McIntyre loses the Shortley family, that Astor "only serves to reflect [Mrs. McIntyre's] thoughts" (67). Carter Martin labels Astor "a primitive" (93), comparable to the mentally disabled Bishop of *The Violent Bear It Away* and Lucynell of "The Life You Save May Be Your Own." There have been a very few critics who have taken a more positive view of Astor. Daniel Lesgoirres and Linda Munk have discussed Astor as representing a positive religious value. Janet Egleson Dunleavy says that Astor thinks about the situation on the farm more perceptively than Mrs. Shortley does (199). Robert Coles expresses a similar sentiment (22), though he also concedes that the word "shiftless" is applicable to Astor (28). John Roos praises Astor as being "associated with light" and "associated with speech" (292), though Roos finds Father Flynn equally worthy of praise. My goal now is to build on these positive statements about Astor and defend him thoroughly against attack.

One possible charge against Astor is that he is an inefficient worker. I have two basic responses to this charge. First, it is to be expected that an old man with poor eyesight, one who is offered constant insult and poor wages, should not be expected to break any records as a worker. My other—and more serious—response is that we *do* see Astor at work, as when we are told that he "stopped work" (*CW* 285) to witness the arrival of the Guizacs. We witness his slow but steady cleaning of a barn (305), and Mrs. McIntyre notices the moment when there is a pause to the sound of "shoveling" done by Astor and Sulk (323). As the Shortleys leave at the end of Part 1, we see Astor walking toward the farm at approximately 4 a.m., on time to help with the early morning milking (304). The Judge and Mrs. Shortley seem to agree that Astor does his best (299), and even Mrs. McIntyre, when she decides to fire Mr. Shortley rather than Astor and Sulk, complains that Blacks "lie and steal" (302), not that Astor and Sulk fail to work.

There might be a reason to complain about Astor and Sulk's running a still on the farm, but this is a minor fault, and Robert Donahoo has made very clear that in *The Violent Bear It Away*, which O'Connor was composing while she was composing "The Displaced Person," moonshine is a pathway to enlightenment. We should blame Astor for his still no more than we blame Old Tarwater for his still. There might also be a complaint based on the fact that, when Mrs. McIntyre is about to have her grand confrontation with Mr. Guizac over his plan to marry his cousin to Sulk, we are told that Mr. Guizac is alone because "…the Negro had not arrived" for work (*CW* 313). But I believe this reference to lateness probably refers to Sulk, who is shown assisting Mr. Guizac at other points.

To my mind, the most significant charge against Astor as a worker comes from his being "pleased to see Mr. Shortley back" toward the end of the story, because Mr. Shortley expected less work from Blacks (*CW* 319). One might reply, as Robert Coles has, that a reluctance to work hard is "a…pitiable but necessary safety valve for people who get precious little for anything they do, no matter how strenuous" (28). Perhaps a better defense of Astor comes out of thinking about what it is like to work with Mr. Guizac. When Sulk is working with the Displaced Person, as Mrs. McIntyre watches, Mr. Guizac "pushed the colored boy out of the way and attached the wagon to the cutter himself, gesticulating with a bright angry face when he wanted the hammer or the screwdriver. Nothing was done quick enough to suit him. The Negroes made him nervous" (*CW* 293; emphasis added). Note the shift from singular to plural here, from talk about Sulk to a conclusion about "The Negroes." It seems that the story's supposed Christ figure might be attributing to Astor any fault he imagines in Sulk. Why would Astor enjoy working with Guizac if anger is expressed over even a simple request for a tool?

In spite of Astor's reasons not to want to work with Mr. Guizac, I think we can conclude that Astor is generally nice to him. When the Displaced Persons arrive on the farm, Astor shakes hands with Mr. Guizac (*CW* 298). And, as John Roos points out (283), Astor suggests to Mrs. Shortley that the Guizacs should be able to find, and have already found, a home on the farm: they are not forever displaced, because "If they here, they somewhere" (*CW* 290), a sentiment that Sulk seconds. When Mrs. Shortley presents Mr. Guizac as a malevolent force that will displace the Blacks, Astor attempts to defuse Sulk's tension over her comments (297), and even when Astor suggests to Mrs. McIntyre that something is going on between Sulk and Mr. Guizac, Astor does not say that Mr. Guizac is doing something wrong, just that he is different (307).

Of course, if one wants to charge that Astor is not good enough to Mr. Guizac, a place to start the case against Astor is to say that he tells Mrs. Shortley about the deal between Guizac and Sulk (*CW* 299). Jan Nordby Gretlund makes a most challenging critique of Astor, I believe, by saying "It is hard to believe that he would not have put a quick end to Sulk's plans" (204). Although Mrs. Shortley never gets around to telling on Mr. Guizac, surely Astor thinks she will put an end to the scheme to marry Sulk to Mr. Guizac's cousin. I propose that Astor's expectation is a reasonable one. My defense of Astor's behavior here is that he is being very, very careful, for which I cannot blame him. As Robert Coles has pointed out, it must have amazed Astor to see the special treatment Mr. Guizac received on his arrival (15). I also believe that Astor's primary motivation is probably to protect Sulk, who is, after all, having some of his wages—$3 each week (*CW* 311)—taken from him by Mr. Guizac. If one needs more reassurance that Astor is not out to get Mr. Guizac, recall that Astor is nowhere to be found when Mr. Guizac is murdered.

And as Michael Faulknor reminds me, Astor never criticizes Guizac ("Beyond" 6).

There is much to be said on Astor's behalf in relation to how he deals with the White women on the farm. He consistently deflects Mrs. Shortley's assaults, but he does pay careful attention to what she says, especially when she reports on Mrs. McIntyre's opinions of him (*CW* 290). When it comes to how Astor responds to Mrs. McIntyre, I cannot claim that his strategies succeed, but I think he does the best he can and that he attempts to lead Mrs. McIntyre in a good direction. He tries to laugh off her racist insults (290), and he tries to offer her corrective suggestions about some of her classist (307) and racist (306) assumptions. He does have some success, as when Mrs. McIntyre "caught exactly what he meant her to catch in his tone" when he says, "…me and you…is still here" (*CW* 305). Other times, in a "veiled" and "polite" manner, he offers Mrs. McIntyre advice, and—far from being overly docile—he pushes her so far that, as he is pretending to talk to himself, Mrs. McIntyre feels so effectively challenged that "…she had got up suddenly and slammed the window down so hard that he had fallen backwards off his feet" (308). His careful attempts to improve her behavior even extend to his trying to show her that she should retain the farm's peacocks (308–09). When Mrs. McIntyre complains that she has struggled with "the constant drain of a tribe of moody unpredictable Negroes" (309), her complaint can be interpreted as unintended praise. Why shouldn't Astor be moody, and why shouldn't he let it show? I say that it is a good thing that Astor has managed to give Mrs. McIntyre some surprises over the years.

I suppose that one reason Astor is not generally considered a hero is that he almost disappears from the story before he disappears from the farm. If he offers grace, it is grace resisted. What do we expect him to do at the end—hold Mrs. McIntyre's hand? While George A. Kilcourse has praised Astor's "wisdom" (198), Kilcourse also charges Astor with abandoning Mrs. McIntyre at the end of the story (206). I think it is a mistake to expect Astor to befriend at the end his White boss. The final line we have to explain Astor's disappearance from the farm suggests his commitment to two of the story's values: community and work. We are told that "The old man Astor could not work without company" (*CW* 316). John Roos similarly claims that Astor needs "friendly speech" (294). He needs Sulk, but Sulk leaves.

Perhaps we want Astor to struggle for more thorough change. To this request I would reply that we do at least see a hint that Astor could endorse a revolutionary change, one expressed, of course, in a modest fashion. Think about Astor's quoting to Mrs. McIntyre some of the sentiments of the Judge, the husband that she still respects: "The old Negro had known the Judge. 'Judge say he long for the day when he be too poor to pay [an n-word] to work,' he said. 'Say when that day come, the world be back on its feet'" (*CW* 326). The strategy here could be considered very clever, balancing an acceptance of an insult (in the form of the n-word) with a call for the end to a system based on bosses' paying wages. (I'll note again that John Roos agrees with this reading [293].) Astor's strategy does not work, I should probably admit again, but I still believe he receives O'Connor's endorsement. Michael Faulknor suggests that Astor is at his best with his straightforward statement to Mrs. McIntyre that "Black and white…is the same" (*CW* 236; Faulknor, "Beyond" 5), and Faulknor also points out that Astor's use of the Judge's saying turns out to be correct, if we believe that the world is indeed back on its feet at the end when Mrs. McIntyre is no longer paying Astor and Sulk to work on her farm.

I am going to end this section the way I tell my students to end their papers, with a bit about what difference the argument makes. So what if Astor's nice? I have two main answers. First, I think we tend to assume that O'Connor accepted many of the racist attitudes and stereotypes of her time. O'Connor herself, I should mention, does little to defend the person who was the basis for Astor. In *The Habit of Being*, a letter written only a year after "The Displaced Person" was collected in *A Good Man Is Hard to Find and Other Stories*, O'Connor herself suggests that Astor *is* rather foolish: "The two colored people in 'The Displaced Person' are on the farm now. The old man is 84 but vertical or more or less so. He doesn't see too good and the other day he fertilized some of my mother's bulbs with worm medicine for the calves. I can only see them from the outside" (19 May, 1956, *HB* 159). In another, later letter, from 1963, O'Connor says she is wary about having someone adapt her writing into a play that would result in the sort of thing this article does: "turning one of my colored idiots into a hero" (9 Nov. 1963, *HB* 547). One might also note here that Brad Gooch, who says Astor is based on a farm worker at Andalusia named Henry, finds the character Astor unpleasantly comparable to Stepin Fetchit (243). Nevertheless, I think that O'Connor, in her fiction, was inclined to be very critical of racism, leading the reader toward conclusions that O'Connor as a reader of her own fiction was sometimes inclined to resist. Perhaps the problem is that the story tricks us into seeing Astor the way characters within the story see him. Sarah Gordon discusses the passage in which Mrs. McIntyre views Astor as if sliced, by the sun, into thirds (*CW* 305), and Gordon says that the passage shows that the boss "is incapable of seeing the whole man" (188). I'm trying here to propose that the work asks us to see the whole man, even if the author herself sometimes did not do so. In a letter dated 3 Nov. 1963, years after "The Displaced Person," O'Connor gives a suggestion of the sort of complexity she could appreciate in black workers at Andalusia: "...they lie like artists" (*GT* 287).

My second way to explain significance has to do with action. As I said earlier, this story basically condemns paralysis and inaction. Another side to my understanding of the story is that while one should work for change, one should also, like Astor, strive only for as much as one can get away with. In O'Connor studies, we tend to love to talk about O'Connor as having strong, even radical beliefs, but it is possible to read "The Displaced Person" as supporting moderation. Most of the criticism that has said something on behalf of Astor has come at the story from a theological perspective, though John Roos, with whom I most nearly agree, is a political science professor. I want to add that Astor's attitude, of trying to promote reform slowly and carefully, is also valid from a very practical, very secular, angle. I'll end with a reminder to you, a quotation you probably know from O'Connor herself, one that I think expresses part of her story's meaning: "The uneducated Southern Negro is not the clown he's made out to be. He's a man of very elaborate manners and great formality which he uses superbly for his own protection and to insure his own privacy" (*Conversations* 104).

My innocent graduate student Michael Faulknor found himself getting involved in this project when he took my course in Spring 2018 on how to be a graduate student in English. I tried to keep my mouth shut as Faulknor wrote a research paper on Astor and Sulk. I got lucky as my student taught me some things, especially about Sulk. Faulknor began his paper by taking on Ralph Wood, who says "Astor and Sulk, the two good-for-nothing farmhands...are so scandalized by the excellence that Mr. Guizac brings to Mrs. McIntyre's farm that they conspire with her and her white-trash tenants to get rid of him" (Wood 142; Faulknor, "Beyond" 1). Faulknor makes a good case that neither of the Black workers would choose to enter into a conspiracy with Whites.

What else has Faulknor made me reconsider? Perhaps when Sulk is caught stealing the turkey, it is a step in a moral awakening for him

(Faulknor, Consultations). Perhaps when Sulk starts giving money to Mr. Guizac, his motive is genuinely charitable (Faulknor, "Beyond" 8). Notice, as Faulknor does, that when Mrs. McIntyre tells Sulk she will get his money back from Mr. Guizac and return the money to Sulk (*CW* 244), Sulk does not thank her. When Mrs. McIntyre asked Sulk what he is doing with a photo of the cousin, he did not say "I'm contributing to saving her." Making no attempt to hide the photo (which he might do if he believed his behavior was wrong), he says, "She going to mah me" (*CW* 311). Why would he say that when he also says, "I don't reckon she goin to come nohow" (311)? A couple of possibilities occur to me. O'Connor characters say kooky things at crucial moments; I have the same explanation for Mrs. McIntyre's statement that "Christ was just another D. P." (320). Or more seriously, I'd say Sulk is simply endorsing, safely, what Mr. Guizac has told him. Or perhaps Sulk feels that he must avoid admitting to his charity, since to do so might point out the clear failure of charity on the part of Mrs. McIntyre. Sulk may be learning what I think Astor knows, that one can only get away with so much. (Faulknor is also inclined to ask about the extent to which Mr. Guizac may intentionally be trying to teach Sulk such a lesson.)

A final point in Faulknor's defense of Sulk has to do with the murder scene. Sulk is present, and he does not save Guizac. How shall we defend Sulk as we read these words?:

> She heard the brake on the large tractor slip and, looking up, she saw it move forward, calculating its own path. Later she remembered that she had seen the Negro jump silently out of the way as if a spring in the earth had released him and that she had seen Mr. Shortley turn his head with incredible slowness and stare silently over his shoulder and that she had started to shout to the Displaced Person but that she had not. She had felt her eyes and Mr. Shortley's eyes and the Negro's eyes come together in one look that froze them in collusion forever, and she had heard the little noise the Pole made as the tractor wheel broke his backbone. The two men ran forward to help and she fainted. (*CW* 325–26)

Notice that the passage is from Mrs. McIntyre's point of view, and that she would wish to imagine that guilt is to be widely shared. Notice also that Sulk, and even Shortley, "ran forward to help" Guizac, while she fails to do so. It's hard to see Sulk as thoroughly heroic here, but to be heroic would require him to contradict what he could easily see as the intentions of his White female boss and his White male supervisor. Perhaps all we can expect of Sulk here is self-preservation. I am inclined to recall that as Sulk escapes, it is, to Mrs. McIntyre, "as if a spring in the earth had released him." Perhaps even Mrs. McIntyre realizes that the calamity is going to have the indirect effect of freeing Sulk from the tangled web of collusion that the farm has always been.

A final thought: In my position as a leader of O'Connor Studies at Georgia College, I regularly meet with visitors, including lots of school groups, and I am regularly asked about the level to which O'Connor was racist. I was once asked such a question while standing in Andalusia's Hill House, where some Black workers lived, and I could not recall any evidence that O'Connor ever entered the Hill House. My general answer about O'Connor's racism is that she was less racist than most White people of her time, and more racist than she realized, and that she knew racism was a personal problem—knew it was one of her sins—and then I insist that O'Connor's fiction is always anti-racist. My thesis here about "The Displaced Person" is consistent with that stance. At the same time, I would agree that O'Connor makes treating Astor and Sulk positively an easier job for herself by remaining somewhat distant from them. She sees Astor and Sulk "from the outside," even as she tries to get a glimpse of a "whole man." O'Connor never narrates from the point of view of Astor or Sulk, perhaps because she realizes her ignorance, perhaps because she fears what she might uncover. Do we ever, for example, have a hint about the sexual urges of Astor or Sulk? Does O'Connor take for granted that Sulk longs for a White woman? Or is she tricking her racist American readers into making such an assumption? Maybe both. But O'Connor stops at a point where a contemporary writer might charge, or blunder, right on in. I would suggest that O'Connor, in maintaining a respectful distance from Astor and Sulk, is practicing what we now sometimes call political correctness, and I also think O'Connor was doing the best she could.

WORKS CITED

Coles, Robert. *Flannery O'Connor's South*. Baton Rouge, Louisiana State University Press, 1980.

Donahoo, Robert. "Making Moonshine: O'Connor's Use of Regional Culture in *The Violent Bear It Away*." *Flannery O'Connor Review*, vol. 16, 2018, pp. 1–14.

Dunleavy, Janet Egleson. "A Particular History: Black and White in Flannery O'Connor's Short Fiction." *Critical Essays on Flannery O'Connor*, edited by Melvin J. Friedman and Beverly Lyon Clark. Boston, Hall, 1985, pp. 186–202.

Faulknor, Michael. "Beyond Bystanders: Examining Astor and Sulk in 'The Displaced Person.'" Spring 2018. Research Methods, Georgia College, student paper.
_____. Consultations with Marshall Bruce Gentry via e-mail and annotations. Apr. 2019, Nov. 2019, Dec. 2020.
Gentry, Marshall Bruce. "Criminal Neglect in Flannery O'Connor's Fiction." *The Centrality of Crime Fiction in American Literary Culture*, edited by Alfred Bendixen and Olivia Carr Edenfield. New York, Routledge, 2017, pp. 185–206. Routledge Interdisciplinary Perspectives on Literature.
Gooch, Brad. *Flannery: A Life of Flannery O'Connor*. New York, Little, 2009.
Gordon, Sarah. *Flannery O'Connor: The Obedient Imagination*. Athens, University of Georgia Press, 2000.
Gretlund, Jan Nordby. "The Side of the Road: Flannery O'Connor's Social Sensibility." *Realist of Distances: Flannery O'Connor Revisited*, edited by Karl-Heinz Westarp and Jan Nordby Gretlund. Aarhus, Den., Aarhus University Press, 1987, pp. 197–207.
Kilcourse, George A., Jr. *Flannery O'Connor's Religious Imagination: A World with Everything Off Balance*. New York, Paulist, 2001.
Lesgoirres, Daniel. "'The Displaced Person' ou 'Le Christ Recrucifé.'" *Delta*, vol. 2, Mar. 1976, pp. 75–87.
Martin, Carter W. *The True Country: Themes in the Fiction of Flannery O'Connor*. Nashville, Vanderbilt University Press, 1969.
Munk, Linda. "Understanding Understatement: Biblical Typology and 'The Displaced Person.'" *Journal of Literature and Theology*, vol. 2, no. 2, 1988, pp. 237–53.
O'Connor, Flannery. *Conversations with Flannery O'Connor*, edited by Rosemary M. Magee. Jackson, University Press of Mississippi, 1987.
_____. *Flannery O'Connor: Collected Works*, edited by Sally Fitzgerald. New York, Library of America, 1988. "The Displaced Person" is on pp. 285–327.
_____. *The Habit of Being: Letters*, edited by Sally Fitzgerald. New York, Farrar, 1979.
_____. Unpublished manuscripts. Flannery O'Connor Collection, Special Collections, Georgia College Library and Instructional Technology Center, Milledgeville.
O'Connor, Flannery, et al. *Good Things out of Nazareth: The Uncollected Letters of Flannery O'Connor and Friends*, edited by Benjamin B. Alexander. New York, Convergent-Random, 2019.
Paulson, Suzanne Morrow. *Flannery O'Connor: A Study of the Short Fiction*. Boston, Twayne-Hall, 1988.
Roos, John. "Flannery O'Connor and Political Community in 'The Displaced Person.'" *A Political Companion to Flannery O'Connor*, edited by Henry T. Edmondson III. Lexington, University Press of Kentucky, 2017, pp. 278–302.
Wood, Ralph C. *Flannery O'Connor and the Christ-Haunted South*. Grand Rapids, MI, Eerdmans, 2004.

O'Connor as Miscegenationist

A variety of positions on the topic of O'Connor and race have been presented reasonably. I can agree with Timothy P. Caron that O'Connor's southern religiosity ironically led her into problems on the subject of race, or with Julie Armstrong's Whiteness-studies approach to O'Connor's works, in which Armstrong finds some stereotyping. Angela Alaimo O'Donnell's book-length study of race and O'Connor reasonably says, "Though O'Connor's art often constitutes a victory over her own prejudices, that victory is a partial one" (8). I also agree with Margaret Earley Whitt when she suggests that O'Connor's racial views became increasingly enlightened, and with Ralph C. Wood on the subject of race when he says that whatever O'Connor's personal struggles with racial issues, her Catholicism guided her fiction toward an enlightened stance. I appreciate Wood's pointing out "the anthropologists' claim that everyone is at least the forty-fifth cousin of everyone else" (93). Perhaps we can all agree that O'Connor struggled with race, that she was less enlightened that she should have been, and that she was more enlightened than a lot of people.

In this reconsideration of O'Connor and race, I intend to avoid what some justifiably consider an unfair shortcut—references to O'Connor's letters, essays, and interviews. Instead I will focus on the fiction. My thesis, which I think is original, is that Flannery O'Connor, a "White" writer of Irish ethnicity, writes as a miscegenationist,[1] that she advocates race-mixing more than she would be comfortable acknowledg-

---

[1] The title of this essay, which may appear outlandish, uses a word that comes from a Civil War hoax: a couple of journalists apparently tried to sabotage Abraham Lincoln's re-election in 1864 by trying to trick him (and other Republicans) into endorsing their pamphlet which created the term "miscegenation" and praised race-mixing as a panacea. See "Miscegenation, a Story" and *Miscegenation: The Theory*, which was apparently written by Croly and Wakeman.

ing. For those who find my claim as startling as I have at times—after all, the Supreme Court did not throw out state laws against miscegenation until after O'Connor's death—let me review three sources of encouragement.

One is a book I once attempted to gain permission to publish: Clif Boyer, formerly of the Georgia College Library, prepared a double-columned, single-spaced index—of well over two-hundred pages—to O'Connor's *The Complete Stories*. While waiting for permission for Boyer to quote in this index virtually every word of *The Complete Stories*, I would flip through the index from time to time, and I remain impressed by O'Connor's color palette, her use of complex colors, compound or hyphenated colors such as, of course, rat-colored (*CS* 83), but also chocolate purple (88), dead-silver (294), dried yellow (93), fox-colored (314), freezing-blue (289), gold sawdust (242), gray-purple (241), "a green that was almost black or a black that was almost green" (99), green-gold (164), mole-colored (96), monkey white (61), polluted lemon yellow (85), sticky-looking brown (277), sweet-potato-colored (169), toast-colored (285), tobacco-colored (218). Of course one might say that O'Connor had a sharp eye for shades of color because she was a painter and a visual writer. But did she learn to notice and enjoy colors mixed and in flux because she was a writer, or was she a good writer because she was inclined to mix colors, to notice the mixing of color all around her? I assume O'Connor noticed a mistake constantly being made—the separating into mere black and white of a wide range of colors, racial and otherwise. (I am emphasizing Black-White race-mixing here, though it is also true of course that O'Connor notices the mixing of Native Americans with other races.) When O'Connor describes skin, she seems to enjoy noting gradations of color, mixes, changes: burnt-brown (*CS* 121), cinnamon (215), coffee (254), gray (415), purple (414), red (198), tan (255), yellowish (198). O'Connor records the ways "White" skin isn't white, the ways that changes in skin from white to other colors often mark the emotion of revelation: "White" skin in O'Connor is mottled (41) or speckled (161). Mr. McIntyre is "clay pink" (218), Mr. Cheatam "nearly the same color as the unpaved roads" (237). "White" people are given names like Ruby, Red Sam, Tanner. I particularly like the way O'Connor makes white an unnatural color in this description: Old Tarwater's "skin between the pockmarks grew pink and then purple and then white and the pockmarks appeared to jump from one spot to another" (301). And notice how many colors Julian's mother's face is in "Everything That Rises Must Converge": "her florid face" (485) becomes "an angry red" (492), then "unnaturally red" (495), and then she is "purple-faced" (495) and seems "almost gray" (495), and then Julian's mother's face is transformed into "a face he had never seen before" just before the "tide of darkness seemed to be sweeping her" away from Julian (500). It is in that final darkness that Julian and his mother converge.

Another source of encouragement for looking at O'Connor as a race-mixer is an article in which O'Connor is compared to Latino writer Richard Rodriguez. Farrell O'Gorman proposes what he (and Rodriguez) call a "brown" reading of O'Connor. O'Gorman stops just short of saying that O'Connor endorses race-mixing, apparently because for O'Connor to do that would be to take a political stand (45n11). But O'Gorman and Rodriguez agree on an erotic impulse in O'Connor's art that has something to do with relations between different races.[2] In a sense, I am proposing that, while O'Connor would sign no petition, she endorsed miscegenation in all sorts of ways, however apolitically, symbolically, fantastically. I will avoid repeating O'Gorman's readings here, but it is clear that O'Gorman and Rodriguez show us how O'Connor's Catholicism could give her interesting insights on race.

A third source of encouragement for treating O'Connor as a race-mixer is Patricia Yaeger's *Dirt and Desire*, because for Yaeger, so much of southern women's writing is about race, even—or especially—when the writing is about everydayness. There are many inspiring ideas in Yaeger's book, but most relevant here are those in which Yaeger builds on "the historical association of African Americans with earth or dirt" (37) and on the idea that "...in modern southern culture, both white and black women have been fastened to dirt—defined as its source and charged with its removal" (275). For Yaeger, race is the elephant in the living room that southerners fascinatingly try to ignore, and ignoring the topic in a certain way becomes a way to talk about the subject. While White women writers "use dirt to explore the possibilities in a fantasied self-blackening," according to Yaeger, "...black women use dirt as a means of transcendence, a way of changing the meaning of blackness altogether"

---

[2] Rodriguez says all sorts of interesting things in his book *Brown*, such as his assertions that "The future is brown..." (35); "I do not hesitate to say into a microphone what everyone knows, what no one says. *Most American blacks are not black*" (134); and "White is an impulse to remain ignorant of history" (139).

(275). I am inclined to accept the suggestion that O'Connor's references to dirt imply an indirect discussion of race.

Before I go any further with my attempt to reveal support of miscegenation in O'Connor's fiction, I should explain what I assume is going on in Flannery O'Connor's psyche. I have already noted that I find things in the fiction that would make O'Connor, generally a gradualist on the subject of civil rights, uncomfortable. How can this be? My answer has to do with how the parts of the psyche other than the conscious intellect are involved in the creation of fiction. Some literary criticism is written as if everything O'Connor ever wrote were a sort of term paper, in which everything there is intended and almost everything has its documentable source. I assume that when O'Connor writes fiction, she communicates ideas and feelings from all sorts of places in her psyche. She probably would not have become a great writer if she had not been comfortable with the idea that there are important things in her fiction of which she is completely unaware.

These assumptions about O'Connor's psyche come from watching my wife, the poet Alice Friman, as she composes poems and as she teaches. One of Alice's basic lectures as she teaches poetry and creative writing is particularly applicable to the study of O'Connor. This lecture is based on Alice's adaptation of something called the Johari Window, created back in the 1950s by Joseph Luft and Harry Ingram while researching group dynamics.[3] Here, as I understand it, is Alice's version of the Johari Window, which she uses to talk about where poetry comes from and how to tap into that great well of mystery that is the self:

> Imagine a window divided into four panes.
> The first pane conveys things about the writer that the writer knows and that others know too.
> The second pane conveys things about the writer that the writer knows but that others do not know. This one is about the writer's secrets.
> The third pane conveys things about the writer that the writer does not know but that others do know. This is about the writer's blinders.
> The fourth, and most important, pane conveys things about the writer that others do not know and that even the writer does not know.

---

[3] For one of many explanations of the Johari Window, see http://www.businessballs.com/johariwindowmodel.htm.

The creators of the Johari Window, who are not highlighting art, apparently consider it healthy to have the first pane grow more important, to increase awareness all around and reduce what is hidden. In a writing class, Alice's lecture leads to the conclusion that the course involves learning about oneself and one's classmates because in order to become a writer, one must avoid shying away from the possibility of revealing oneself. As paradoxical as it may seem, creative writing comes primarily from and through the fourth pane. One needs to be prepared to work at getting in touch with memories, desires, fears. All four kinds of communication happen in creative writing, whether one likes it or not. Artistry is a matter of coordinating and controlling (just enough) the different sorts of communication—*not* of shutting down any of them. We communicate things we do not know we are giving away. We communicate through what we hide. We communicate mystery.

So while I think O'Connor may have been aware of *some* of what I believe exists in her fiction, her full awareness is far from necessary. I also assume that some *part* of O'Connor's psyche wished to communicate another substantial portion of what I am pointing out in this essay.

My claim about miscegenation is supported in the fiction almost explicitly in a couple of places. For example, there is the explicit promotion of miscegenation by a heroic, arguably Christlike character—Mr. Guizac, the displaced person. Then there is the title "Everything That Rises Must Converge." One need not make this title a double entendre to say that the story suggests different races must and should converge. So the point for debate is really whether there is a sexual convergence involved. When Julian thinks about presenting a "suspiciously Negroid" fiancé to shock his mother (*CW* 494), are we to see such a relationship as a sign of hope for the future? Are we, on the other hand, to think that O'Connor has some sympathy for the claim pronounced by Julian's mother, that Blacks can "rise, yes, but on their own side of the fence" (488)? According to Julian's mother, for Blacks to rise on the same side of the fence as Whites is the same as intermarriage, for she almost immediately adds, "Suppose we were half white. We would certainly have mixed feelings." When Julian answers "I have mixed feelings now" (488), is O'Connor praising or blaming this mixedness about race-mixing? What are the motives behind the miscegenationist fantasizing here?

I would like now to imagine some opposition to my idea that O'Connor endorses literally the mixing of races. Perhaps the joining of races occurs at an abstract, nonphysical level. Maybe Julian's fantasy of interracial marriage is motivated so much by a desire to shock that all value disappears from his imagined miscegenation. A Bible passage cited regularly cited in discussions of various othernesses in O'Connor's works suggests that O'Connor might not literally think of race-mixing when she thinks of convergence. Here is Galatians 3:27–28:

> For as many of you as have been baptized in Christ, have put on Christ.
> There is neither Jew nor Greek: there is neither bond nor free: there is neither male nor female. For you are all one in Christ Jesus.

What does this mean practically for a writer of O'Connor's persuasions? Did Flannery O'Connor see a saved character as beyond all differences, as able or required to drop all earthy distinctions? When Mrs. Shortley asks about the Polish Guizacs, "You reckon they'll know what colors even is?" (*CW* 287), does this imagined ignorance carry a hint of the virtue of color-blindness? Sometimes I think O'Connor goes for such a treatment. There is Hazel Motes, finally an emptied, washed-out character if ever there was one: beyond gender, beyond race, beyond sect, beyond humanity. Even his clothes lose their color in the end. Or I think of Ruby Turpin, who sees finally "that even [her] virtues were being burned away" (*CW* 654). I understand why some readers might feel Ruby's vision makes her temporarily leave behind any racial characteristics; her moment of redemption might change her in a way that has nothing to do with the habits she will return to after the story ends, of being a very White lady with ongoing racial prejudices.

But back to the passage from Galatians. I think it makes more sense to say that for a color-obsessed, visual writer like O'Connor, the best way to put into fiction the notion of overcoming differences is to combine races rather than to ignore race. Instead of reading O'Connor as saying that her characters could stop being members of any race, it makes more sense to read her as saying her characters could combine colors, could experience more than one race. I think that we find this suggestion again and again in O'Connor, amazingly in spite of the fact that no O'Connor character ever explicitly states a desire to become racially mixed or to intermarry.

Now for examples: I am going to dash through a series of works here, suggestively and speculatively rather than thoroughly. Back to "The

Displaced Person": We might have doubts about whether O'Connor really endorses a marriage between Mr. Guizac's relative and the yellow-skinned farmhand Sulk. Maybe we are simply to note Sulk's generosity and Mrs. McIntyre's lack of generosity. The more interesting endorsement of miscegenation in this story, to my mind, has to do with Mrs. Shortley, who knows Mr. Guizac to be the great miscegenator, who imagines him to be promoting mixing, not only on the farm but also throughout the English language (because Polish is a dirty language and it dirties the body of English words). Mrs. Shortley does nothing to stop Guizac. Her moment of religious insight coincides with her realization that her refusal to tell Mrs. McIntyre about Mr. Guizac makes him more likely to succeed with his plan for miscegenation. Her orgasmic death scene thus suggests her own participation in Mr. Guizac's browning the world.

"Greenleaf": Once we accept Patricia Yaeger's notion that dirt (even in Georgia) is symbolically Black, Mrs. Greenleaf's religious mud-wallowing becomes a sexual union with a Black Jesus, a union the story endorses. And the Greenleaf bull, which is amazingly described as "squirrel-colored" (*CS* 253) and attributed to a Black owner—at least until Mrs. May learns the bull belongs to the Greenleaf boys—is surely by the end of the story a miscegenator who disturbs "the breeding schedule" (*CW* 504)—as well as being Christ, of course. The goring can be interpreted as a redemptive miscegenation.

Back to "Revelation": Along with this story's final image of Mrs. Turpin's burning, there are numerous suggestions that race-mixing is a bridge to heaven. "[Y]ou have to have a little of everything" (*CW* 638), Mrs. Turpin claims proudly, and there is probably some connection between this source of pride and her sense that she is always just about to become Black, a sense she has most noticeably in her dream fantasy of being offered a choice by Jesus about whether to be born Black, and in her dream of the collapse of the hierarchy of races and classes, through the muddying action suggested by the words "moiling and roiling" (636). I would also say that most of the story's talk about animals suggests a concern with race-mixing. Caring for pigs is equated by a character in the story with loving Blacks, and O'Connor uses this equation. Mrs. Turpin's insistence that her pigs are clean and upstanding ironically confirms the equation of pig and Black—or of the pig and race-mixing. And when Mrs. Turpin goes to the pigpen at the story's end, she sees shoats whose color is suggestive of some mixing: "tan with liver-colored spots"

(651). Her husband Claud's earlier descriptions of "white-face cattle" (636) and "white-faced niggers" (641)—both supposedly bred into higher status—reinforces the use of animals to talk about race. So when Mrs. Turpin asks God "How am I a hog and me both?" (652)—even though Mary Grace called her only a hog—I see Mrs. Turpin embracing a revelation of herself as mixed in all sorts of ways, including race.

Here is one more speculation: does purple in this story hint at miscegenation? Another way that Mrs. Turpin becomes non-White is through her wound. Mary Grace's attack makes Mrs. Turpin's face red at first (*CW* 646), then later a green shade of blue (648), so one might conclude that her face has a stage at least of purple. Mrs. Turpin's husband Claud, the man whose jokes link race and animal, the man whose White brains could easily be scattered over a highway with the brains of Blacks (653), is said to have a purple swelling on his leg (633) from a cow's kick, and he is kicked once again on the leg during the story (646) by Mary Grace, whose acne-blue face (635) turns "almost purple" with anger just before she begins her attack (644). What I am speculating my way toward is that Mr. and Mrs. Turpin as purple parents figuratively give birth to purple Mary Grace—or perhaps that Mary Grace and Mr. Turpin introduce Ruby to her purple shading—and that all of them know they are somewhere between White and Black. The fact that Mrs. Turpin contemplates baby pigs and a pregnant sow in the pigpen suggests that her own potential as a mother is on her mind here.[4] The punch line to this speculative train of thought, I hope, is that after shifting purple away from its traditional association with royalty, O'Connor redeems the color by making her use of it—in relation to the Turpins and Mary Grace—key to the final revelation. What starts this greatest revelation is literally "a purple streak in the sky" (653). It may seem that all my emphasis on figurative language overstates the suggestions of physical race-mixing, but let me finish this discussion by recalling that the story satirizes Mrs. Turpin when she imagines race superficially, when she thinks she could be "herself but black" without significant change (636). To some extent, the story insists the race talk be real.

On to "A Circle in the Fire": Yaeger suggests that Whites can be the source "of pollution" in racial terms, as in this story (262; 296n6). If one accepts that the boys' destruction of the farm triggers the female

---

[4] William Meyer, Jr. introduced me to this idea.

characters' redemption, along with the idea that Mrs. Cope experiences race-mixing as the boys nakedly set fires, then we have something of a fresh explanation for that puzzling line about Mrs. Cope having a look that "might have belonged to anybody, a Negro or a European or to Powell [one of the boys] himself" (*CW* 251). These three angels of redemption can burn away parts of Mrs. Cope in a fashion suggestive of Mrs. Turpin's burning, but that does not prevent Mrs. Cope's crossing the racial line, profoundly, by being polluted by three boys who are, ironically, freshly washed.

Back to "Everything That Rises Must Converge": Everybody in this story is potentially everyone else's double. Racial barriers are crossed constantly. The color purple works here to equate Julian's mother and the Black mother through their hats, and the mothers swap sons. What I might add to discussions of race in this story is inspired by Leanne E. Smith, who points out that "...it is the [Black mother's] pocketbook, more than the hat, that...bluntly teaches a lesson that Julian wants his mother to learn about changing societal norms" (49). The purple crowns, I would agree, are less important than the mothers' contrasting pocketbooks. Julian's mother has a pocketbook that once dispensed nickels but now only pennies (*CW* 498), and at the end of the story she drops and forgets the purse (499). The Black mother has "a mammoth red pocketbook that bulged throughout as if it were stuffed with rocks" (495). Usually the Black woman's pocketbook is treated by critics as a political statement, but I would also suggest—even if one has not recently reread the section of "The Comforts of Home" about Sarah Ham's sexual pocketbook—that both purses in "Everything That Rises Must Converge" can also impress one as being about sexual power. Julian's mother, with her fantasies of being close to Blackness in the person of her mammy, is on her way out; the Black mother, who suggests crossing racial lines through the clothes she chooses for herself and for her son, also suggests that part of her power to make her choices comes from sexuality. The Black mother suggests miscegenation so strongly that she makes us see how superficially Julian is able to think about it. When the Black mother first displeases Julian by sitting beside him, we are told "He could not see anything but the red pocketbook upright on the bulging green thighs" (496). Julian's response, of course, is to wrench his focus as soon as possible away from the pocketbook and toward the identical hats. Julian cannot face—until perhaps the very end of the story—what convergence must be.

While we are on the subject of O'Connor's making Black women into sex symbols, let me address "The Artificial Nigger," where Nelson encounters a Black woman whom he asks for directions. Nelson might see her primarily as a maternal figure, but she is also sexual, and he quickly feels "as if he were reeling down through a pitchblack tunnel" (*CW* 223). This tunnel image suggests not only the sewers of Atlanta and a pathway to hell but also surely the woman's womb, the woman's vagina. So I agree that her sexual symbolism is something O'Connor is using. It is all one-sided, of course—in no sense does the story imply that the Black woman desires anything about Nelson—but the conclusion seems unavoidable that this story is saying Nelson would be better off if he could stay in touch with Blacks, could return to his birthplace, which, as Mr. Head reminds him, is a city full of Blacks. I now typically read this story in conjunction with *The Violent Bear It Away*, where, after the White boy returns to his country home, it is even clearer that he will have to return to the city, probably to confront Black people constantly. Yaeger notes as significant the fact that young Tarwater finally "smears his face with dirt" (265; *CW* 478), suggesting perhaps a bit of "racial protest" (Yaeger 265). One has to infer from a story like "The Artificial Nigger" the full range of discoveries that await Tarwater back in the city.

"The Enduring Chill": Here Asbury fantasizes about communion with Black workers in a way that would cause "the difference between black and white [to be] absorbed into nothing" (*CW* 558). Not quite the right fantasy, Asbury: too abstract, too bloodless. His Leda-and-the-swan moment at the story's end is successful, but primarily because of an earlier symbolically miscegenationist fantasy played out in more clearly physical terms. It is important that in one of Asbury's dreams, he imagines being brought back to life by a "violently-spotted" cow who is "softly licking his head as if it were a block of salt" (564). This seemingly silly detail sets up the crucial basis for Asbury's enduring chill: the source is Bang's, a venereal disease of cows, which Asbury contracted by drinking milk in hopes of achieving communion with Blacks.

"Judgment Day": Throughout this story I feel O'Connor wants to allow Tanner to cross the racial line in a way the old man cannot consciously admit. The physical argument for miscegenation that I find most persuasive in this story is Dr. Foley, the wave-of-the-future, multiracial owner of the land on which Tanner squats with his Black friend Coleman Parrum. Dr. Foley "was only part black. The rest was Indian and white" (*CW* 680). Tanner knows that his own actions require acceptance of Dr. Foley as a symbol of necessary convergence, and Tanner finally decides, probably along with his author, that there is value in working for Foley, thus becoming "a nigger's white nigger" (685). Of course Tanner learns this lesson, becomes "tanner," by living in New York City, symbolically the land of miscegenation.

Is it perverse to compare Tanner's desire to cross the color line with Enoch Emery's? If, as Timothy P. Caron has suggested, Gonga the Gorilla is a symbol of the Black race (39), I am prepared to agree that Enoch wants to become Black as he turns himself into Gonga, even if Enoch does not understand this desire. One way I differ from Caron—and from most readers, I must admit—is on the extent to which I think O'Connor is satirizing Enoch. I believe that insofar as Hazel Motes is the protagonist emptied of race in *Wise Blood*, Enoch Emery is the character embodying miscegenation in *Wise Blood*, perhaps fully successfully.

I have heard people I respect say we have overdone our talking about race. I have tried to suggest here that race, rather than being a tangential topic for O'Connor, is intertwined with all the rest of her important themes. One could continue on the train of thought I have been riding in this article, perhaps in a religious direction. Maybe we should read O. E. Parker as a character who crosses the color line as he colors himself; of course this reading makes the face of Christ the final step in Parker's transition to a different race status. Or maybe we should follow John D. Sykes, Jr., who sees in "A Temple of the Holy Ghost" evidence that for O'Connor, Christ is always of "two 'natures'" (89). If we agree with Sykes that Christ is like O'Connor's hermaphrodite, then it may be that combining opposites in all sorts of ways is a path toward the sacred. Seeing the divine as essentially a matter of mixture makes me think that it may even be appropriate to reconsider the significance of those multicolored peacocks.

On the other hand, I should note that the course of my speculations here makes it easy to overstate the value of miscegenation in O'Connor's fiction. Certainly the history of racial oppression gives ample evidence of race-mixing that both results purely from, and reinforces, White racist domination. And there is ample evidence of race-mixing that has resulted in little or no benefit to humankind, or that benefits only Whites. Critic bell hooks tells the story of overhearing a conversation, among White boys in New Haven, Connecticut, about the value of having sex with "as many girls from other racial/ethnic groups as they could 'catch' before graduation" (23).[5] One of their misguided goals, according to hooks, was "to make themselves over, to leave behind white 'innocence' and enter the world of 'experience'" (23). O'Connor created such a young man in Julian of "Everything That Rises Must Converge," I think, and probably was critical of his motives. But there is still the possibility that O'Connor's talk about race-mixing is motivated primarily by a desire to benefit Whites. One might look at O'Connor's endorsement of miscegenation as primarily biological, with insufficient attention to changing behavior.

I return eventually—and repeatedly—to the idea that, however much O'Connor may have endorsed miscegenation in the various ways I have been sketchily speculating about here, those endorsements tend toward the indirect, the veiled, the cautious. When O'Connor thought about her own racial awareness, she probably saw in herself a bit of the impracticality of Asbury Fox in "The Enduring Chill"—somebody who means well but who needs years of work. O'Connor knew there were answers she did not have. We are left with this question: to what extent shall we see O'Connor's writing as simply timid, and to what extent shall we also see her writing as surreptitious?

A postscript: When I first read Paul Elie's important 2020 article "Everything That Rises," I thought that he might consider this article of mine an example of a tendency among "O'Connor lovers" of which Elie disapproves, the tendency to "downplay" (84) the racism in O'Connor's letters. While I agree with Elie that O'Connor's racist comments need to be taken fully into account, I also think that if one begins a consideration of O'Connor's fiction with the conclusion that she deserves to be labeled a racist, it becomes harder to appreciate the sort of thinking about race on O'Connor's part that this article attempts to reveal.

WORKS CITED

Armstrong, Julie. "Blinded by Whiteness: Revisiting Flannery O'Connor and Race." *Flannery O'Connor Review*, vol. 1, 2001–02, pp. 77–86.

Boyer, Clif. *Flannery O'Connor:* The Complete Stories *Index*. Flannery O'Connor Collection, Special Collections, Georgia College Library and Instructional Technology Center, Milledgeville, unpublished manuscript.

---

[5] I thank Beauty Bragg for introducing me to hooks's essay.

Caron, Timothy P. *Struggles over the Word: Race and Religion in O'Connor, Faulkner, Hurston, and Wright*. Macon, Mercer University Press, 2000.

[Croly, David Goodman, and George Wakeman.] *Miscegenation: The Theory of the Blending of the Races, Applied to the American White Man and Negro*. New York, H. Dexter, Hamilton and Co., 1864.

Elie, Paul. "Everything That Rises." *The New Yorker*, 22 June, 2020, pp. 82–85.

Friman, Alice. Personal interviews. Conducted by Marshall Bruce Gentry, 5 Apr. 2005 and 25 May 2020.

hooks, bell. "Eating the Other: Desire and Resistance." *Black Looks: Race and Representation*, Boston, South End, 1992, pp. 21–39.

http://www.businessballs.com/johariwindowmodel.htm. This is one of many websites that describe the basics of the Johari Window. Accessed 18 May 2008.

"Miscegenation, a Story of Racial Intimacy." *African American Registry*, https://aaregistry.org/story/miscegenation-a-story-of-racial-intimacy/. Accessed 27 Aug. 2021.

O'Connor, Flannery. *The Complete Stories*. New York, Farrar, 1971.

———. *Flannery O'Connor: Collected Works*, edited by Sally Fitzgerald. New York, Library of America, 1988.

O'Donnell, Angela Alaimo. *Radical Ambivalence: Race in Flannery O'Connor*. New York, Fordham University Press, 2020.

O'Gorman, Farrell. "White, Black, and Brown: Reading O'Connor After Richard Rodriguez." *Flannery O'Connor Review*, vol. 4, 2006, pp. 32–49.

Rodriguez, Richard. *Brown: The Last Discovery of America*. New York, Viking, 2002.

Smith, Leanne E. "Head to Toe: Deliberate Dressing and Accentuated Accessories in Flannery O'Connor's 'Revelation,' 'A Late Encounter with the Enemy,' and 'Everything That Rises Must Converge.'" *Flannery O'Connor Review*, vol. 6, 2008, pp. 40–55.

Sykes, John D., Jr. "Two Natures: Chalcedon and Coming-of-Age in O'Connor's 'A Temple of the Holy Ghost.'" *Flannery O'Connor Review*, vol. 5, 2007, pp. 89–98.

Whitt, Margaret Earley. "1963, a Pivotal Year: Flannery O'Connor and the Civil Rights Movement." *Flannery O'Connor Review*, vol. 3, 2005, pp. 59–72.

Wood, Ralph C. *Flannery O'Connor and the Christ-Haunted South*. Grand Rapids, MI, Eerdmans, 2004.

Yaeger, Patricia [S.] *Dirt and Desire: Reconstructing Southern Women's Writing, 1930–1990*. Chicago, University of Chicago Press, 2000.

Flannery O'Connor's Attacks on Omniscience

In her introduction to *Three by Flannery O'Connor*, Sally Fitzgerald suggests that O'Connor based her first major work, the novel *Wise Blood*, on Eliot's modernist classic *The Waste Land* (ix–x). Although Fitzgerald admits that O'Connor later moved away from "the substructure she was relying on from Eliot" (xi) for *Wise Blood*, Fitzgerald perhaps likes comparing O'Connor to Eliot because to do so reinforces the value of a traditionally religious approach to O'Connor, an approach that emphasizes O'Connor's conservatism and orthodoxy. Therefore, while it makes some sense to call O'Connor a modernist, it is debatable whether calling her a modernist necessarily opens her works to new insights instead of simply reaffirming a standard reading. We might also question the correctness of labeling O'Connor a modernist for other reasons. In a letter dated 28 Aug. 1955, written when she arrived at the University of Iowa to attend graduate school, O'Connor states, "I had never heard of Faulkner, Kafka, Joyce, much less read them" (*CW* 950). Apparently these authors were not as influential as a book O'Connor calls "The Humerous Tales of EAPoe" (950).

Consider also the negative references to modernism in O'Connor's story "The Enduring Chill": the attempts by the protagonist, Asbury, to fashion himself after Kafka—by writing a letter to his mother like Kafka's to his father—or after Yeats—by misquoting "The Second Coming" as he describes his plight (*CW* 544)—receive the narrator's ridicule, and we are told that a priest named Father Finn is able to brush off a reference to James Joyce "as if he were bothered by gnats" (565). However, when we look at "The Enduring Chill" and other works by O'Connor as involving an attack on omniscience (rather than as attempts at omniscient narration that do not quite work out), we see them as better works of literature.

Edward Kessler treats "The Enduring Chill" at length as a failed story that he contrasts to Flaubert's successful "A Simple Heart" ("Un Coeur Simple"); O'Connor's story fails, according to Kessler, because O'Connor refuses to allow a reader a variety of alternatives for interpreting the meaning of the waterstain symbol central to the story (126–36).

Kessler's reading results from his equation of the narrative voice with O'Connor herself. Other critics who discuss this story also equate O'Connor and her narrator. Suzanne Morrow Paulson calls the ending of "The Enduring Chill" one of those rare passages in which O'Connor mistakenly "seemed to plan explicit authorial intrusion" (11). A survey of O'Connor criticism shows that it is quite common to assume that the O'Connor narrator speaks for her, despite problems noted by those who make that assumption. Jack Ashley, while admitting that the O'Connor narrator can be "shockingly hostile to the characters" and can display "Olympian snobbery and pungent condescension" (77), still calls the O'Connor narrator "omniscient, unlimited, and within the microcosm of the story, infinite" (74), comparable to the narrators of classic nineteenth- and eighteenth-century novels. Ashley says that the narrator's voice is that of "the prophet" (80), despite the "paradox that O'Connor's characters who most live inwardly in their private worlds of moral and emotional subjectivism are most savagely judged" (78). Thomas O. Sloane says that in performing literature he finds it interesting to discover ways in which a narrator becomes "a talker whose voice reveals, belies, sometimes even betrays the author" (2), and he considers the O'Connor narrator to be "a surrogate, a substitute or echo, of that primary voice we call the author or 'implied' author" (3). Sloane says that the narrator provides the religious level to the final passage of "The Enduring Chill" (20), but he suspects that sometimes "…readers will…distance themselves from the narrator when no distance is intended" (21).

Such an approach becomes more questionable as it moves toward the increasingly popular step of attributing sainthood to O'Connor. Sloane implies that O'Connor is a "true prophet…whose voice sounds through the narrator" (5). Later Sloane says, referring to O'Connor's narrator, "She alone, of all the major presences in O'Connor, is complete, confident, at times serene, and above all far-sighted" (6). Reviews of O'Connor's *Collected Works* seem particularly inclined to canonize O'Connor in a religious sense as well as a literary one. For example, although Mark Caldwell, writing for the *Philadelphia Inquirer*, sees some things to criticize in her works, he also says that "like her God," O'Connor "is a prophet rather than a comforter" (F9). Mary Jo Salter seems to accept the idea that O'Connor plays God successfully: Salter asks, "Isn't there something in the notion that the more merciless the author, the more he or she may reveal our dependence on the (not always evident) mercy of the first Author?" (36). And the review of *Flannery*

O'Connor: Collected Works in *The Flannery O'Connor Bulletin* calls O'Connor "a transcendently important figure" (Wood 92).

O'Connor herself wrote in a letter, "You have to be able to dominate the existence that you characterize" (30 Sept. 1955, *CW* 959), but it seems that her narrator's domination of the characters often fails. Shirley Foster notes the establishment of "a complicity between implied narrator and reader, in which the latter feels able to recognize—and anticipate—the former's intent," and Foster also notes that the reader's "assumptions...are destroyed" (261) in work after work. Although Foster says that at times "O'Connor provides what appear to be deliberately false clues" (265) and that it may seem "as if the author takes delight in turning on her audience a mocking vindictiveness" (271), Foster never argues for the reader's right to interpretation or characters' rights to their own ways. But while Foster comes to conclusions nearly opposite those of this author, she does lay the groundwork for a reading in which the O'Connor narrator is the most wrongheaded one. In discussing "The Enduring Chill," Foster insightfully claims that Mrs. Fox and Asbury achieve "a triumph" despite the expectation the reader has acquired from the narrator of a "wholly deflationary conclusion" (268). In his perceptive discussion of "The Enduring Chill," Jefferson Humphries notes that O'Connor "knew very well" that "a text is supposed to" blur the "distinction...between...writer and reader" (130). On the other hand, we might say that O'Connor forces the reader to rethink the narrator's interpretations. In "The Enduring Chill," it is true that the narrator repeatedly encourages a reading in which Asbury is forced into submission to the Holy Ghost, but the story is also filled with details that resist such an interpretation. If we consider the "omniscient" narrator to be wearing blinders, if we consider Asbury the artist unconsciously bent on destroying his own illusions, then O'Connor is not producing clumsy fiction.

Consider also one of the major finds in *Flannery O'Connor: Collected Works*: the final revision of "The Turkey" into a story called "An Afternoon in the Woods" (a story O'Connor considered including in the collection *A Good Man Is Hard to Find and Other Stories*) in which at one point the young male protagonist, here called Mason, thinks that he engages in conversation with the Devil and then even with God. When Mason catches a Turkey, we read the following:

> He stopped, realizing suddenly that what had happened was a clear call to the ministry.

"Yaaa," the voice said, "now you have to be a preacher, wise guy."

He shifted the turkey slightly on his shoulder. Like Billy Ghrame, he thought, flying to Europe all the time.

"Naaa, like the fat gold glick at the Methodist church in town," said the voice.

No, like that priest that founded Boys' Town, he said. I'll found a town for boys that are going bad. The appropriateness of this struck him with force and he began to imagine a line of boys that he had reformed, walking after him through the woods. Come on, boys, he said, God has given us a turkey.

You gave us a good bird, he said to God.

Only the best for a valuable man, God said. Glad to have you on my side, Mason. (*CW* 769)

As we learn here to trust the "voice of God" even less than that of the Devil, this passage teaches us to question whether *any* authoritative voice may be found in an O'Connor story. Critics who are inclined to equate O'Connor's devil with The Devil rather than with a character's obscure expression of repressed desires should have an interesting time explaining the peculiar presence of a "voice of God" in this passage. John Burt is correct in his essay "What You Can't Talk About" when he suspects from time to time that the voice of the author/narrator seems to be headed toward error. Burt says of the MFA story "The Turkey" that if we consider it incorrect for the protagonist "to project meanings onto natural events and to assume that catching the turkey shows how he stands with God, then it is also wrong for the author to project meaning onto those same events, to say that they prove either that God's ways are mysterious or that there is no God" (129). The typical O'Connor narrator is constantly projecting meanings we can and should question.

One might expect that discussions of films based on O'Connor's works would be forced to notice the gap between the narrator's view of the proceedings and what the reader may make of the characters' lives, but there is often confusion about what to make of that gap. Jacqueline Taylor says that the film version of "The Displaced Person" leaves us "baffled" by the "peculiar behavior" of Mrs. Shortley, even as she notes, perceptively, that Mrs. Shortley's "failure has sociological rather than spiritual implications" when we leave out the narrator's guidance (6). I have argued elsewhere (in *Flannery O'Connor's Religion of the Grotesque*) that in relation to Mrs. Shortley and many other O'Connor characters, the narrator is overly authoritarian, and that the point of many works by O'Connor is in her characters' achievement of redemption by devices her typical narrator mocks in vain. Perhaps that claim about O'Connor's narration can be extended by considering gender to be of crucial significance to O'Connor's handling of narration.

Louise Westling's *Sacred Groves and Ravaged Gardens* goes to such lengths to expose a feminist undercurrent (however repressed) in O'Connor's writings that it once seemed to me that perhaps O'Connor's reputation had grown due to her "*anti*-feminism" (Gentry, Review 108). But we need not think that O'Connor is as patriarchal and traditional as she seems when we read the recent books emphasizing her Catholicism or the reviews of *Flannery O'Connor: Collected Works*. Another article by Westling suggests a tentative solution to what could be considered a dilemma. In an essay on O'Connor's correspondence with the mysterious person called "A," Westling stresses the importance of O'Connor's association of authorship with men, to the point that "Flannery O'Connor's persona as author seems always to be male" ("Revelations" 19). This is an insightful comment by Westling, who also notes that O'Connor "always referred to the writer as 'he'" and (based on evidence in some of O'Connor's letters) that she thought of "herself almost as her father's double." One may speculate that Mary Flannery O'Connor dropped her first name when she entered college because she liked the ambiguity of gender contained in her middle name, and one should consider the advice O'Connor accepted from Caroline Gordon, that an omniscient narrator "never speaks like anyone but Dr. Johnson" (qtd. in *CW* 923). But while Westling considers O'Connor's allegiance to be almost always with the male, perhaps it would be more accurate to say that in her fiction O'Connor creates a male narrator whose power, authority, and omniscience are overthrown. While we may agree with Westling that many of O'Connor's letters display "an ambivalence about being a woman which twisted many of her powerful stories away from the shapes and effects she intended" ("Revelations" 15), we should also quickly add that the tension in O'Connor's authorial psyche about identifying with the male or the female intensifies the effects of many of her works.

Perhaps Sally Fitzgerald was too inclined to make O'Connor fit some sort of definition of normalcy in relation to gender. One of the previously unpublished letters that Fitzgerald selected for inclusion in the Library of America volume *Flannery O'Connor: Collected Works* insists that "…lesbianism I regard…as any other form of uncleanness" (13 Sept.

1954, 925). Fitzgerald also reveals that O'Connor had a Marine sergeant as a "close friend" in college (Chronology 1240) and that she fell in love with a "Danish-born, Harcourt Brace textbook representative" in 1953 (Chronology 1246). While nothing prevents our using these details to reopen the question of why there seems to be so little romance in O'Connor's works, hopefully we will not simply take data about O'Connor's loves as the tidy conclusion to our speculation about her sense of herself as female. We should also resist any temptation to substitute O'Connor's childhood for her female adulthood. Part of the drive to purchase O'Connor's house in Savannah involved the collection of memories about O'Connor's childhood, a topic that is adorably safe for a fund-raising campaign (Brown 9). Visitors to the O'Connor Collection in Milledgeville, and readers of Fickett and Gilbert's treatment of O'Connor's life may feel that, at times, an idealized version of O'Connor as child is being sold.

Sometimes it seems necessary for a woman writer to reject gender in order to reach the highest, most petrifying levels of acceptance. When Marguerite Yourcenar was elected an Immortal in the French Academy, part of what made her acceptable to this most traditional of literary bodies was the attitude pronounced by Maurice Rheims: "Madame Yourcenar is not a woman, but an object of literature, a monument. Otherwise, I'm against women at the Académie Française" (qtd. in McDonald 42). O'Connor's position in the culture may not be all that different from that of Yourcenar if those of us who study her ignore the gender issue in the interest of making her a classic. O'Connor's attitude to all of this would probably bear some resemblance to that of the little girl in "A Temple of the Holy Ghost," who felt sure that "She could never be a saint, but she thought she could be a martyr if they killed her quick" (*CW* 204). We should be wary of the possibility that we may kill O'Connor when we think we are honoring her.

Now it may be possible, perhaps even more than Louise Westling was inclined to do, to label O'Connor's consciousness some sort of feminist one. My train of thought suggests a new sense in which we may feel that a Mrs. Shortley or a Mrs. May or a Hulga Hopewell do more than suffer a male narrator's punishments. But an emphasis on gender would also shed new light on works primarily about characters who are male. We may have an explanation, in O'Connor's feelings on gender, for the use of both the more feminine "Hazel" and the more masculine "Haze" for the protagonist of *Wise Blood*. Perhaps it is the character's female side that saves him from the plight to which the male narrator condemns him. Perhaps we have a new explanation for the fact that the ending of *The Violent Bear It Away* involves a sexual penetration. Perhaps the end of "An Afternoon in the Woods," in which Mason (whose real name, ironically, is Manley) is chased by "Something Awful...with its arms rigid and its fingers ready to clutch" (*CW* 772), is to suggest flight from sexual pursuit. And, in "The Enduring Chill," perhaps it is because of Asbury Fox's unconscious attraction to some aspect of his mother's life (probably her closeness to the rhythms of the natural world) that he is able to triumph over a thoroughly masculine narrator. We may also see Asbury as achieving the status of Yeats's Leda in relation to the god as bird at the end of the story. Asbury manages to duplicate Yeats's "Leda and the Swan," it seems, becoming a female, a Leda raped by the god. And just as Yeats asks whether Leda "puts on his knowledge with his power" as she is raped, Asbury takes on knowledge and power even at the moment of what might look like the physical body's most profound submission to masculine omniscience. Perhaps it is precisely *because* he becomes like a female that Asbury achieves a victory.

Although Sandra M. Gilbert and Susan Gubar in *The War of the Words* only mention "Good Country People" among O'Connor's works, and then only to call it a story about a woman "punished for unfeminine arrogance" (112), perhaps we can relate O'Connor meaningfully to their thesis in that study. If, as they say, modernism can be considered "for men as much as for women a product of the sexual battle" of the modernist period (xii), then we might conclude that the battle in O'Connor's works between a masculine narrator and female or feminized characters is at the heart of one of the literary culture's most important struggles. Perhaps in O'Connor's works we see the gender battle producing the attacks on omniscience that make an author seem to be a modernist.

WORKS CITED

Ashley, Jack Dillard. "Throwing the Big Book: The Narrator Voice in Flannery O'Connor's Stories." *Realist of Distances: Flannery O'Connor Revisited*, edited by Karl-Heinz Westarp and Jan Nordby Gretlund. Aarhus, Den., Aarhus University Press, 1987, pp. 73–81.

Brown, Hugh. "Flannery O'Connor's Girlhood Remembered." *Southern Cross*, 6 July 1989, p. 9.

Burt, John. "What You Can't Talk About." *Flannery O'Connor*, edited by Harold Bloom. New York, Chelsea, 1986, pp. 125–43.

Caldwell, Mark. "The Dark Forces of Flannery O'Connor." Review of *Flannery O'Connor: Collected Works. Philadelphia Inquirer*, 9 Oct. 1988. Microform. Reprinted in [*Newsbank*] *Review of the Arts: Literature Index*, 1988, fiche 121, grids F8-9.

Fickett, Harold, and Douglas R. Gilbert. *Flannery O'Connor: Images of Grace*. Grand Rapids, MI, Eerdmans, 1986.

Fitzgerald, Sally. Chronology. *Flannery O'Connor: Collected Works*. New York, Library of America, 1988, pp. 1237–56.

———. Introduction. *Three by Flannery O'Connor*. Signet Classic ed., New York, NAL, 1983, pp. vii–xxxiv.

Foster, Shirley. "Flannery O'Connor's Short Stories: The Assault on the Reader." *Journal of American Studies*, vol. 20, no. 2, 1986, pp. 259–72.

Gentry, Marshall Bruce. *Flannery O'Connor's Religion of the Grotesque*. Jackson, University Press of Mississippi, 1986.

———. Review of *Sacred Groves and Ravaged Gardens: The Fiction of Eudora Welty, Carson McCullers, and Flannery O'Connor*, by Louise Westling. *South Central Review*, vol. 2, no. 4, 1985, pp. 106–08.

Gilbert, Sandra M., and Susan Gubar. *The War of the Words*. Vol. 1 of *No Man's Land: The Place of the Woman Writer in the Twentieth Century*. New Haven, Yale University Press, 1988. 2 vols.

Humphries, Jefferson. *The Otherness Within: Gnostic Readings in Marcel Proust, Flannery O'Connor, and François Villon*. Baton Rouge, Louisiana State University Press, 1983.

Kessler, Edward. *Flannery O'Connor and the Language of Apocalypse*. Princeton, Princeton University Press, 1986.

McDonald, Marci. "A Success That's Rather Academic." *Maclean's*, 17 Mar. 1980, pp. 40, 42.

O'Connor, Flannery. *Flannery O'Connor: Collected Works*, edited by Sally Fitzgerald. New York, Library of America, 1988.

Paulson, Suzanne Morrow. *Flannery O'Connor: A Study of the Short Fiction*. Boston, Twayne-Hall, 1988.

Salter, Mary Jo. "Seeing and Believing." Review of *Flannery O'Connor: Collected Works. New Republic*, 24 Apr. 1989, pp. 34–38.

Sloane, Thomas O. "The Strategies of Authorial Presence: Narrators and Regionalism in Flannery O'Connor and Eudora Welty." *Literature in Performance*, vol. 2, no. 1, 1981, pp. 1–25.

Taylor, Jacqueline. "Narrative Strategies in Fiction and Film: Flannery O'Connor's 'The Displaced Person.'" *Literature in Performance*, vol. 2, no. 2, 1982, pp. 1–11.

Westling, Louise. "Flannery O'Connor's Revelations to 'A.'" *Southern Humanities Review*, vol. 20, 1986, pp. 15–22.

———. *Sacred Groves and Ravaged Gardens: The Fiction of Eudora Welty, Carson McCullers, and Flannery O'Connor*. Athens, University of Georgia Press, 1985.

Wood, Ralph C. Review of *Flannery O'Connor: Collected Works. The Flannery O'Connor Bulletin*, vol. 17, 1988, pp. 92–97.

Gender Dialogue in O'Connor

Men and women battle constantly in O'Connor's works, but apparently critics have been reluctant to question or analyze what probably seems obvious: that men always win. Even when Bakhtinian dialogism in O'Connor is being discussed, the battle between the authoritarian narrator and the rebellious characters has been described as a conflict based on differences in religious viewpoint, not specifically on gender. Perhaps this critical silence exists because Bakhtin seems to have a blind spot regarding feminism (Booth 154).[1] I believe that women win frequently, however. After arguing that the typical O'Connor narrator is a rigidly patriarchal female who promotes gender separation, I will show that O'Connor characters frequently find redemption as they move toward androgyny. The feminine becomes a source for the characters' rebellion, for voices

---

[1] Bakhtin's most important texts for an understanding of dialogism are "Discourse in the Novel" and *Problems of Dostoevsky's Poetics*. In *Flannery O'Connor's Religion of the Grotesque*, I have discussed the relevance of Bakhtin's theories on the grotesque (in *Rabelais and His World*) and on novelistic narration to the study of O'Connor, arguing that her stories typically dramatize battles between an excessively authoritarian narrator and grotesque characters engaged in unconscious strategies for redeeming themselves, strategies the narrator mocks in vain. This essay reconsiders the argument in my "Flannery O'Connor's Attacks on Omniscience," where I suggest that the battles may be seen as gender disputes as well, with the narrator a male and the typical character a female (or feminized male). Although I am now inclined to label the typical O'Connor narrator female rather than male, I still want to insist that she uses her narrator to express a point of view she wants to transcend. There are important differences between O'Connor and the narrators in her fiction. See *Flannery O'Connor's Religion of the Grotesque* (6–9) for my discussion of how Bakhtin's theories of novelistic narration can be most usefully adapted to the study of O'Connor. For a discussion of feminist attacks on Booth's feminism, see Bauer (173–74).

that compete with the narrator's voice for authority. In the course of a given work, while maintaining a battle against the narrator, a female character discovers strengths that are masculine (especially by patriarchal standards), or a male character discovers his female side and the advantages of the feminine.

O'Connor typically claimed that she did not care much about gender. To Betty Hester (her correspondent called "A"), O'Connor wrote on 22 Sept. 1956: "On the subject of the feminist business, I just never think...of qualities which are specifically feminine or masculine. I suppose I divide people into two classes: the Irksome and the Non-Irksome without regard to sex. Yes and there are the Medium Irksome and the Rare Irksome" (*HB* 176). Louise Westling has argued that O'Connor allied herself with masculine authority more than with other women ("Revelations" 19). After reading Westling's arguments about O'Connor's complicated sense of her own gender, one can easily conclude that when O'Connor's fiction is dialogic, gender is one of the areas of dispute, and one is likely to take seriously O'Connor's concession to Hester, in a letter dated 2 Aug. 1955: "You are right that I won't ever be able entirely to understand my own work or even my own motivations" (*HB* 92; *CW* 944).

Frederick Crews, who portrays O'Connor as an overly conscious crafter of stories that fit the academic model of her time (144–45), says that "nowhere" in her fiction does he find O'Connor's irony directed at her narrators (150), so perhaps it is worthwhile to consider a couple of examples in which mockery of a narrator is fairly explicit. In a letter to Sally Fitzgerald and Robert Fitzgerald dated 20 Dec. 1952, O'Connor ridicules one of the local farm wives who narrates the story of another farm wife. I quote the passage with Sally Fitzgerald's editorial insertions in *The Habit of Being* (a passage revised slightly for its publication in *CW* 905–06):

> Mrs. P. [farm wife] met Mrs. O. [former farm wife] wandering around downtown yesterday. They didn't take to each other atall but Mrs. P. never loses an opportunity to get any information about anything whatsoever so she stopped her and asked if Mr. O. was working *yet*. Well, says [his wife] (whine), dairy work is so regular, we decided he better just had get him a job where he could work when he wanted to. Mrs. P. has not got over this yet. She never will. She manages to repeat it every day in [Mrs. O.'s] tone of voice. (50)

Here ridicule is directed at a narrator for repeating with malicious glee the words of another. At the same time, however, we notice O'Connor's own glee in repeating the words of both these women. Surely she is also poking fun at herself for her own delight in recording and ridiculing others' speech. This passage from a letter is comparable to a passage in "The Displaced Person," where Mrs. McIntyre complains to Mrs. Shortley about all the "sorry people" (*CW* 293) whom Mrs. McIntyre has had on her farm. Mrs. Shortley refuses to acknowledge the insult to herself, thinking, "Neither of them approved of trash" (293). Most readers with whom I have discussed this passage see satire directed not just at Mrs. Shortley but also at Mrs. McIntyre for her spitefulness; I question whether the O'Connor narrator can be excused for expressing a similar attitude with one more narrational layer of distance from the characters.

The early story "The Crop" provides another example of a narrator within the story who can be seen as ridiculed throughout, Miss Willerton. As Ruth Fennick has pointed out, after creating a sharecropper and his wife and starting a fight between them in a story she is writing, Miss Willerton enters her own story, "adopting the role of God (or His angel)," and she "strikes down the evil wife and rescues Lot from imminent death" (47). Miss Willerton may be laughable, but one reason the reader is amused is instructive: humor results because Miss Willerton cannot maintain her commitment to this implausible wish fulfillment she creates, *not* because she momentarily becomes the equal of her characters. Her fantasy of entering her own story is the only point at which Miss Willerton indeed seems to show potential as a writer; when she goes to the grocery store at the end of "The Crop" and once again considers herself superior to people like the characters she has created (*CW* 739–40), Miss Willerton deserves ridicule once again.

These two clearly ridiculous narrators, the farm wife Mrs. P. and Miss Willerton, are, of course, both women, and when I in the past have described an O'Connor character as a version of the typical O'Connor narrator, that character was another female, Sarah Ruth Cates from "Parker's Back" (*Religion* 80). This woman disapproves of cars (*CW* 655) and even considers "churches...idolatrous" (663); like the typical O'Connor narrator, she is "forever sniffing up sin" (655). Robert H. Brinkmeyer, Jr., however, has pointed to a male character, Julian in "Everything That Rises Must Converge," as one who resembles the O'Connor narrator: "In their efforts to show people up, both Julian and the narrator distort and demean; they manipulate to teach a lesson, simplifying the complexity of human experience to validate their own—but no one else's—integrity. A central irony of the story lies in this mirroring of Julian and the narrator, for because of their close identification, Julian's downfall implicitly signals the narrator's even if the narrator remains unaware of it" (72).

Most of O'Connor's writers are male, and most of her writers receive ridicule; along with Julian, one thinks of Asbury Fox in "The Enduring Chill," Thomas in "The Comforts of Home," Calhoun in "The Partridge Festival" (though Calhoun does have a female counterpart, Mary Elizabeth), and Rayber in *The Violent Bear It Away*. But O'Connor's women also frequently tell stories, orally rather than in writing. The issue of whether the typical O'Connor narrator is male or female can be resolved, I believe, through the positing of a composite figure: a female narrator espousing patriarchal, masculine values.

I should provide an explanation about the narration in the stories I have been discussing. I do not wish to claim that Miss Willerton succeeds in dialogically rivaling her narrator for authority in "The Crop"; I can consider Miss Willerton as much of a joke as Ruth Fennick does. Miss Willerton's failure to win the reader's sympathy is one reason this story looks like an apprentice story. In "Everything That Rises Must Converge," the narrator resembles a woman as much as a man. The narrator's satire is like the lightning bolt of judgment delivered by the Black mother who hits and perhaps kills Julian's mother for patronizing the Black child.

In most of O'Connor's works, narrators who represent patriarchal authority have their authority undercut; the characters they mock are capable of strength and self-transformation that the narrators underestimate and misinterpret. The battle is more complicated than a matter of male patriarchy in the narrator versus female rebellion in the characters. Dale M. Bauer, in discussing the ways Bakhtin opens his theories to feminist uses of them, says, "The feminist struggle is not one between a conscious 'awakened' or natural voice *and* the voice of patriarchy 'out there.' Rather, precisely because we all internalize the authoritative voice of patriarchy, we must struggle to refashion inherited social discourses into words which rearticulate intentions (here feminist ones) other than normative and disciplinary ones" (2). Surely all of O'Connor's characters have internalized the voice of patriarchal authority; that is why their strategies for redemption, their battles against the narrator's authoritarian and totally conscious patriarchy, must be carried on unconsciously. If O'Connor's characters understood their rebellion against patriarchy, they generally would not want to rebel, and they could not rebel even if they did want to.

Two more examples of characters who resemble the typical O'Connor narrator are Mrs. Pritchard of "A Circle in the Fire" and Mrs. Freeman of "Good Country People." These characters do not use theology to rationalize their malicious glee for narration, but its lack may simply indicate that theology is not necessarily the ultimate basis of the narrator's persona. Mrs. Pritchard is willing to "go thirty miles for the satisfaction of seeing anybody laid away" (*CW* 232), and she can easily imagine the landscape "flattened to nothing" (235). She feels "satisfaction" when she says to Sally Virginia Cope (who thinks herself capable of handling three delinquent boys), "They'd handle you" (244). Mrs. Pritchard smiles in "an omniscient rewarded way" when she reports misfortune (245), she cannot "stand an anticlimax" (246), and she is "charged" by the story's climactic fire (250). Mrs. Freeman, equally fond of the grotesque, also resembles the O'Connor narrator in never admitting she is wrong while telling a story; she mechanically follows her tale, her eyes "turn[ing] as the story turn[s]" (263). It is also interesting that the narrator of "Good Country People" starts referring to Joy Hopewell as Hulga at precisely the point at which we are told that Mrs. Freeman enjoyed taking the liberty of calling her Hulga (266).

Perhaps the best example of a character who resembles the O'Connor narrator is one who does bring in the religious dimension: the nun at the end of "A Temple of the Holy Ghost." Although the nun never speaks, she literally forces patriarchy into the face of the young female protagonist, "mashing the side of [the child's] face into the crucifix hitched onto [the nun's] belt" after swoop[ing] down on her mischievously and nearly smother[ing] her in the black habit" (*CW* 209). As if the association of the nun with negative aspects of patriarchy is not obvious, the child protagonist recalls her mother's statement that the nuns at the convent school "keep a grip on" the "necks" of their female students so that the young girls will not "think about boys" more than is allowable (197).

Regarding the typical narrator as a female spokesman for patriarchy clarifies the ways that O'Connor characters rebel. In work after work, her characters resist the patriarchal authority represented by the narrator, finding their own unorthodox routes to redemption. One form of resistance has to do with gender. While narrators promote gender differences, satirizing women who are masculine and men who are feminine, the characters move toward androgyny, toward being both male and female. Such dialogue was surely important for O'Connor personally, for her position in society made her understand what it is to be both dominant and marginal. Her class made her position in Milledgeville very respectable, and her personal dogmatism allied her with religious authority, but she also knew the limits that could be imposed on her by her gender, her disability, even in some contexts her southernness.[2] Consider what is must have been like for O'Connor to face her community's expectation that she would want to be a southern belle. And, of course, what we know of O'Connor's mother makes it plausible that she would be a female voice for patriarchal authority in O'Connor's life and thus a model for a female narrator. Mrs. O'Connor exercised control over her daughter's entire adult life, and apparently she was the constant dispenser of judgments the daughter wanted both to accept and reject. As Thelma J. Shinn says, "The alternatives to growth for [O'Connor's] women are a hated dependency on mothers or a perpetual but socially sanctioned dependency on a heavenly Father" (90). In stories in which the patriarchal female narrator is victorious and succeeds in imposing monologic control over the text's potentially disruptive voices, O'Connor's female characters find themselves subject to the authority of both the mother and the father.

In her study of correspondence between O'Connor and Hester, Louise Westling has thoroughly demonstrated that O'Connor was properly open to the raising of questions about gender in her fiction ("Revelations"). And O'Connor did tell Hester, in a letter dated 6 Sept. 1955, "Of course I do not connect the Church exclusively with the Patriarchal Ideal" (*HB* 99; *CW* 952). But in *Sacred Groves and Ravaged Gardens*, Westling's study of the traditional association of southern womanhood with the landscape, she concludes that O'Connor could not "envision any positive, active life for women" (176). Shinn states a similar view: "O'Connor's presentation of women is very pessimistic, even hostile. The only women who offer any values are the Southern ladies, and their truths have become empty clichés" (90).

---

[2] Nancy Glazener refers to "the peculiar position of women who (if they are bourgeois) can be both dominant and marginal" (129).

Claire Kahane finds in "A Temple of the Holy Ghost" a sort of solution to gender issues for O'Connor in which the intersex sideshow performer promises "a symbolic resolution to the problem of gender limitation" ("Gothic" 350). For Louise Westling, "A Temple of the Holy Ghost" is something of a copout ("Revelations" 18), but for Kahane, the sideshow performer "restor[es] to women at least conceptually the breadth of human potential" ("Gothic" 350). The child protagonist learns to value that sinful pride that makes her mockingly imitate the Baptist preacher in town (*CW* 204), in spite of her conscious sense that the rules of the church forbid such malicious glee in using another's words and that the rules of the community forbid any rudeness on the part of little ladies. Insofar as "A Temple of the Holy Ghost" is inspired by Carson McCullers's dream of powerful androgynous females, as Westling and Kahane have demonstrated (*Sacred* 138–43; "Gothic" 347–50), it may seem an exceptional story for O'Connor. In a letter to Beverly Brunson dated 13 Sept. 1954, O'Connor surprisingly rejects the idea that the story has to do with sex or even with power for women: "The point is of course in the resignation of suffering which is one of the fruits of the Holy Ghost; not to any element of sex or sexlessness" (*CW* 925). The child character in "A Circle in the Fire," Sally Virginia Cope, has fantasies of masculine strength that are even more explicitly drawn than are the fantasies of the child in "A Temple of the Holy Ghost." Although Sally Virginia cross-dresses and carries toy pistols, she is finally unable to solve the problems presented by the three boys who threaten to destroy her mother's farm.

O'Connor also creates many other female characters who achieve masculine strength. Ruby Turpin of "Revelation," Mrs. Shortley of "The Displaced Person," and perhaps even Mrs. May of "Greenleaf" and Sally Virginia's mother, Mrs. Cope, in "A Circle in the Fire," are good examples of females overcoming patriarchal authority through private strategies. Each may appear to suffer a chastening in the course of the story, but they can also be read as creators of alternate, unorthodox, personal religious systems that give them as much control over their lives as men have over theirs. It is no coincidence that many of O'Connor's female characters have taken the "man's place" on a farm.

Many female characters in O'Connor's fiction are associated with masculine divinity. This pattern is surprising; one might expect O'Connor to compare women to female divinity, and occasionally the image of the Virgin Mary does come up. Sabbath Lily Hawks in *Wise*

Blood, after a night of fornication with Hazel Motes, presents herself as the Madonna, carrying a stolen, shrunken mummy and telling Hazel, "Call me Momma now" (*CW* 106). Sarah Ruth Cates's pregnancy mystifies O. E. Parker in "Parker's Back" as if she had been impregnated supernaturally. The sideshow performer in "A Temple of the Holy Ghost" wears a blue dress and submissively says, as the Virgin could, "This is the way [God] wanted me to be and I ain't disputing His way" (*CW* 206). Sally Virginia Cope has a rather appropriate age and the perfect middle name. And Lucynell Crater in "The Life You Save May Be Your Own" is called "the sweetest girl in the world" and "an angel of Gawd" (176, 181).

But such characters are ultimately the objects of effective satire as they are victimized by men or stuck in unenlightened positions. Such characters as Mrs. Greenleaf or Mrs. May in "Greenleaf" or the child in "A Temple of the Holy Ghost" might be exceptions to the pattern. However, in general, I think O'Connor resists equating her heroic female characters with the Virgin/Madonna because of her deep disgust for the prescribed repression and bland perfection of the southern belle, that corruption of and substitution for the Virgin Mary. Kathryn Lee Seidel discusses the background for such an equation of the belle and Mary, saying, "Repression is the requisite personality trait for the girl who wishes to be the madonna-angel of male fantasy" (67), and the "exaggerated notion of the belle's purity is a Protestant analogue for the inviolateness of the Virgin Mary" (140).

Rather than risk the possibility of seeming to honor southern womanhood in the form of the belle, O'Connor made many of her females into versions of Christ and other male religious figures. Consider the similarity of Sarah Ruth Cates's eyes to those of Jesus, the prophetic abilities of Mrs. Shortley in "The Displaced Person" and of Ruby Turpin in "Revelation," Joy/Hulga's identification with the god Vulcan in "Good Country People," Mary Fortune Pitts's identification with the Christ-like trees in "A View of the Woods," the equation of Hazel Motes's mother with Jesus in *Wise Blood*, and the female child preacher in *The Violent Bear It Away*, Lucette Carmody, who is obsessed with Jesus. Even in "A Temple of the Holy Ghost," where the child protagonist identifies with the Madonna-like sideshow performer, the story's final image, of a sun like "an elevated Host drenched in blood" (*CW* 209), suggests an equation of the child's maturing body with the body of Christ. Although I accept Martha Chew's persuasive argument that O'Connor's characterization of Lucynell Crater is an attack on the "traditional role of the Southern woman" (17), I also believe that O'Connor's hatred of the belle led her to find ways to affirm women who are able to take on positive masculine attributes.

Two problematic figures, Ruby Hill of "A Stroke of Good Fortune" and Joy/Hulga Hopewell of "Good Country People," for whom the battle with narrational authority is less successful, require special attention. One might construct a reading of O'Connor's works in which the association of females with masculine divinity is taken as always justly and purely satirical. These two stories might seem to prove the case indirectly by demonstrating that two women who try to become like men deserve punishment precisely because they ought to be purely feminine. Perhaps "A Stroke of Good Fortune" deserves to be attacked; Karen Fitts has proposed that this story should be taught so that teachers can expose and refute O'Connor's patriarchal biases. Critics like Westling and Kahane are inclined to emphasize that the protagonist, Ruby Hill, can achieve a remarkable amount of reader sympathy in the course of her defeat. I would argue that neither story is typical of O'Connor. Ruby Hill ridiculously dreams of self-destruction rather than of freedom and power. Perhaps Joy/Hulga's fantasies of herself as a goddess submissive to a man (Hulga-become-Joy/Venus submissive to Manley Pointer as Mars) may be too patriarchal, finally; perhaps Hulga is an androgynous character guilty of dreaming that she can become a belle. More likely, the narrator punishes Joy/Hulga because the character is simply too close to home for O'Connor. A strategy for self-transformation by a character, if it is to work, probably has to remain beyond the conscious reach of that character. In order for O'Connor to understand, well enough to write a short story, the psyche of a character so like herself, perhaps she could not allow that character's unconscious strategy to succeed.

It is even more interesting to discover that gender ambiguity seems to allow males to achieve redemption more easily than females in O'Connor. Many of her male characters achieve redemption, it seems, because their personal strategies involve assuming what they perceive as females roles. The feminization of men became more pronounced and more valuable over the course of O'Connor's career. In the posthumous collection *Everything That Rises Must Converge*, gender is one of the things that must converge. Asbury, for example, finally manages to imagine himself in the position of a victorious Leda about to be raped by a godly bird. Although Asbury misquotes Yeats early in that story, he apparently remembers the possibility in "Leda and the Swan" that Leda "put[s] on" the god's "knowledge with his power."[3] Similarly, we may read "The Comforts of Home" as a story in which Thomas, far from succumbing to masculine advice from his father, botches his consciously intended plans for incriminating a woman in order to demonstrate to himself how much he has in common with Sarah Ham and with his mother.[4] Despite serious efforts to achieve redemption, other male characters may ultimately fail because they finally reject the femaleness with which they engage in dialogue. Examples are Mr. Fortune in "A View of the Woods," Julian of "Everything That Rises Must Converge," and Sheppard in "The Lame Shall Enter First," characters who ought at least to admit their similarity to women rather than trying to force females to become masculine. Mr. Fortune ends up killing his granddaughter, and Julian might be considered responsible for the death of his mother in a manner less transformative than that in the scene in which Thomas kills his mother.

Before considering "The Lame Shall Enter First," we must examine the novel *The Violent Bear It Away*, in which the protagonist, Tarwater, is ready to become a child evangelist after he is raped; it is certainly possible for the rape of a man by a man to have nothing to do with women, but we can also say that within the set of ideas about gender that one might expect Tarwater to have, part of the insult of rape is that it puts him in the position of being dominated, a position he would associate with being feminized. O'Connor apparently intended the rape scene to dramatize pure evil; Jean W. Cash has published and analyzed an uncollected letter dated 27 Aug. 1962 in which O'Connor says the scene "can only be understood in religious terms" (69). But a statement of conscious intent does not eliminate other, less conscious meanings for the scene, as O'Connor herself admitted. Certainly Old Tarwater taught the boy that bad people are asses and whores (*CW* 355); Tarwater probably thinks his rape makes him both. And the rapist, whom Tarwater wholly or partly creates, is a stereotype of effeminacy. It is probably significant that when Tarwater does become a prophet as the novel ends, his role model is

---

[3] Patricia S. Yaeger argues, in a Bakhtinian reading of Eudora Welty, that Welty turns the patriarchal values of Yeats's poems upside down in *The Golden Apples*. I see a similar feminist inversion of Yeats in "The Enduring Chill."

[4] See "The Hand of the Writer in 'The Comforts of Home.'"

most likely a female. Lucette Carmody, the evangelist Tarwater hears in the middle of the novel, preaches as a child and preaches in the city so we might say that she is more like what Tarwater will become at the end of the novel than is Old Tarwater.

If *The Violent Bear It Away* is regarded in such a manner, it is easier to know what to make of that devilish story "The Lame Shall Enter First," in which the young male delinquent Rufus (a character clearly related to Tarwater) becomes a substitute for both the son and the wife of the protagonist, Sheppard. When Rufus claims that Sheppard made "Immor'l suggestions!" (*CW* 630), we may recall that Rufus has been given the dead wife's room and has danced about the house in her corset (606) and conclude that Rufus's claim makes some sense. I suggest that the feminization of a male character in this story fails to produce redemption because the story belongs to Sheppard ultimately, not to the feminized Rufus. Robert H. Brinkmeyer, Jr., has called Rufus "a double to the narrator" (97) in this story, but Sheppard is clearly the protagonist. Although I do not think Sheppard desires Rufus sexually, there may be a connection between Sheppard's adoption of the role of purely masculine dominator and the disastrous ending of the story.

O'Connor's first collection has less feminization of males and fewer good men. A good man is hard to find because being masculine gets in the way of being good. In this collection there are many almost purely masculine characters—The Misfit, Mr. Head, Gen. Sash, Mr. Shortley, and of course, that most masculine and vicious of characters, Manley Pointer. It is to this collection that I would apply Josephine Hendin's description of "much of O'Connor's work" as taking place in a world where males "are either old, asleep, dead, diseased, or mutilated, or murderers and thieves" (121). The clearest Christ symbol among O'Connor's male characters, Mr. Guizac of "The Displaced Person," is not feminized. He is clearly masculine from the moment he shocks Mrs. Shortley with a kiss on the hand of Mrs. McIntyre at the beginning of the story. But there are hints of the valuable feminization of males in some of O'Connor's early works. Gabriel in the seldom discussed story "Wildcat" equates the prowling of the wildcat with Gabriel's meeting the Lord and even with Gabriel's feminization: when the wildcat is about, Gabriel is encouraged to stay with women for protection. But the feminized characters in the early works are typically boys, not men. In "An Afternoon in the Woods," the revised version of "The Turkey" that almost made it in the collection *A Good Man Is Hard to Find*, a young character, again named Manley (perhaps the original Manley), is trying hard to become fully masculine but finally imagines himself pursued by a "Something Awful" (*CW* 772) that may dominate, feminize, and rescue him. And in "The River," the protagonist Harry/Bevel in a sense faces a choice between two captors who will dominate him: Mr. Paradise, associated with a dominating pig and the three male children who have sadistically introduced Harry/Bevel to the pig, or that man Mrs. Connin introduced Bevel to, Jesus in the form of "the waiting current...like a long gentle hand" (171) taking Bevel to death by drowning. Surely Harry/Bevel selects the more feminizing choice, though both choices have potential in that direction. If one decides that O'Connor associates childhood with androgyny, one can also develop a reading of the late story "Parker's Back" in which O. E. Parker is feminized as he is redeemed, for when Sarah Ruth Cates beats him with a broom at the end of the story, he cries "like a baby" (675).

Wise Blood handles the protagonist's gender with a high level of complexity. The protagonist is called Hazel, a feminine name, as well as Haze, a more masculine-sounding name. Hazel is drawn powerfully to—indeed, haunted by—memories of his mother and the homestead and landscape she dominated, and he spends much of the novel apparently trying to become another Manley Pointer by preaching blasphemy and dominating and destroying others. An important scene in the novel involves his murder of his double, who is significantly named Solace Layfield. The name suggests a lay in the field and the solace that goes with it. The scene in which Hazel insists that Solace undress before Hazel runs over him with his Essex surely has a sexual dimension.[5] After Hazel watches Solace die, Hazel sees himself adopting a dominated, feminized role, and he senses that such a role is somehow proper for him too. We might conclude that Hazel becomes feminized when he conjures up a patrolman to dominate him and destroy his car. Probably the most positive effect Hazel has on any character is his influence on Mrs. Flood, his landlady, who also makes a woman of him. Even if one is reluctant to make much of the fact that she wants to "penetrate" his "darkness" (*CW* 127), or that she envisions him finally as a "dark tunnel" (131), surely when Mrs. Flood thinks of marrying Hazel after he blinds himself, she

---

[5] For an argument that Hazel and *Wise Blood* are generally asexual, see J. O. Tate.

plans to play the dominant role.[6] I have in the past written that Enoch Emery, Hazel's disciple, and Hazel "follow complementary paths toward redemption" (*Religion* 136), but one aspect of Enoch's private religion seems to be that he is trying to move closer and closer toward masculinity. Perhaps Enoch's putting on of Gonga's ape suit in his final scene demonstrates that Enoch cannot adopt Hazel's androgyny. Perhaps it is his androgyny that makes Haze's rebellion against his narrator's presentation of him effective.[7]

One benefit in examining gender dialogue in O'Connor is that it helps preserve our sense of the O'Connor character's wonderful individuality. Dale M. Bauer warns that in many works with dialogue between genders, the voices of women eventually "die out" (xiv). O'Connor's women and men refuse to become a mass of identical, silenced souls as they work out their redemptions; one might recall Ruby Turpin's vision, at the end of "Revelation," of diverse humanity on a ladder to heaven, still odd, still grotesque, still "shouting and clapping" (*CS* 654). As Michael Holquist says, society for Bakhtin is "a simultaneity of uniqueness" (153), a description that also fits O'Connor's fictional world. Another interesting aspect of this approach is that the narrator becomes, like most O'Connor characters, somewhat "freakish": the narrator is a patriarchal female who tries to deny to characters the very compassion desired by the narrator as well as by the real Flannery O'Connor. In considering the complexity of the narrator, one recalls Parker's "suspicion" about Sarah Ruth Cates, that maybe "…she actually liked everything she said she didn't" (*CW* 655), along with the line in "Good Country People" about the pleasant Mrs. Hopewell, who "had no bad qualities of her own but she was able to use other people's in such a constructive way that she never felt the lack" (264).

---

[6] Compare the "long penetrating look" Manley gives Joy/Hulga in "Good Country People" (*CW* 281) or the "white penetrating stares" (236) the three boys turn on Mrs. Cope in "A Circle in the Fire." Claire Kahane has made a strong case that Hazel's self-blinding finally achieves his desired escape from women and all they represent in the novel ("Comic" 116–17).

[7] Mary Frances HopKins provides a thorough analysis of the specific stylistic techniques by which *Wise Blood* becomes dialogic, but HopKins never considers the narrator's authority to be called into question.

Although it is important to separate O'Connor's narrator from O'Connor herself, the narrator generally reflects parts of O'Connor's own character that she wanted to transform. In a study on the Bakhtinian carnivalesque and grotesque (among other things), Peter Stallybrass and Allon White make a generalization that suggests the extent to which the O'Connor narrator might also be involved in something like the characters' search for redemption through a shift in gender: "A recurrent pattern emerges: the 'top' attempts to reject and eliminate the 'bottom' for reasons of prestige and status, only to discover, not only that it is in some way frequently dependent upon that low-Other…but also that the top *includes* that low symbolically, as a primary eroticized constituent of its own fantasy life" (5).

None of my argument is intended to suggest that O'Connor's conscious intentions were markedly different from what she said they were. O'Connor would not have written what she did if she were not an orthodox Catholic. But whereas Louise Westling argues that O'Connor's "ambivalence about being a woman" ("Revelations" 15) interfered with her art, I believe O'Connor produced her best art when her emotions caused her works to overflow their containers, cracking the molds intended to control and shape them. As Claire Kahane has suggested, even the nun in "A Temple of the Holy Ghost" suggests a Catholic version of intersex status ("Gothic" 350).

O'Connor's apparent definition of woman as that which is dominated may be very troubling, though I would answer that she understood fully the extent to which women receive unfair treatment. I prefer to raise gender questions about O'Connor's fiction (and what perhaps must follow, more analysis of O'Connor's sense of her own gender) to the inclination on the part of some critics to demonstrate that she was perfectly "normal" in order to "save" her from investigations of gender issues. Rather than concluding tidily our investigations of O'Connor's sense of herself as female with details about her occasional close male friend, I would rather claim that she was willing to sympathize and identify with all of her characters, to investigate the mysteries of gender and the need for androgyny, even if doing so might make her very uncomfortable.

WORKS CITED

Bakhtin, M[ikhail] M[ikhailovich]. "Discourse in the Novel." *The Dialogic Imagination: Four Essays*, edited by Michael Holquist, translated by Caryl Emerson and Michael Holquist. Austin, University of Texas Press, 1981, pp. 259–422.

———. *Problems of Dostoevsky's Poetics*, edited and translated by Caryl Emerson. Minneapolis, University of Minnesota Press, 1984.

———. *Rabelais and His World*, translated by Héléne Iswolsky. Cambridge, MIT Press, 1968.

Bauer, Dale M. *Feminist Dialogics: A Theory of Failed Community*. Albany, Albany State University of New York Press, 1988.

Booth, Wayne C. "Freedom of Interpretation: Bakhtin and the Challenge of Feminist Criticism." *Critical Inquiry*, vol. 9, no. 1, 1982, pp. 45–76. Reprinted in *Bakhtin: Essays and Dialogues on His Work*, edited by Gary Saul Morson. Chicago, University of Chicago Press, 1986, pp. 145–76.

Brinkmeyer, Robert H., Jr. *The Art and Vision of Flannery O'Connor*. Baton Rouge, Louisiana State University Press, 1989.

Cash, Jean W. "O'Connor on *The Violent Bear It Away*: An Unpublished Letter." *English Language Notes*, vol. 26, no. 4, 1989, pp. 67–71.

Chew, Martha. "Flannery O'Connor's Double-Edged Satire: The Idiot Daughter Versus the Lady Ph.D." *The Southern Quarterly*, vol. 19, no. 2, 1981, pp. 17–25.

Crews, Frederick. "The Critics Bear It Away." *The Critics Bear It Away: American Fiction and the Academy*, New York, Random, 1992, pp. 143–67.

Fennick, Ruth. "First Harvest: Flannery O'Connor's 'The Crop.'" *English Journal*, vol. 74, no. 2, Feb. 1985, pp. 45–50.

Fitts, Karen. "Politics and Pedagogy: The Womb as Contest Property in Flannery O'Connor's 'A Stroke of Good Fortune.'" CEA Conference, 28 Mar. 1992, Pittsburgh, PA. Conference presentation.

Gentry, Marshall Bruce. "Flannery O'Connor's Attacks on Omniscience." *The Southern Quarterly*, vol. 29, no. 3, 1991, pp. 53–61.

———. *Flannery O'Connor's Religion of the Grotesque*. Jackson, University Press of Mississippi, 1986.

———. "The Hand of the Writer in 'The Comforts of Home.'" *The Flannery O'Connor Bulletin*, vol. 20, 1991, pp. 61–72.

Glazener, Nancy. "Dialogic Subversion: Bakhtin, the Novel and Gertrude Stein." *Bakhtin and Cultural Theory*, edited by Ken Hirschkop and Davis Shepherd. Manchester, UK, Manchester University Press, 1989, pp.109–29.

Hendin, Josephine. *The World of Flannery O'Connor*. Bloomington, Indiana University Press, 1970.

Holquist, Michael. *Dialogism: Bakhtin and His World*. New York, Routledge, 1990.

HopKins, Mary Frances. "The Rhetoric of Heteroglossia in Flannery O'Connor's *Wise Blood*." *Quarterly Journal of Speech*, vol. 75, 1989, pp. 198–211.

Kahane, Claire. "Comic Vibrations and Self-Construction in Grotesque Literature." *Literature and Psychology*, vol. 29, no. 3, 1979, pp. 114–19.

———. "The Gothic Mirror." *The (M)other Tongue: Essays in Feminist Psychoanalytic Interpretation*, edited by Shirley Nelson Garner, et al. Ithaca, Cornell University Press, 1985, pp. 334–51.

O'Connor, Flannery. *Flannery O'Connor: Collected Works*, edited by Sally Fitzgerald. New York, Library of America, 1988.

———. *The Habit of Being: Letters*, edited by Sally Fitzgerald. New York, Farrar, 1979.

Seidel, Kathryn Lee. *The Southern Belle in the American Novel*. Tampa, University of South Florida Press, 1985.

Shinn, Thelma J. *Radiant Daughters: Fictional American Women.* New York, Greenwood, 1986. Contributions in Women's Studies 66.
Stallybrass, Peter, and Allon White. *The Politics and Poetics of Transgression.* Ithaca, Cornell University Press, 1986.
Tate, J. O. "The Essential Essex." *The Flannery O'Connor Bulletin*, vol. 12, 1983, pp. 47–59.
Westling, Louise. "Flannery O'Connor's Revelations to 'A.'" *Southern Humanities Review*, vol. 20, 1986, pp. 15–22.
———. *Sacred Groves and Ravaged Gardens: The Fiction of Eudora Welty, Carson McCullers, and Flannery O'Connor.* Athens, University of Georgia Press, 1985.
Yaeger, Patricia S. "'Because a Fire Was in My Head': Eudora Welty and the Dialogic Imagination." *PMLA*, vol. 99, 1984, pp. 955–73.

Wise Women, Wise Blood

Looking at the big picture, one could make the case that nothing is fair to women: government, religion, the arts, business, even Women's Studies programs. While Flannery O'Connor might not like for us to say anything nice about relativism, when it comes to treating women fairly, all is relative. All human institutions fall short, but if one wants a site of genuine concern about the evils of sexism, the institution of the novel is as good a place to look as any. Of course, there is also the problem of "And they all lived happily ever after." In many works, marriage is *the* happy ending, the happy version of death, the moment in a plot beyond which we have been trained to believe we need not go. *Wise Blood* clearly refuses this ending for its female characters, and I prefer to see this refusal as a benefit to its female characters rather than as a detraction.

Wise Blood is, at the very least, a novel deeply concerned about unfair treatment of women, since the novel studies the ways in which women struggle mightily against the problems they face, and, more significantly, suggests the possibility that women can recover their ancient power, a power that approaches the divine. An examination of Sabbath Lily Hawks and Mrs. Flood, along with several of the lesser female characters, suggests that the wisdom of the blood alluded to in the novel's title may be an essentially female characteristic of great value. Some readers have interpreted "wise blood" as basically an ironic concept almost totally irrelevant to this novel's larger religious themes. One of my goals here is to clarify the ways in which the novel's title makes sense.

Of course there are images of women in *Wise Blood* that can be considered negative. Some women are old. Some women are ugly. Some women have thoughts and opinions that are untrue or unkind. But these images are to a large extent a matter of O'Connor's attack on southern traditions that require women to live up to unreal standards of youthful beauty, charm, and a sort of safe pleasantness. Alice Walker has praised the works of O'Connor for her "demythifying sentences about white women," saying that when O'Connor started writing about White females in the South, she left "not a whiff of magnolia...in the air" (52). And surely Alice Walker is not the only woman who sees the benefits in what might look like an attack on women. Patricia Yaeger sees "a brilliant fictional strategy" in O'Connor's choice "to remain in the tomboyish role of the angel-aggressive little girl" who can, in all sorts of ways, "attack her society's angels" (96).

One might also think *Wise Blood* is unfair to women because the main male characters, Hazel Motes and Enoch Emery, accept uncritically every hateful prejudice and stereotype about women. If the book lets either (or both) of these characters experience a positive conclusion, are we being asked to excuse their sexism? My answer is no. Although much of what the two protagonists struggle to prove to the world revolves around their obsession with their masculinity, *Wise Blood* requires that both characters modify their gender identity, perhaps even become feminized, in order to experience whatever redemption they achieve.[1] Insofar as these characters reject the feminine at the end of the novel, their redemption is only partial. Susan Srigley argues that Hazel Motes is flawed because he is essentially isolated at the end—and determined to remain isolated. (See Srigley's "Moral Vision" and "Penance and Love.") Conversely, it is the women of *Wise Blood* who offer the opportunity to commune with humanity; even if we believe that Hazel is saintly, he may also be overly reluctant to break out of isolation because he still clings to sexist assumptions.

In the novel's first chapter, Hazel Motes clearly does not like any of the women he meets on the train, and many readers are tempted, despite Hazel's obnoxiousness, to accept all his negative images of women. But should we? The narrator proceeds as if basically without hope for the world presented here, and if anything good comes out of any of the novel's people, it will come as a surprise not only to us and the characters but also—especially—to the narrator. Therefore, in search of something more than a bleak satire directed against the hopeless, one sorts through the narrator's data looking for value. And one can indeed find value, especially in the women. In many instances, the details that the narrator provides as evidence of female triviality and even depravity can be reinterpreted as evidence of their wise blood.

---

[1] For two important readings of gender in *Wise Blood* that relate to the reading presented here, see Barounis and Daniel.

Let us examine the initial negativity toward Mrs. Wally Bee Hitchcock, the first woman Hazel meets on the train. Here is how she is described by the narrator: "She was a fat woman with pink collars and cuffs and pear-shaped legs that slanted off the train seat and didn't reach the floor" (*CW* 3). The cult of the southern belle is under attack, and we must laugh along with the narrator here to some extent. Hazel jokes to himself later about her age, and perhaps the narrator encourages us to laugh with him at this point too (5). But are we to accept satire as giving us the whole truth about Mrs. Hitchcock?

Although she is criticized as both childish and elderly, Mrs. Hitchcock makes some reasonable observations. We might expect wisdom from her if we consider her maiden name, Weatherman (*CW* 5), as an indication that she pays attention to the sky; we should recall that at the opening of chapter 3, the narrator criticizes those who fail to look up to the heavens. When Mrs. Hitchcock first encounters Hazel on the train, she accurately considers him a poor young hick who is ill-prepared to go anywhere but home (3). She aggressively studies Hazel's eyes, searching for meaning in them. When she first follows his intense gaze to try to figure him out, she notes "a child" and "the porter" (3)—neither of which strikes her as likely to attract Hazel's stare. When he looks down the aisle a second time, we are told that "What he was looking at was the porter" (4). After this line, in which the reader is receiving information at the same time that Mrs. Hitchcock figures it out, she tries to change the subject (probably a good choice), whereas the narrator, for purposes of satire, provides a flashback to Hazel's first meeting the porter.

What is to be said about the child whom Hazel ignores and whom Mrs. Hitchcock notices? One perhaps surprising contrast between Mrs. Hitchcock and Hazel is between her reasonable orientation toward the future versus Hazel's unproductive orientation toward the past. His famous attack on her—"I reckon you think you been redeemed" (*CW* 6)— is a reply to her comment that her reason for traveling is to reconnect with a married daughter and with three grandchildren who know her only well enough to call her "Mammadoll." For Hazel, apparently, her illusion of redemption has to do with her thought about connecting with children. And Hazel cares very little about children—even his two dead brothers, one of whom died in infancy, the other at age seven: "[W]hen they shut [his brother's coffin], Haze ran and opened it up again. They said it was because he was heartbroken to part with his brother, but it was not; it was because he had thought, what if he had been in it and they had shut it on him" (10).

While Mrs. Hitchcock may seem to deserve satire for passively absorbing Hazel's abuse, she may also be admired for trying to engage him in conversation. Of course, we may think that she is ridiculous because she uses clichés: "There's no place like home" (*CW* 4), "...time flies" (6), and "...life [is] an inspiration" (6). But clichés can be read as nonthreatening statements meant to establish and reinforce bonds.[2] Although clichés do not work here, Mrs. Hitchcock does not give up easily: she persists in telling her story, that she too is leaving home for someplace else that she prefers, looking for a world in the future in which people are connected; Hazel, in contrast, looks forward to a future he has little sense of, based on an unchosen break from a past he wishes he could recover. The rest of the novel urges Hazel toward some of Mrs. Hitchcock's attitude. This is not to claim that Mrs. Hitchcock becomes the novel's hero, but that even the novel's minor female characters have hidden potential.

The narrator continues to adopt an attitude toward women that is perhaps even more negative than Hazel's. When Hazel goes to the dining car, he is seated "with three youngish women" that the narrator tells us are "dressed like parrots" (*CW* 7). He proceeds to trade insults with them but does not want to look at them directly; for as long as he can, he merely stares at the neck of the woman across from him. It is the narrator who pays attention enough to satirize them through the parrot comparison. Mrs. Hitchcock also seems the butt of a joke, in an almost slapstick scene, when the passengers are entering sleeping berths—even though in this instance she is satirized for standing up for herself, in contrast to the earlier passage in which she was satirized for being passive.

> Going around the corner [Hazel] ran into something heavy and pink; it gasped and muttered, "Clumsy!" It was Mrs. Hitchcock in a pink wrapper, with her hair in knots around her head. She looked at him with her eyes nearly squinted shut. The knobs framed her face like dark toadstools. She tried to get past him and he tried to let her but they were both moving the same way each time. Her face became purplish except for little white marks over

---

[2] Carole K. Harris associates clichés in O'Connor's works with the strengthening of bonds among people.

it that didn't heat up. She drew herself stiff and stopped and said, "What IS the matter with you?" (8)

Here we see the narrator joining in with Hazel's negative view of female characters and going beyond Hazel, who presumably would not pay attention to her head sufficiently to come up with the comparison to toadstools. Such excessive malice on the part of the narrator may alert us to the need for a reconsideration of the character.

Mrs. Leora Watts, the prostitute, who, like Mrs. Hitchcock in her wrapper, is introduced as a large woman in stereotypical pink, needs to be reconsidered as well. As Sarah Gordon points out, Hazel "never sees her in any fully human way" (105), so we may choose to do that work. Like Mrs. Hitchcock, Mrs. Watts stares at Hazel penetratingly (*CW* 17).[3] As much as she seems to be a resident of Eliot's wasteland, she also reaches accurate conclusions about Hazel: that Hazel is laughable (33), and that Hazel, like his hat, is "Jesus-seeing" (34). Hazel finally leaves Mrs. Watts because "He wanted someone he could teach something to..." (62), and Hazel realizes that he cannot teach Mrs. Watts anything. He surely thinks she is unable to learn, but there may also be a sense in which she has virtues he lacks. Hazel had learned of Mrs. Watts from a bathroom wall that labels her friendly, and in a town that consistently disappoints Enoch Emery, Mrs. Watts is one of the few friendly people. The narrator quotes her line about not caring whether Hazel is a preacher (18) in order to satirize her, but she is still quite clearly willing to accept everyone. One of the novel's most ironic lines is Hazel's rhetorical question "What do I need with Jesus?" along with his explanation, "I got Leora Watts" (31); my argument here suggests we might indeed see some godly qualities in Mrs. Watts. Alongside the satire the narrator directs at her, then, we can perhaps see in Mrs. Watts some of the power—and perhaps at least a pinpoint of light—of the sort that is suggested by her name.

As with Mrs. Hitchcock and Mrs. Watts, there seems to be much to dislike about Hazel's mother, but this initial impression also merits re-

---

[3] The term "penetrate," used to describe what women try to do to Hazel's face, may suggest that the women are playing a masculine role rather than being women. The term carries some suggestion of the narrator's consistent mockery of women's behavior, but it also suggests a more positive possibility: that women are taking back some of the patriarchy's power and putting men into the passive position stereotypically labeled female.

thinking. From the start of the novel, Hazel associates his mother with a chifforobe in the kitchen, her one valuable possession, and, more significantly, with vision, weak or strong: he carries her glasses and wears them to keep from being able to read the Bible for too long at a stretch (*CW* 12). The novel's opening chapter ends with a scene demonstrating his identification with his mother, who is filled with dissatisfaction at the prospect of her own death (14). Hazel will finally learn to be satisfied with his death—he is, after all, to some extent, a suicide—so he does move beyond the attitude he associates with his mother. If his mother is what Hazel rejects, must we reject her? I think not. While we might suspect that Hazel is justified in fearing her when, while talking about Jesus, "She hit him across the legs with [a] stick..." (36), we might also conclude that this expression of her repressed anger is actually a rather slight one: her husband is far from a prize, and she may be remembering the lost son who wandered off to see a mowing machine, only to be cut in half (10). Hazel's mother in the published novel, beyond a few details such as these, is largely a function of Hazel's view of her, a view distorted by both love and fear. (A thorough rethinking of Hazel's mother of the sort I call for here has been performed by Catherine Bowlin, who has made a persuasive argument that Annie Lee Jackson, Hazel's mother in the manuscripts of *Wise Blood*, is perhaps the key figure in the novel.)

Robert Donahoo has made an impressive case that O'Connor's descriptions of women's plights have much in common with the picture of women presented, a decade after the publication of *Wise Blood*, in a major feminist text, Betty Friedan's *The Feminine Mystique*. Donahoo sees Sabbath Lily Hawks and Leora Watts, Hazel's mother and Mrs. Flood, as illustrations of Friedan's ideas—"victims of the feminine mystique rather than victims of the author's misogyny" (24). To supplement Donahoo's case about these characters' plights, I emphasize here what the female characters accomplish.[4]

A major argument against my thesis that *Wise Blood* is fair to women is that the novel *almost* turned out much fairer—that the novel before its final form *seems* to be fairer. Sarah Gordon and Katherine Hemple Prown have analyzed the manuscripts of *Wise Blood* and concluded that O'Connor's drafts give a larger role to women (Sabbath, especially, and

---

[4] I am grateful to Robert Donahoo for reading a draft of this essay and making a number of valuable suggestions.

also Hazel's mother and sister, and others) than the finished novel does. Gordon and Prown discuss the extensive back-stories O'Connor considered for several of these characters. The main implication for Gordon is that O'Connor expunged the feminist prophetic voice she once planned to give the novel (102). Prown says that the women of the published novel are "relatively harmless," but that this quality results from "their relative unimportance to the narrative as a whole" (119).[5]

It may seem obvious that *Wise Blood* would indeed be fairer to women if it told more of their stories. Hazel's mother is given a maiden name of Annie Lee Jackson (file 29) and, significantly, a sexual background in some of the drafts, perhaps making her more human. But there is also plenty of evidence that points in the other direction. Some of the background information on the characters makes it more difficult to regard them positively. For example, the mother's potential back-story suggests a severely troubled soul who makes her own problems worse: in one manuscript, she submitted to marriage to punish herself for the sin of becoming pregnant (file 29); in another draft, she has an orgasm while in bed with her son Hazel (file 91a). If some of this material had made it into the finished novel, we might have a clearer sense of why Hazel is so quick to imagine his mother in the same sort of box he had seen a naked woman in at the carnival strip show. In the published version, the mother's question, "What you seen?" (*CW* 35), along with her ability to see Hazel through a tree, suggests, less troublingly, the sort of supernatural wisdom that children often attribute to mothers.

Seemingly more significant is the manuscript material about Sabbath, who, as Gordon puts it, "for a time at least, occupied a central place in the novel and on whom a great visionary burden was placed" (98). In some of the drafts Sabbath is a prophetess who has seen God in tears (file 71a). It is suggested that she has the novel's wise blood (file 136). And there is reference to a text written to describe how Jesus caused Sabbath's religious victory (file 141a). Fascinating as some of this abandoned manuscript material is, I believe that if O'Connor had used more of this material in the published

---

[5] See Gordon's chapter "Literary Lessons: The Male Gaze, the Figure Woman" (83–130) and Prown's chapter "Flannery O'Connor and the Problem of Female Authorship: The Manuscripts as Evidence" (111–57) for thoughtful, thorough analyses that arrive at conclusions quite different from mine about the significance of the *Wise Blood* manuscripts.

novel, her ultimate claims about women, though more direct, perhaps, would be less intriguing.

My reason for claiming that *Wise Blood* became fairer to women even as it said less about them is based on a basic shift in how the characters regard each other. In many of the manuscripts, the basic plan is for Hazel to find his path to redemption by studying women. Reading file 71b, in which Hazel studies in some detail the facial features of Sabbath, one is struck to recall how rarely Hazel looks at women in the published novel. In the final version, as Sabbath tries to seduce Hazel in the woods, "He train[s] his eyes into her neck" (*CW* 70), a strategy similar to his focusing on a woman's neck in the dining car (7). He is avoiding looking at women directly. O'Connor's intent, at the manuscript stage, to have Hazel transform himself through studying Sabbath is made explicit in a handwritten note at the end of file 141a. Such a strategy—of making women what a man studies in order to become wise—could reduce the novel's women to props, and, in one manuscript, there is a suggestion that Sabbath would need to kill herself for this plot sequence to come about believably (file 22a).[6]

As she revised *Wise Blood*, O'Connor made a profound switch: while Hazel Motes is still something of a student of faces (most notably of the face of the fake blind man, Asa Hawks), Hazel typically refuses to study women and take wisdom from them. Women, on the other hand, are consistently intent upon studying the face of Hazel Motes; and, for the most part, they tend to learn from their studies. With Mrs. Flood, for example, one can claim that wise blood, in the form of female wisdom, is movingly recovered. The shift is away from studying females to create male saintliness and toward studying male saintliness to recreate female divinity. I do not question

---

[6] O'Connor did not abandon this sort of material entirely. In Lucette Carmody in *The Violent Bear It Away*, one finds a version of a female prophet figure, and in the late story "Parker's Back," O'Connor returns to the premise of having a man find religion by studying a religious woman's face. Within the published version of *Wise Blood*, we might also see in the Welfare woman a version of the religious female who could serve to enlighten a man who studies her, namely Enoch Emery; perhaps her mistake with Enoch is in sending him away to that Bible academy. Additional hypotheses worth testing are that as O'Connor revised *Wise Blood*, she worked to distance herself from the influence of what was apparently her favorite Faulkner novel, *As I Lay Dying*, and that she worked to distance herself and Sabbath from Erskine Caldwell and the female preacher Bessie Rice in *Tobacco Road*.

Prown's evidence that the Writers' Workshop at the University of Iowa taught O'Connor to write like a man (37–43); I simply want to add that O'Connor also figured out, in a surreptitious fashion, how to write like a wise woman.[7]

O'Connor's women in *Wise Blood* tend to be peelers. In one sense, this can be a putdown of women. The potato peeler salesman tells Enoch Emery to buy a peeler "to keep him company" (*CW* 20), and this claim might be regarded as simple praise for a commercial product, but the salesman's come-on also has another meaning he does not intend: the salesman is reducing women to peelers, to the consumerist society's machines for serving men. The peeler as a concept (also significant because O'Connor used the title "The Peeler" when she published an early version of a portion of *Wise Blood*) is also relevant to women because, to attract men, women are regularly stripping themselves: the woman at the carnival, Mrs. Watts, the woman at the swimming pool who follows Hazel into the museum, and Sabbath.

But women in *Wise Blood* are also peelers in the sense that they try, more consistently than men do, to peel away layers of pretense, falseness, obfuscation. *Wise Blood* is full of women studying Hazel, successfully penetrating some of his mystery. The woman at the city park's pool, a peeling female whom Hazel does briefly examine (*CW* 47), provides a particularly interesting insight. She follows Hazel to the museum and practically forces him to look at her face—positioned "over" Hazel's—in the glass of the museum case that holds the mummy (56). Hazel's rejection of the woman—he immediately flees—makes him resemble the shrunken man, suggesting that the woman represents possibilities that Hazel avoids at his peril: "When Haze saw her face on the glass, his neck jerked back and he made a noise. It might have come from the man inside the case" (56). That the museum is a site where Hazel could have accessed some wisdom from women—perhaps wisdom of an ancient sort, even—is also suggested by the description of the entrance to the muse-

---

[7] One more point about studying manuscripts: the mere fact that a topic is treated at greater length in manuscript does not prove that it was downplayed in the final manuscript. O'Connor created an explicitly Catholic character for *Wise Blood* named Shrike (file 71c), and there is an attribution of wise blood to a Mrs. Shrike (file 141a), but nobody would claim that Flannery O'Connor downplayed Catholicism as she revised her novel to exclude these characters.

um: "...between each column there was an eyeless stone woman" (55). Whatever wisdom we find later in Mrs. Flood—who eventually tries to make herself see by being eyeless, "staring with her eyes shut" (131)—is foreshadowed at the museum.

My argument is that the feminism of the novel took on a subtler but more effective form as O'Connor completed her novel. The voice of Sabbath Lily Hawks only occasionally sounds religious in the published version, and some readers consider her totally corrupt, perhaps because she is a female. I believe, however, that Sabbath is ultimately a sympathetic character, and it is profoundly significant that the novel does not finish her story. She is abandoned by the novel's narrator, in a sense, as if she were no longer worth troubling ourselves over, but she is also therefore freed. In the finished novel, the more seriously religious role is transferred from Sabbath to the older Mrs. Flood. And symbolically, from the landlady is finally released a flood of a mature woman's wise blood.

Sabbath Lily Hawks is consistently the victim of all the novel's men—her father Asa, as well as Hazel and Enoch. She is prematurely accused of giving Hazel the "fast eye" (*CW* 27), and Hazel is quick to conclude that, because she is a bastard, "...her case was hopeless" (69). Enoch ridicules her looks after she beds Hazel: "I see why he has to put theter washrag over his eyes..." (103). Asa's treatment of her always verges on abusiveness, as when he orders her to accept the potato peeler from Hazel: "You put it in your sack and shut up before I hit you" (27). Furthermore, as she suggests to Hazel, she believes her God rejects her: "...and do you know what? A bastard shall not enter the kingdom of heaven!" (66–67).

Despite all the meanness directed at her, Sabbath uses survival strategies that we can to some extent admire. She has learned that what is valued in her culture is religious talk about sinful women, and so (rather like the novel's narrator), she produces such talk. Twice she tries to impress Hazel Motes with startling sermonettes—about a dead baby staring through a chimney at its evil mother (28) and about a mistreated child who provokes her evil grandmother to kill her or to commit suicide (69).[8] One might be tempted to dismiss these speeches as simply evidence that Sabbath is one more of the novel's phony preachers, like her father or

---

[8] Douglas Robillard, Jr., believes that the grandmother kills the child (71). I see ambiguity about who dies in the passage.

Onnie Jay Holy. Sabbath herself can refer dismissively to "Preacher talk" (*CW* 107), so we know that she knows there is a tendency toward falsity in such talk. I consider Sabbath no more blameworthy than that other character who preaches because there seems to be no alternative—Solace Layfield. What saves Sabbath from mere phoniness is that her sermons do probably have a personal experience—even a personal pain—behind them. In comparison to Onnie Jay Holy, who glibly demands pity by proclaiming that "Not even my own dear old mother loved me..." (85), Sabbath is not so completely self-serving.

There is evidence in the *Wise Blood* manuscripts that Sabbath's stories have a personal level to them (file 144a), and Ralph Wood has pushed to an extreme the possibility that Sabbath is in her own stories. Wood interprets the passage about the dead child staring through the chimney as suggesting that Sabbath killed her own child, perhaps the product of incest with the abusive Asa Hawks (238). Amid his speculation, Wood is confident that O'Connor's point is to attack "the sexual abandonment that would begin in the 1960s and then become a world pandemic" of abortion (238). Sabbath knows that the baby "had Jesus" (*CW* 28), and according to Wood, we therefore know Sabbath has a "pained conscience" reminding her that the baby has "life that its killers could not kill" (239). Then when Sabbath tells the story of an abusive grandmother (*CW* 69), Wood speculates that "Perhaps this abused and unwanted child was Sabbath herself, and perhaps she has perpetuated the cycle of destruction by aborting her own baby" (240). The grandmother does not love her child, is, in fact, made sick by the child's goodness, and the child drives the grandmother to murder or suicide by telling her that the child sees her "in hell-fire, swoll and burning" (*CW* 69).

I prefer a different take on how Sabbath enters her stories. The emotional content is valid even though the details of her stories are far-fetched, even though Sabbath's mother died shortly after giving birth to her (*CW* 66), and even though there are no details available about Sabbath's grandmother. What strikes me as genuine is that, like the children in Sabbath's stories, she obviously feels abandoned, ignored, unloved—and *Wise Blood* consistently justifies those feelings. Sabbath tells her tales to try to get somebody to pay attention to her, and, like the child "locked up in a chicken crate" (69), she clearly feels desperate enough to use meanness on others.[9] Her sense of desperation seems justified when one notices how little Hazel reacts to her tale of the evil grandmother. And Sabbath's sense that she is unloved becomes especially poignant when one considers the moral she draws from her tale of the dead baby hanging in a chimney: that "good looks" are insufficient—they "ain't enough" (*CW* 29). Sabbath surely feels that she is ugly and probably also that, even if she were not ugly, no amount of comeliness would be enough to make anyone love her.

Despite all her pain, Sabbath is possessed of an energetic personality, an impressive life force, a sense of humor—all of which have been ignored by critics as thoroughly as they are ignored by Hazel. Sabbath notes her invisibility: when she climbs from the back of Hazel's car where she has been hiding, she says "I been here all the time…and you never known it" (*CW* 66). She speaks with a tone more inviting than complaining. At several points, against the odds, Sabbath seems loving. She likes Hazel's eyes (61, 95), there is more than manipulation in her intentions when she claims that she can "save" Hazel because "I got a church in my heart where Jesus is King" (68), and even in the novel's final pages, as Sabbath is dismissed once more, there are things to be said on her behalf. After Hazel's self-blinding, the narrator tells us, looking through Mrs. Flood's eyes, that Sabbath develops "the disposition of a yellow jacket" (121). Has Sabbath proven that she is despicable, merely the "harpy" Mrs. Flood calls her (121), according to the novel as a whole? I think not. She is desperate, yes, trying still to get something out of Hazel, whom she has concluded—I think accurately—is "honest-to-Jesus" (121), and Hazel himself assures us that what Sabbath wants from him is not money (121). There is room to speculate about what Sabbath might want from the blind Hazel.

The novel's final words about Sabbath are that Mrs. Flood is considering putting her into "a detention home" (*CW* 121). Where does this leave Sabbath? She has not yet reached the sweet age of sixteen, but she has energy and good street sense. And I would also attribute to her the ability to love. Consider the moment when she receives the museum mummy. Even before she tries to use the mummy to declare herself an

---

[9] See Thimme (85) and Martin for color photographs of the comparable crib (the "kiddie coop") in which Flannery O'Connor herself was kept in her childhood home.

Eve/Mary figure who is bonded to Hazel, she has an interesting response to the mummy itself: "She might have sat there for ten minutes, without a thought, held by whatever it was that was familiar about him. She had never known anyone who looked like him before, but there was something in him of everyone she had ever known, as if they had all been rolled into one person and killed and shrunk and dried" (104). This scene is often interpreted as an indication of her blindness, her failure to see corruption; I recommend that we consider instead the wealth of evidence that Sabbath recognizes fully how very corrupt her world is. When she refers to "everyone she has ever known" being "rolled into one person" before being "killed," she has every reason to react with revengeful glee—to treat it the way Hazel soon will, by slamming it against a wall. Instead, she reacts with a startlingly positive feeling: "'Well I declare,' she murmured, 'you're right cute, ain't you?'" (104). This may not quite reach the level of compassionate wisdom exhibited by the grandmother in "A Good Man Is Hard to Find" when she reaches out to The Misfit, but when Sabbath tells Hazel "I might have fixed him!" (106) following Hazel's violence against the mummy, we see that she still has hope about the possibility of connecting with an adult she can treat as a child.

A key point about Sabbath is that O'Connor does not have the novel give a final ending to Sabbath's story. She remains alive and free, ready to restart her life. The negative impression we are given about her in her final paragraphs may be attributed in part to the narrator's bias, in part to what will become clear later: that Mrs. Flood sees her as a rival who must be dismissed so that Mrs. Flood can continue the complex, mysterious work she needs to do.

The most deeply significant female character in *Wise Blood* other than Sabbath is Mrs. Flood, and my argument is that she may experience an even more believable redemption than does Hazel Motes. Certainly, she first appears in the novel as a rather ordinary and corrupt human being, mercenary and selfish. But as she studies the mystery represented by Hazel Motes, she overcomes her limitations, embarks on a spiritual voyage, and reaches out with love toward another human being. Perhaps more significantly, she is the novel's most significant figure for the audience of the novel, so that the reader of *Wise Blood* is being taught to experience what she experiences, to identify with her more than with Hazel. I believe that one meaning of Mrs. Flood's name is that she unleashes a flood—at least for the reader—of the wise blood referred to in the novel's title. Without claiming a specific source or influence, I would like to point out the possibility that O'Connor could have been aware, however vaguely, of the tradition of the Great Mother, in which the phrase "wise blood" would likely refer to the menstrual blood of female divinities (Barbara Walker 636).[10]

It should be noted that feminist critics have disagreed about the presence of a divine female principle in O'Connor's works. Louise Westling, after surveying the power of female divinity through history (159–61), concludes that O'Connor "probably was not...familiar with the extensive history of the Great Mother's worship as [Westling describes it], because much of the archeological evidence has been discovered and publicized in the years since her death" (161). Westling sees O'Connor typically punishing her female characters "with a finality which restores a balance with the dominant values of the world in which we all must live" (174); in other words, O'Connor always eventually allies herself with the patriarchy.

On the other hand, in Cynthia Seel's recent archetypal reading of O'Connor, "O'Connor's characters...recover feminine potential as they undergo trials" (2). After citing Westling's views, Seel counters that "...the feminine principle in O'Connor's fiction exists as a transcendent positive force..." (2). My inclination is to argue that O'Connor's published texts support the sort of reading Seel has produced, despite what we might suspect that O'Connor herself, as an orthodox Catholic, would probably say about such readings. As O'Connor worked out for herself the question of what it might mean to become a female writer, she surely was asking herself what the ideal status of women within religion might become.

There are early hints of Mrs. Flood's connection to ancient wisdom. Although Mrs. Flood is introduced by the narrator as "resembling the mop she carried upside-down" (*CW* 60), we have seen another comparison to a mop a few pages earlier: the owl that Hazel takes very seriously at the zoo is also described as looking "like a piece of mop" (54). Beneath the satire here, we may be reminded of classical associations of owls with divine females—the most famous being Athena. Other details possibly

---

[10] In one Norse myth, for example, Odin "stole...'wise blood' from [a] cauldron...in the keeping of the Earth-goddess..." and, in another myth, "...Odin gave up one of his eyes for the privilege of drinking from the feminine Fount of Wisdom..." (Barbara Walker 735).

worth rethinking are those about Mrs. Flood's head: she has "a nose that had been called Grecian" and "hair clustered like grapes" (124). Perhaps we should recall the stone women of the classical park museum (55) and see in Mrs. Flood a new version of the female who is more impressive when she is blind.

A passage about Enoch comes close to describing wise blood as female:

> [H]e was certain when he woke up that today was the day he was going to know on. His blood was rushing around like a woman who cleans up the house after the company has come, and he was surly and rebellious. When he realized that today was the day, he decided not to get up. He didn't want to justify his daddy's blood, he didn't want to be always having to do something that something else wanted him to do, that he didn't know what it was and that was always dangerous.
>
> Naturally, his blood was not going to put up with any attitude like this. He was at the zoo by nine-thirty, only a half-hour later than he was supposed to be. All morning his mind was not on the gate he was supposed to guard but was chasing around after his blood, like a boy with a mop and a bucket, beating something here and sloshing down something there, without a second's rest. (*CW* 76)

Whereas Enoch associates his wise blood with his father, that is a misunderstanding on Enoch's part. It makes more sense here to associate his wise blood, that supervisor of mopping, with the power of female authority. O'Connor's imagery suggests that the divine female has been reduced in modern times to the status of a cleaning lady, but the cleaning lady is ready for a promotion. Mrs. Flood is described as acting "as if she had once owned the earth and been dispossessed of it" (120)—and this is usually taken as merely a sarcastic comment by a narrator intent on diagnosing her pretension. But might not the idea that she once owned the earth be a clue to a mythic reading in which we take Mrs. Flood more seriously? Surely the surname Flood implies a connection to ancient myths about floods.

As Hazel is blinding himself—with a bucket of water from Mrs. Flood's house, water to which he adds quicklime—Mrs. Flood thinks, we are told, that "She was not religious or morbid, for which every day she thanked her stars" (*CW* 119). And yet she does become morbid, and the stars that she imagines will indeed make her religious. That her morbidity comes to her as a surprise is made apparent at the beginning of the next (and final) chapter: "...she didn't like to look at the mess he had made in his eye sockets. At least she didn't think she did. If she didn't keep her mind going on something else when he was near her, she would find herself leaning forward, staring into his face as if she expected to see something she hadn't seen before" (120).

Mrs. Flood, a static character to some readers, actually goes through profound development. She may never stop worrying about money, putting things into terms stemming from feeling cheated of it—a trait that allows the narrator to satirize her throughout—but she learns to be genuinely interested in Hazel and then even to love him. What becomes love clearly starts as something else: "She thought of benefits that might accrue to his widow should he leave one" (*CW* 124). And even without hoping for his death, she thinks for a while that she could benefit from marrying him because she could "have him committed to the state institution for the insane" (127). But a more compassionate alternative takes over: "...gradually her plan had become to marry him and keep him. Watching his face had become a habit with her; she wanted to penetrate the darkness behind it and see for herself what was there" (127). Consequently, by the time she pronounces her understated, very practical-sounding proposal—"...there's only one thing for you and me to do. Get married. I wouldn't do it under any ordinary condition but I would do it for a blind man and a sick one" (128)—her practical tone is hiding her truest, deepest feeling.

Like Sabbath talking about the church in her heart, Mrs. Flood means it, and hopes love will bloom, when she declares her feeling: "'I got a place for you in my heart, Mr. Motes,' she said and felt it shaking like a bird cage; she didn't know whether he was coming toward her to embrace her or not" (*CW* 129). Like Sabbath, she mixes her statements of love with harsher statements, but the harsh comments are those of self-defense. Her true feeling is in her tears at night, and even the narrator seems forced to admit that "She wanted to run out into the rain and cold and hunt him and find him huddled in some half-sheltered place and bring him back and say, Mr. Motes, Mr. Motes, you can stay here forever, or the two of us will go where you're going, the two of us will go" (129–30). When Hazel is returned by the police, she adds a similarly sincere expression of feeling, reinforced by her taking Hazel's hand: "'I knew you'd come back,' she said. 'And I've been waiting for you. And you needn't to pay any more rent but have it free here, any way you like, upstairs or down. Just however you want it and with me to wait on you, or if you want to go on somewhere, we'll both go" (131).

By the novel's final line, Mrs. Flood, through her study of Hazel's face with "[t]he outline of a skull...plain under his skin" and "burned eye sockets...lead[ing] into the dark tunnel where he had disappeared" (*CW* 131), is creating her own religious sense, recreating her divinity with its ancient basis, despite Hazel's long-term, uncompassionate inattention toward anyone other than himself. Mrs. Flood feels as if she is "blocked at the entrance," unable to "begin" (131), but these sentiments are the distortions of the intellect. Mrs. Flood knows without knowing she knows; the reader of the novel may achieve an understanding of wise blood that is more thorough than what any of the characters ever achieves within the novel. *Wise Blood* ends with an image of the essential tie between wise blood and female attributes that transcend intellect.

While Donahoo has written that *Wise Blood* "refuses to project any positive outcome to Mrs. Flood's decision" to choose "self-hood reliant on Haze" (26), I believe that Mrs. Flood transcends Hazel, who "rudely" tells her, "You can't see" (*CW* 125)—as if he agreed with the narrator that the woman's case is forever hopeless. When one regards Mrs. Flood's rather mean statements about Sabbath in the context of Mrs. Flood's conclusive new beginning, I believe it makes sense to see Mrs. Flood as being like Hazel in relation to Solace Layfield or Enoch Emery in relation to Gonga—as a novelistic protagonist who must reject the old self's double in order to remake the self. Unlike Solace and the man who originally wears the Gonga suit, however, Sabbath is clearly not killed. Perhaps Mrs. Flood sends Sabbath, her Eve/Mary, into the world of work at the detention home, but Sabbath has every opportunity, according to this novel, to rediscover the wise blood that Mrs. Flood has and may even eventually understand.

WORKS CITED

Barounis, Cynthia. "Reading Through Spectacle(s): Flannery O'Connor and the Politics of Drag." *Flannery O'Connor Review*, vol. 5, 2007, pp. 99–118.

Bowlin, Catherine L. "'In Case His Vision Should Ever Become Dim': Annie Lee Jackson's Wise Blood." 2016. Georgia College, MA thesis.

Daniel, Scott. "Gender-Bending Innuendo and Mystical Theology in O'Connor's *Wise Blood*." *Flannery O'Connor Review*, vol. 4, 2006, pp. 110–21.

Donahoo, Robert. "O'Connor and *The Feminine Mystique*: 'The Limitations That Reality Imposed.'" *"On the Subject of the Feminist Business"*: *Re-Reading Flannery O'Connor*, edited by Teresa Caruso, New York, Peter Lang, 2004, pp. 9–28.

Gordon, Sarah. *Flannery O'Connor: The Obedient Imagination*. Athens, University of Georgia Press, 2000.
Harris, Carole K. "The Echoing Afterlife of Clichés in Flannery O'Connor's 'Good Country People.'" *Flannery O'Connor Review*, vol. 5, 2007, pp. 56–66.
Martin, Marcelina. Photographs featuring O'Connor family's "kiddie coop." *A Literary Guide to Flannery O'Connor's Georgia*, by Sarah Gordon, et al., Athens, University of Georgia Press, 2008, pp. 6, 8.
O'Connor, Flannery. Unpublished manuscripts. Flannery O'Connor Collection, Special Collections, Georgia College Library and Instructional Technology Center, Milledgeville.
———. *Wise Blood*. *Flannery O'Connor: Collected Works*, edited by Sally Fitzgerald. New York, Library of America, 1988, pp. 1–131.
Prown, Katherine Hemple. *Revising Flannery O'Connor: Southern Literary Culture and the Problem of Female Authorship*. Charlottesville, University Press of Virginia, 2001.
Robillard, Douglas, Jr. "The Mystery of Children's Suffering in *Wise Blood* and *A Memoir of Mary Ann*." *Flannery O'Connor Review*, vol. 7, 2009, pp. 69–77.
Seel, Cynthia L. *Ritual Performance in the Fiction of Flannery O'Connor*. Rochester, NY, Camden House, 2001.
Srigley, Susan. "Moral Vision and the Grotesque: *Wise Blood*." *Flannery O'Connor's Sacramental Art*. Notre Dame, IN, University of Notre Dame Press, 2004, pp. 55–89.
———. "Penance and Love in *Wise Blood*: Seeing Redemption?" *Flannery O'Connor Review*, vol. 7, 2009, pp. 94–100.
Thimme, Jane. "Photographs from the O'Connor Childhood Home in Savannah." *Flannery O'Connor Review*, vol. 5, 2007, pp. 82–88.
Walker, Alice. "Beyond the Peacock: The Reconstruction of Flannery O'Connor." *In Search of Our Mothers' Gardens: Womanist Prose*, New York, Harcourt, 1983, pp. 42–59.
Walker, Barbara G. *The Woman's Encyclopedia of Myths and Secrets*. New York, HarperCollins, 1983.
Westling, Louise. *Sacred Groves and Ravaged Gardens: The Fiction of Eudora Welty, Carson McCullers, and Flannery O'Connor*. Athens, University of Georgia Press, 1985.
Wood, Ralph C. *Flannery O'Connor and the Christ-Haunted South*. Grand Rapids, MI, Eerdmans, 2004.
Yaeger, Patricia S. "The Woman without Any Bones: Anti-Angel Aggression in *Wise Blood*." *New Essays on* Wise Blood, edited by Michael Kreyling. New York, Cambridge University Press, 1995, pp. 91–116.

Flannery O'Connor's Child Bishops

with Elaine E. Whitaker

Relating Flannery O'Connor and the medieval is hardly new, the approach having been used in full-length studies by Anthony Di Renzo and Rufel F. Ramos. O'Connor biographer Brad Gooch has published an essay about reasons to consider O'Connor medieval, starting with her comment that she had a "thirteenth century" sensibility. Yet medievalism is both more than and different from these sources. As operationalized by Leslie Workman, it is "the ongoing process of recreating, reinventing, and reenacting medieval culture in postmedieval times."[1] How then does the concept of medievalism provide an additional lens for O'Connor's art?

Studies of Flannery O'Connor contribute to the study of medievalism when one accepts the premise that the medieval period was characterized by respect for *authoritas*. Its defining feature was acceptance of received tradition, whether classical or religious. O'Connor was raised within and consistently observed her Roman Catholic faith, calling herself a Thomist.[2] In turn, the concept of medievalism brings to the art of O'Connor not only the tool of grotesquery but also an understanding that hierarchal value systems invite and ritualize significant revolt. Overseers of such systems provide rituals to ameliorate perceived and perhaps real oppression, while still acculturating new members. O'Connor's participation in medievalism fascinatingly informs her treatment of one such group—fictional children. Specifically, it is possible to map several of O'Connor's plots that involve juvenile characters onto the medieval idea of the boy bishop, a practice that extended beyond gender restrictions. Examining O'Connor's works in relation to the medieval boy-bishop

---

[1] Quoted by Elizabeth Emery and Richard Utz 2; see also Karl Fugelso 53–61.

[2] See her 20 Apr. 1961 letter to John Hawkes, *CW* 1149.

tradition makes clearer the extent to which O'Connor empowers children, both male and female.

The medieval church's annual identification of boy and, in isolated cases, girl bishops fits into its liturgical calendar of seasons, allowing annual recapitulation of birth, death, and resurrection. Cathedrals or abbeys that elected to have child bishops did so during the seasons of Advent and Christmastide. Selection or election might occur on Saint Nicholas day, December 6, and be effective for a period not to extend beyond Epiphany. In other words, a child bishop replaced their adult counterparts during a fixed festival season when both daylight and the patience of students was shortest. During this season of reversals, youth were allowed almost all privileges.[3] The medieval scholar Neil MacKenzie has found a particularly fascinating instance in which an archbishop observed boys playing in his courtyard and noted that a "little boy" (10) who was playing bishop had performed a valid baptism.

Following O'Connor's construction of children and youth from an early draft of *Wise Blood* through her first short story collection provides evidence that O'Connor experiments with and perfects the festal breaches of order that are allowed medieval child bishops. The lowly character named Sabbath in *Wise Blood* was, in many of O'Connor's drafts, a totally

---

[3] See E. K. Chambers as well as Neil MacKenzie, *The Medieval Boy Bishops* and "Boy into Bishop." Evidence of the existence of a season when boys and girls had their own vestments comes from the inventories and records of expenditures in the Records of Early English Drama series. Generally, those identified would minimally have made a first communion but not yet have experienced puberty. A typical child bishop would be around twelve years old. What these young people did during the season of reversal has been addressed by Chambers and, more recently, by MacKenzie. They sponsored feasts, made diocesan visits, preached sermons, and, although they typically could not consecrate or celebrate the Sacraments, they had ample opportunities to chant during the service. Thus, a good singing voice was such a conspicuous asset that the head of the boy choristers was a likely candidate to be boy bishop. The duration of a boy bishop's reign was estimated by Chambers as between three and eight days. MacKenzie has found support for nuns to elect a young girl (*Medieval* 93) during this season. Boy-bishop sermons were written by adults, including Erasmus. One of these is very well documented, rhetorically, and includes explication of the text from which O'Connor derived the title for her second novel, *The Violent Bear It Away*: Matt. 11:12 (MacKenzie, *Medieval* 63).

sincere prophet figure who experienced visions. O'Connor revised Sabbath away from this early conception but may have put some of the early Sabbath into *The Violent Bear It Away* as the powerful Lucette Carmody, a character much younger than Sabbath.

Several of the short stories found in O'Connor's first collection, *A Good Man Is Hard to Find and Other Stories*, contain child bishops. Even the title story contains a girl and a boy on a trip analogous to the diocesan pilgrimage and festal banquet associated with the reign of a medieval boy bishop. Although without as much control as O'Connor will later accord some of her child characters, June Star in "A Good Man Is Hard to Find" succeeds in acting temporarily as a star, performing "her tap routine" (*CW* 141) at the barbecue place where her family eats their last meal, and each child is quite pleased that they have "had an ACCIDENT" (145) on their pilgrimage. While John Wesley and June Star may be no more than holy innocents, the outlines of a child bishop's temporary entitlement emerge in the collection's second story, "The River." Here an unusually young character, Harry Ashfield, renames himself after a nineteen-year-old evangelist, Bevel Summers, and ultimately drowns himself. The drowning of a boy bishop is not unprecedented, as the corpse of such a child was once observed in his miniature bishop's robes floating in the Seine (MacKenzie, *Medieval* 1). In Harry/Bevel's case, the self-baptism is only successful when his coat takes on sufficient water to submerge him beyond rescue. It is the same coat where he had hidden a children's religious book that he had stolen from the home of his sitter. Like a medieval boy bishop as described by MacKenzie, Harry/Bevel Ashfield reacts to his sense of oppression by performing a baptism. Just as a boy bishop's performance of the rite of baptism could be ruled valid (MacKenzie, *Medieval* 19-20), so too might Harry/Bevel's self-baptism, even though—or perhaps precisely because—he has received his religious training from a book called "The Life of Jesus Christ for Readers under Twelve" (*CW* 160). While there may be flaws in Harry's plan to baptize himself, it is not unusual for O'Connor's evangelical characters to depart from orthodoxy without authorial disapproval. Many interpreters of this story have Harry/Bevel running away from his secular parents and toward the religiosity of his babysitter, Mrs. Connin, and the preacher who first baptizes Harry. However, the boy-bishop tradition should open our eyes to the ways in which Harry/Bevel rejects *all* of the religious authorities he has encountered—not just the authority of his parents. At the story's end, Harry/Bevel heads to the river on a day when he knows he will not find Mrs. Connin at home (169), and he does not want to reconnect with Rev. Summers either: "He intended not to fool with preachers any more…" (170). There is a fair amount of room for debate about whether Connin and Rev. Summers are good religious guides, but even if they are perfect, Harry/Bevel clearly wants to establish his own authority, and the boy-bishop tradition encourages our being open to that. Like a medieval boy bishop who, if he died while in office, would be buried in his vestments (Mackenzie, *Medieval* xii), Harry/Bevel drowns while still wearing his coat.

Probably the majority of the stories in O'Connor's collection *A Good Man* have some version of a boy or girl bishop. Consider the young hitchhiker at the end of "The Life You Save May Be Your Own," the boy who accepts none of Mr. Shiftlet's nonsense about the wonderful mother who "taught him his first prayers at her knee" (*CW* 182) and whom Shiftlet calls "a angel of Gawd" (183). The hitchhiker destroys Mr. Shiftlet's sentimental authority with an outburst delivered as he jumps from Shiftlet's car: "You go to the devil!…My old woman is a flea bag and yours is a stinking pole cat!" (183). The result of this outburst is that Mr. Shiftlet prays, and his prayer might even be sincere. In the subsequent story, "A Stroke of Good Fortune," the pistol-packing boy certainly overthrows the authority of Ruby Hill. Even if this "six-year-old boy who lived on the fifth floor" (187) does seem a bit young for the task of diocesan visitations on the building's spiral staircase, given his fetal-sounding name, Hartley Gilfeet's weapon on Ruby's chair unseats her.

An example of a girl bishop is the unnamed child in the next story, "A Temple of the Holy Ghost." Oppressed by family, including her only slightly older cousins who attend school at a convent, the child sometimes doubts her own religiosity: "She could never be a saint, but she thought she could be a martyr if they killed her quick" (*CW* 204). Nevertheless, this girl bishop achieves a valid Catholic insight into the unity of body and spirit as she reinterprets the story she has been told about an intersex worker in a freak show at the local fair. Her story includes passages about singing—a key element in the boy-bishop tradition, for boy bishops were often selected from the church choir. Additionally, the story ends with the child being embraced by a nun. One might also consider the boys who sing hymns in this story as Protestant versions of the boy bishop.

Then there is Nelson, the boy in the story O'Connor called her favorite, "The Artificial Nigger." The child consistently overthrows the moral authority of his grandfather, Mr. Head. Although Nelson seems to give in to Mr. Head at the story's end, claiming that he will never again go to Atlanta (*CW* 231), it surely makes more sense to see Nelson as a boy bishop whose term of authority has ended—and who will likely regain his subversive authority in another form as he grows up.

The subsequent story, "A Circle in the Fire," features both boy and girl bishops. Three boys from Atlanta visit a farm and announce, like boy bishops, their general authority—over both the owner and her farm. As in the medieval pattern, the characters Powell Boyd, Garfield Smith, and W. T. Harper require the generosity of those they visit while in the boy-bishop role, and they feel free to do harm to the place they are visiting. Attention to the boy-bishop tradition helps make sense of the story's controversial last line, in which they are described, at least from the point of view of Sally Virginia Cope, as "prophets...dancing in the fiery furnace, in the circle the angel had cleared for them" (*CW* 251). The boys do not always have to be taken as religious authorities, only at certain times. The girl bishop in this story is Sally Virginia, who also works throughout the story to overturn the authority of her outspokenly pious mother, thus earning her surname, Cope. Coping, of course, is what adults try to do in the face of subversive children, but it is also a term for a piece of clothing worn by clergy. In this story, Sally Virginia becomes fully deserving of her cope.

Four years lapse between the first publication of *A Good Man* and O'Connor's completion of the first draft of her second novel, *The Violent Bear It Away*. By its final draft, she has reached a new level of complexity on the empowerment of children. The novel's title comes from a passage in the gospel of Matthew that was the subject of one of the surviving sermons delivered by a medieval boy bishop. *The Violent Bear It Away* contains multiple iterations of what Mikhail Bakhtin called the "characteristic logic [of carnival], the peculiar logic of the 'inside out' (*á l'envers*), of the 'turnabout,' of a continual shifting from top to bottom, from front to rear, of numerous parodies and travesties, humiliations, profanations, comic crownings and uncrownings" (11). Most obvious as the novel's focal character is Frances Marion Tarwater. The agenda for his boy bishopric has been carefully prepared for him by his great uncle Mason Tarwater, whose stories have molded his reality. Young Tarwater feels oppressed by schooling and counters with moments of "sass" in which he challenges his great uncle's stories. In *Violent*, lineage acts as an oppressive hierarchy through Tarwater's knowledge of "two complete histories, the history of the world, beginning with Adam, and the history of the schoolteacher" (*CW* 366), Tarwater's uncle Rayber. It is a complex family tree that leaves him born out of wedlock to "a whore" (366). His boy bishopric begins at the death of his great uncle when he becomes "drunk as a coot" (396) and sets fire to property rather than following the great uncle's explicit instructions for Christian burial. Indulgence in alcohol, a cause for Tarwater's prior punishment by his great uncle, remains to this day a mark of carnival, and Robert Donahoo has argued thoroughly that *The Violent Bear It Away* is a hymn to moonshine. Tarwater's torching and his travel between urban and rural locations are both features of actual boy bishropics. Tarwater's bishopric ends when he realizes that his great uncle has already received Christian burial despite his efforts to avoid providing it. The reversion to established order manifests itself through the efforts of the traditionally lowest characters, the African-American Buford Munson, and the woman at the store who disciplines Tarwater by refusing to sell him a grape soda, symbolically excommunicating him. In the calendar of the church year, all boy bishoprics end—ideally, but not always, in progress toward adulthood.

The contention that multiple boy bishops exist in *The Violent Bear It Away* emerges most clearly when Tarwater's uncle Rayber takes his son Bishop and Tarwater to Cherokee Lodge toward the end of the novel. At the lodge's registration desk, Tarwater asserts the authority to name himself. In the Church, a bishop is presented for ordination using his full name and, in subsequent references, only his Christian name. During the registration scene at Cherokee, the young Tarwater is intent on correcting Rayber's attempt to sign him in as Frank Rayber (*CW* 425); ignoring Rayber, Tarwater completes "his essay on the [registration] card" (426) with his own version of his chosen full name and the words "NOT HIS SON" (428). By bringing Tarwater to the lodge, Rayber has succeeded in putting him forth as a boy bishop with a lake "set down in front of" him (428) and not of his own choosing. Not only does this scene increase the likelihood that Tarwater will act in his capacity as boy bishop, but it also introduces the possibility of agency for the character who bears the maiden name of his mother, Bernice Bishop, as his Christian name.

The character named Bishop, though his very young age and mental disability might seem to disqualify him as able to take on the temporary authority of a boy bishop, is very powerful. O'Connor considered writing from Bishop's point of view (see file 181a) and considered having Bishop speak understandably (see file 182a), but she finally saw more power in a character of near silence and childlike mystery. Bishop has already been the subject of strong critical claims. Karl Martin, for example, has argued that Bishop should be considered the "true protagonist" of the novel because his religious status is superior to that of old Mason Tarwater and because Bishop actually controls the performance of the novel's most significant baptism (158, 181). Martin seems worried that his readers will think he is claiming that Bishop is a Christ symbol (167); less worried about making such a claim, Seth Greer has enthusiastically suggested that Bishop is described the way Christ looks in many of O'Connor's possessions found in the Special Collections library at Emory University (9–10). Martin's argument about Bishop would benefit from the concept of the medieval boy bishop as a way to explain the surprising authority that a boy like Bishop Rayber can demonstrate.[4]

The key to using the concept of the boy-bishop tradition for a new understanding of O'Connor's character named Bishop is probably a scene just before Tarwater simultaneously baptizes and drowns Bishop. The narration at this point basically reflects the point of view of Rayber, who thinks he is in a battle against Tarwater for mastery of Bishop. Startlingly for Rayber, however, Bishop and Tarwater both look "somehow ancient" (*CW* 452) as they head toward the lake where the drowning and baptism will occur. Rayber is surprised to note that Bishop may be more powerful than Tarwater, more able to transform and renew the world:

> Each weed that grew out of the gravel looked like a live green nerve. The world might have been shedding its skin. The two [boys] were in front of him half way down the dock, walking slowly, Tarwater's hand still resting just under Bishop's hat; but it seemed to Rayber that it was Bishop who was doing the leading, that the child had made the capture. He thought with a grim pleasure that sooner or later [Tarwater's] confidence in his own judgment would be brought low. (452)

When Rayber comments that "If anyone controlled Bishop, it would be himself," Rayber may think the word "himself" refers to Rayber, but Rayber's words could also ironically imply that Bishop himself might control what happens to Bishop. Note also that when Rayber

---

[4] For another reading of Bishop in *The Violent Bear It Away* that is compatible with the reading in this essay, see Chen.

hears "an unmistakable bellow" (455) coming from the lake, he seems to assume that the noise comes from the struggling Bishop as he resists drowning. But there is ambiguity here. Rayber also has a moment in which the bellowing appears "to come from inside" Rayber (456), and the reader is never quite sure who produces the noise. Perhaps it is Tarwater, who, like Rayber, is amazed into feeling like bellowing over the surprising power that Bishop takes on in this scene. Rayber has more in common with both Tarwater and Bishop than we usually acknowledge, for he too had a boy-bishop phase at fourteen in which, after having been singled out as special by Old Tarwater, he tries to overthrow the old man's authority (396). The rest of Rayber's life may be interpreted as a matter of living out the effects of having been a boy bishop.

Another way to apply the boy-bishop tradition to *The Violent Bear It Away* is to examine O'Connor's creation of a girl bishop, in the person of the child evangelist Lucette Carmody, whose sermon is heard by Rayber and Tarwater. Rayber has followed Tarwater in his nighttime procession through the city, with Tarwater almost invariably walking in front of his uncle, as Gary M. Ciuba has observed (134). Leading in a way that required others to follow is precisely what a medieval boy bishop would do during his reign. At one point, Tarwater enters a store-front church where Lucette Carmody, a female of eleven or twelve years who has been six years in ministry, is witnessing. She wears a shortened version of her mother's cape and gown. Rayber observes Lucette through a window, hoping to assert control over Tarwater by debunking the occasion. When Rayber sees Lucette, however, he quickly qualifies his skepticism, sure that the girl is "not a fraud" (*CW* 411), that Lucette believes sincerely (412). O'Connor critics have regularly discussed Rayber as a version of Dostoyevsky's Ivan Karamazov, who wants nothing to do with a God who allows the mistreatment of children.[5] If O'Connor was thinking of Dostoyevsky, Lucette Carmody delivers O'Connor's knockout punch to Ivan Karamazov. The girl bishop, empowered by the spotlight in a store-front church, has no use for the "pity" Rayber is sure she sees in his face when their eyes meet. Lucette preaches about the power of Christ as a child, and then she singles out Rayber for personal condemnation: "I see a damned soul before my eye!" (*CW* 415). Lucette overstates her case, but

---

[5] See, for example, Jessica Lynice Hooten Wilson.

as O'Connor famously said, "to the hard of hearing you shout" (*MM* 34). Lucette has to make clear that she neither needs nor wants Rayber's pity.

As was mentioned earlier, Lucette Carmody could be considered a reimagining of Sabbath Lily Hawks in *Wise Blood*, and unpublished novel manuscripts support this view. As O'Connor revised Sabbath Lily, the character became somewhat more calculating, and less powerful. With Lucette, we might say nearly the opposite. File 172 in the O'Connor Collection at Georgia College shows a Lucette forced to preach because of physical abuse by her mother. When Lucette breaks off her sermon and leaves the stage, she is still a sincere believer: she says Jesus has scolded her for being insufficiently authentic. Still, she seems ready to give up preaching, if her father would run away with her and start a dancing career. The final, published version of Lucette is more consistently committed to her preaching than is the character in the draft, and the ultimate difference between Lucette and Sabbath may well be that O'Connor was able to believe the younger female preacher could have more power than an older one. Her youth makes Lucette a better candidate for girl-bishop status.[6]

Additional language indicative of a pattern of reversals occurs sporadically throughout the novel, to the point that one might wonder if O'Connor deliberately added references to the carnivalesque. Among these instances are Tarwater's walk "*backwards* from the spot" (*CW* 475, italics added) of his great uncle's burial cross as he formally begins his career as a prophet; his "odd smile, like some strange *inverted* sign of grief" (397, italics added); his loss of his hat in the city after "let[ting] his face hang out *upsidedown* over the floating speckled street" (347, italics added) below the lawyer's office; Rayber's dream of covering "the same territory *backwards* in his sleep" (397, italics added); a recapitulation of this dream sequence as a chase "through an interminable alley that twist-

---

[6] Another interesting sign of an original conception of Lucette is in file 175c. Here, in some manuscript material for *The Violent Bear It Away* that resembles an early O'Connor story, "The Artificial Nigger," as Tarwater and Old Tarwater are returning home on a train after a day in the city, a train conductor says that Tarwater might want to return to the city someday in order to see some of what he had missed. There are movies, shops, fancy buildings and signs, sporting events, and even a young female preacher (12). Such a description hardly prepares for the power and sincerity of the final version of Lucette Carmody.

ed suddenly back on itself and reversed the roles of pursuer and pursued" (417); the gender reversal of "comic recognition" (396) that occurs when Rayber puts Tarwater into Bernice Bishop Rayber's pink bedroom; the newspaper photo that shows Bishop's resuscitator as "striped bottom forward" (419); Tarwater's word for the unconscious or subconscious, "underhead" (436); Rayber's memory of his first trip to Powderhead in which, "When he had been on this road the first time, he had ridden it [facing] backwards" (443) in a wagon; the moon at Cherokee Lodge that "might have been the sun rising on the *upsidedown* half of the world" (454, italics added); and the half of his clothing Tarwater has put "on backwards and did not notice" (472) following his rape.

Only one of O'Connor's late stories, "The Lame Shall Enter First," a later version of the Rayber-Tarwater relationship in *The Violent Bear It Away*, clearly contains a boy bishop character. Rufus Johnson, Tarwater's double, has constructed himself unabashedly as both a disabled person and as a bastard, not the typical medieval boy bishop but nevertheless a powerful figure with historical precedent. That both Francis Marion Tarwater and Rufus Johnson in "The Lame Shall Enter First" produce the effect that was produced by boy bishops—and that led to the eventual prohibition of boy bishops—is most obvious in the characters' interactions respectively with Tarwater's uncle Rayber and with Sheppard. Like boy bishops, each is initially selected for the role he plays and is invited to live in the space previously occupied solely by the selector. Toward the end of each plot, the selector becomes weary of the reversal. Rayber comes to feel "pressure" that is "intolerable" from Tarwater, dreads the possibility of additional time "spent coping with the boy's cold intractability," and no longer wishes "to rehabilitate him" (*CW* 453). Similarly, Sheppard completely loses patience when Rufus Johnson baits him by eating pages of scripture. Sheppard angrily orders him to leave the dinner table and is momentarily relieved that Rufus is leaving the house (628).

The late candidates for girl-bishop status seem problematic, since they are nearly driven toward insanity by the experience (think college student Mary Grace in "Revelation," who heads to the asylum after her moment of authority) or killed in the experience (think Mary Fortune Pitts, who dies with her grandfather in "A View of the Woods"). This shortage of girl power is surprising when one considers O'Connor's serious contemplation of the life of Mary Ann Long—surely a candidate for a sort of girl-bishop status—in O'Connor's introduction to *A Memoir of Mary Ann*.

It is informative to end with an early story, "An Afternoon in the Woods," a story that almost made it into O'Connor's first published collection. A revision of a story called "The Turkey" in O'Connor's MFA thesis, "Afternoon" is fascinating as a story about a boy bishop. The main character, named Manley, is desperate to overturn the authority of his family, and his major strategy is to imagine that God has chosen Manley, that "…He wanted him on His side" (*CW* 768), and therefore that God has presented Manley with a wild turkey. Manley decides that "…what had happened was a clear call to the ministry," and he even manages to make God talk to him: "Only the best for a valuable man, God said" (769). But then, as Manley imagines himself in a position of religious authority, complete with "a roman collar" (770), "three country boys" come along to steal Manley's turkey, thus overturning the fresh authority of the new boy bishop. The story ends with Manley running home, feeling as if he is chased by "Something Awful" (772). This ending might undercut the boy's foolish illusion that he can have religious authority, but it may also indicate how very powerful are the forces that a boy bishop can stir up.

Flannery O'Connor was herself a precocious child, and her seriousness about the importance of childhood in general is well known. Even if she was less than fully aware of the medieval tradition of boy and girl bishops, her attitudes align impressively with a tradition of the medieval Church. If some of the claims about a particular character discussed in this article may seem a bit overstated, the evidence is still clear that O'Connor was always confident that her child characters are potentially quite powerful.

WORKS CITED

Bakhtin, M[ikhail] M[ikhailovich]. *Rabelais and His World*, translated by Hélène Iswolsky. Cambridge, MA, MIT Press, 1968.

Chambers, E. K. *The Medieval Stage*. London, Oxford University Press, 1903. 2 vols.

Chen, Connie. "The Deaths of Bishop Rayber: Drowning Normalcy in *The Violent Bear It Away*." *Flannery O'Connor Review*, vol. 18, 2020, pp. 108–25.

Ciuba, Gary M. *Desire, Violence, and Divinity in Modern Southern Fiction: Katherine Anne Porter, Flannery O'Connor, Cormac McCarthy, Walker Percy*. Baton Rouge, Louisiana State University Press, 2007. Southern Literary Studies.

Di Renzo, Anthony. *American Gargoyles: Flannery O'Connor and the Medieval Grotesque*. Carbondale, Southern Illinois University Press, 1993.

Donahoo, Robert. "Making Moonshine: Flannery O'Connor's Use of Regional Culture in *The Violent Bear It Away*." *Flannery O'Connor Review*, vol. 16, 2018, pp. 1–14.

Emery, Elizabeth, and Richard Utz, editors. *Medievalism: Key Critical Terms*. Cambridge, UK, D. S. Brewer, 2014.

Fugelso, Karl. "Continuity." *Medievalism: Key Critical Terms*, edited by Elizabeth Emery and Richard Utz. Cambridge, UK, D. S. Brewer, 2014, pp. 53–61.

Gooch, Brad. "Thirteenth-Century Lady." *Flannery O'Connor Review*, vol. 5, 2007, pp. 23–34.

Greer, Seth Ellis. "A Liturgy for the Ages: Witnessing the Sacraments in Flannery O'Connor's *The Violent Bear It Away*." 2019. University of Virginia, Undergraduate English Honors Thesis.

MacKenzie, Neil. "Boy into Bishop." *History Today*, vol. 37, no. 12, Dec. 1987, pp. 10–16.

_____. *The Medieval Boy Bishops*. Leicester, UK, Matador, 2012.

Martin, Karl E. "Suffering Violence in the Kingdom of Heaven: *The Violent Bear It Away*." *Dark Faith: New Essays on* The Violent Bear It Away, edited by Susan Srigley. Notre Dame, IN, University of Notre Dame Press, 2012, pp. 157–84.

O'Connor, Flannery. *Flannery O'Connor: Collected Works*, edited by Sally Fitzgerald. New York, Library of America, 1988.

_____. *Mystery and Manners: Occasional Prose*, edited by Sally Fitzgerald and Robert Fitzgerald. New York, Farrar, 1969.

_____. Unpublished manuscripts. Flannery O'Connor Collection, Special Collections, Georgia College Library and Instructional Technology Center, Milledgeville.

Ramos, Rufel F. *"My Kind of Comedy": An Exegetical Reading of Flannery O'Connor as Medieval Drama*. San Bernardino, CA, 2013.

Records of Early English Drama. http://reed.utoronto.ca/print-collections-2/.

[Wilson], Jessica Lynice Hooten. "Demonic Authority of the Autonomous Self in O'Connor and Dostoevsky." *Flannery O'Connor Review*, vol. 8, 2010, pp. 117–29.

The Hand of the Writer in "The Comforts of Home"

A survey of Flannery O'Connor's works might suggest that O'Connor has no respect for the vast majority of writers. O'Connor's narrator ridicules Miss Willerton in "The Crop" as she pretends to understand sharecroppers; Asbury Fox in "The Enduring Chill" as he makes a god of Art; Julian of "Everything That Rises Must Converge," who wants to give up selling typewriters to become a writer; Calhoun and Mary Elizabeth in "The Partridge Festival," who wish to honor a mass murderer through fiction and non-fiction, respectively; and Rayber in *The Violent Bear It Away*, especially when he writes an analysis of Old Tarwater's psyche for an audience of schoolteachers. Early in "The Nature and Aim of Fiction," O'Connor asserts that the basis of her remarks on fiction is St. Thomas's idea "that the artist is concerned with the good of that which is made" (*MM* 65); the true artist, however, is apparently quite rare, for O'Connor adds later in that essay,

> Everywhere I go I'm asked if I think the universities stifle writers. My opinion is that they don't stifle enough of them. There's many a best-seller that could have been prevented by a good teacher. The idea of being a writer attracts a good many shiftless people.... (84–85)

One danger, apparently, is that some writers try to get by on technique alone:

> [Y]ou almost feel that any idiot with a nickel's worth of talent can emerge from a writing class able to write a competent story. In fact, so many people can now write competent stories that the short story as a medium is in danger of dying of competence. We want competence, but competence by itself is deadly. What is needed is the vision to go with it, and you do not get this from a writing class. (86)

Perhaps this problem of "vision" is connected to the fact that in O'Connor's mind any writer inherently commits the error of producing a text that cannot quite be The Text, that cannot duplicate the authority of scripture. One strategy for overcoming this problem appears in "The Comforts of Home," a story that suggests how, when one writes a lie, one may sneak up on truths that the proud consciousness rejects. In general, O'Connor's characters benefit from the fact that they are not entirely competent. Their clumsiness is good for the soul.

The historian named Thomas in "The Comforts of Home" seems to most critics to be as unlikable as any of O'Connor's other writers.[1] In addition to being stodgy, overly dependent on his mother, and uncharitable toward strangers, Thomas seems to accept his father's misogyny. Thomas is so disgusted with the physical body as to deserve the label Manichean.[2] He may also seem predictable as a literary creation. Several critics of the story have called "The Comforts of Home" weak, usually because of its characterization. David Eggenschwiler complains that Thomas is a "flat" character who does not "develop" or "surprise" (83), while Frederick Asals says that the characters seem "overdrawn" (109).[3] Although Thomas is something of a cartoonish character, the excessiveness of his character to some extent helps to produce the complexity of his psyche. In my reading of the story, he works to bring about his own redemption, and O'Connor treats writing—even the writing of untruths—as part of a complex of subversive and redemptive forces. While some writing may be largely controlled by the conscious mind, the process is also an expression of the unconscious. Thomas discovers his own sexuality and irrationality, both of which discoveries result from the uncovering of his female side.

The first step in seeing the positive aspects of writing in this story is to notice that writing is associated with a number of images relating to

---

[1] Sister Bertrande [Meyers] says, for example, that "[o]ne can scarcely curb the inexorable, steadily rising disgust that mounts to the point of nausea and threatens to overflow" (417).

[2] Compare John R. May's argument that "[i]t is not sexuality as such that makes Thomas cringe, but sexual license, perhaps genuine nymphomania" (110).

[3] Kathleen Feeley, however, suggests that O'Connor intended such characterization; Feeley says the characters in O'Connor's story "seem to be *consciously* overdrawn" (37; emphasis added).

The Hand of the Writer in "The Comforts of Home"

the power of the hand. Readers learn little about what Thomas writes, but they do know that, with "pen in hand," Thomas becomes "articulate" and self-confidently powerful (*CW* 580). Throughout the story, as he battles with his mother about the presence in their house of a delinquent girl named Sarah Ham (alias Star Drake), Thomas is usually tongue-tied and unable to follow the repeated advice from his dead father's voice, to put down his foot. When he is able to act, he seems to do so through significant gestures he makes with his hand. For example, he puts a pistol in the pocketbook of Sarah Ham after clumsily accusing her of stealing the gun, and he shoots his mother after he is caught planting the gun. Thomas's scene with the handbag is O'Connor's most overtly Freudian: "He grabbed the red pocketbook. It had a skin-like feel to his touch and as it opened, he caught an unmistakable odor of the girl. Wincing, he thrust in the gun and then drew back. His face burned an ugly dull red" (592). After Sarah catches him and exclaims, "Tomsee put his pistol in my bag!" readers learn that Thomas stands "slightly hunched, his hands hanging helplessly at the wrists as if he [has] just pulled them up out of a pool of blood" (593). By the end of the story, then, the hand of Thomas seems to be an organ at once intellectual, sexual, and potentially destructive.

To understand the potential of the hands of Thomas the writer, readers should next examine a few clues to his psychology and to the ways in which the hand fulfills unconscious desires. On a conscious level, Thomas seems to believe that he has a purely objective interest in the history of his county's first settlers and that his mother's charitable acts toward a "dirty criminal slut" (*CW* 593) are objectionable because they disturb the peace that helps him write. Thomas consciously believes that virtue is essentially moderate and orderly, in contrast to his mother's practice of a generosity that is immoderate and disruptive. He tells himself that "...far from being opposed to virtue, he [sees] it as the principle of order and the only thing that makes life bearable" (575). On an unconscious level, however, he admires and desires the turmoil of his mother's excessive virtue, and he wishes to transform himself to embrace such excess. His attempt to object intellectually to his mother's excessive charity contains a moment of clumsiness, a slip that reveals his unconscious desire. He imagines that if his mother

> [h]ad...been in any degree intellectual, he could have proved to her from early Christian history that no excess of virtue is justified,

that a moderation of good produces likewise a moderation in evil, that if Ant[h]ony of Egypt had stayed at home and attended to his sister, no devils would have plagued him. (575)

This attitude suggests that an excess of good and an excess of evil go together as well; and assuming that Thomas indeed knows about St. Anthony,[4] readers may well conclude that Thomas unconsciously imitates, and even improves upon, the saint's excessiveness. St. Anthony did not abandon his sister; when he gave away his money, he did, after all, keep "enough to support his sister, whom he entrusted to a community of pious women" (Meyer 1:594). By Thomas's own standards, in order for St. Anthony to be a moderate, he would have had to be more personally involved in his sister's upbringing. For Thomas to practice moderation as he himself defines it, then, he would be required to welcome Sarah Ham into his home as a sister. By consciously resisting his mother and Sarah instead of properly attending to them—instead of becoming, like St. Anthony, a "patron...of swineherds" ("Saints" 2464) by caring for a girl named Ham—Thomas chooses a path that makes him even more of a figure of excess than St. Anthony was.[5] Thomas's path also differs from that of St. Anthony in that Thomas does not genuinely desire to defeat those who plague him. Instead, he appears to indulge them, to cooperate with them, even to let them get out of hand, so that the excess of error will produce an excess of virtue.

To assume that Sarah Ham is symbolically a sister to Thomas may seem odd, but several clues suggest that the two may be considered siblings. Both characters manifest self-disgust. Furthermore, Thomas's mother equates the two by repeatedly reminding Thomas and herself that he might have been Sarah. Thomas seems to agree with her, feeling "a deep unbearable loathing for himself as if he were turning slowly into the girl" (*CW* 575). At times, in fact, Thomas seems to understand his similarity to Sarah Ham better than his mother does. Indeed, among the "comforts of home" that his mother mistakenly feels Thomas should be thankful for is the condition of having "no bad inclinations, nothing bad [he was] born with" (582). Later Thomas's mother says that she and her

---

[4] Marian Burns reports that, in a draft of "The Comforts of Home," Thomas "wrote a thesis on Anthony of Egypt" (79).

[5] Frederick Asals has described Thomas's life as a "travesty" of St. Anthony's (115).

son "are not the kind of people who hate" (585–86), the narrator adding that she says it "as if this were an imperfection that had been bred out of them generations ago" (586). The mother does not seem to realize that one reason she is correct in sensing a connection between Thomas and Sarah Ham is precisely that Thomas has the inclination to sin.

Thomas might also be considered Sarah's sibling because the name Thomas means "twin," a word possibly relating to the fact that Sarah creates for herself and Thomas second names—"Star Drake" for herself and "Tomsee" for Thomas. Perhaps the most significant indication that Sarah is Thomas's twin is that she, too, is something of a historian, although her sort of history is the kind that we imagine Thomas consciously avoids—a history built on the lie. Thomas seems to believe that Sarah contaminates his objectivity; when he decides that she has stolen his gun (and my students have shown me that the gun *could* have been stolen by Thomas's mother), what angers Thomas is not the loss of the gun but the thought of Sarah's "hands sliding among his papers" (*CW* 588). For that matter, false texts, often connected with Sarah, fill the story. The sequence of events begins, for example, when Thomas's mother refuses to accept a newspaper account about Sarah, who was jailed for producing a false text: she supposedly wrote a "bad check" (576). Thomas suspects that his mother's report about Sarah's life is incomplete, that it omits horrible details (577). Readers discover that Sarah's personal history is a falsehood anyway and that she learned how to lie and to explain away her inclination to lie when passing "through the hands of several psychiatrists who…put the finishing touches to her education" (578). The culture's institutions cannot define her; she is "not insane enough for the asylum, not criminal enough for the jail, not stable enough for society" (577–78). Sarah does not even accept her own words about herself; the apparent value of the name she chose for herself, "Drake," is undercut by the fact that on the two occasions when she is figuratively in contact with birds—talking with "parakeets" (584) and treating the mother like a "parrot" (580)—Sarah apparently considers birds ridiculous. She seems to be largely a creature of repeatedly inaccurate stereotypes, her face compared to "a comedienne's in a musical comedy" (573) and her laugh to that of "a movie monster" (587).

The more readers notice the lies that fill the story, the more likely they are to suspect that Thomas himself takes part in his own distortion. What is known about Thomas's historical research suggests that his writing departs from objectivity because his motives are subversive. Thomas studies the original settlers of his county, and if readers wonder why he is interested in this subject, they may note that he considers his father an outsider, a squatter who passed for years as a man from the country (*CW* 583). John R. May criticizes Thomas by saying that any "historian of origins should have known that 'squatters' have no title to the place they settle in, least of all to another's mind" (108). I would suggest that Thomas *does* indeed know what May says he *should* know; one motivation for Thomas's work in history may well be to undercut the authority of the father who is squatting in Thomas's mind, to point out the father's lie.

At the same time, however, we see that Thomas seems to believe in parts of his father's advice; in other words, he knows that lies can be successful. Moreover, when Thomas decides to bring the story to a conclusion, he calls in the appropriately named Sheriff Farebrother, whom he considers, perhaps, another false text: the sheriff is "another edition of Thomas's father" (*CW* 585). The sheriff's echoing of Thomas's own ideas also suggests Farebrother's resemblance to Thomas. When Thomas tells the sheriff how to conduct the search of Sarah's room, Farebrother asks, "Want to swap jobs?" (590) O'Connor implies that Thomas can find his own twin all about him, that he is just as devoted to lies as anyone, and that it is ultimately up to him to determine what is true and what is a lie in interpreting his own case. In a moment of crisis Thomas sets himself up to decide that he can make an excess of errors produce an excess of good and that he shares the virtues of some of his twins, the most important of whom is Sarah.

Although Thomas may seem to be surrounded by lies against his will and may seem a victim, we are reminded that he has invited Sarah into the house on at least two occasions. Thomas "had been amused" (*CW* 576) by his mother's plans to visit Sarah and had not insisted that his mother not go to the jail to see her, even though his experience had taught him to expect his mother's activities to have far-reaching effects. After all, his mother's virtues had produced "a sense of devils" (576) in him before. Later, when given an opportunity to agree with his mother that Sarah should not be invited back to the house again, Thomas significantly chooses to say that his mother's activity is what bothers him, not Sarah's presence (583). Part of the significance of the end of the story, in which Thomas is caught red-handed, lies in the fact that Thomas has unconsciously been working to bring about such a reversal for himself.

That Thomas desires what ultimately might seem to be purely disastrous (rather than simply the efficient dismissal of Sarah) is suggested most clearly by the ways in which Thomas fails to follow Farebrother's orders to prepare for the search of Sarah's room. Thomas does not keep himself and the two women out of Farebrother's way; just after hearing the "sofa springs groan" (*CW* 592) as his mother rises from sleep, he starts to put the gun into the handbag; he fails to notice the end of Sarah's shower upstairs; and he puts the gun in a spot other than where he told Farebrother to search. Thomas has even hidden his car in a manner that would suggest that he was about to commit a crime (591).[6]

The precise significance of the reversal Thomas creates for himself may still be difficult to determine. As the lies multiply, Thomas faces the increasingly difficult problem of ascertaining whether any stable values can be found in words, of producing a firm link between error and virtue, between word and deed. His predicament is reminiscent of that of The Misfit, with his desperate plan to gain certainty about his guilt and the grounds for his punishment—"…you get you a signature and sign everything you do and keep a copy of it" (*CW* 151)—or of Mrs. McIntyre in "The Displaced Person," who, despite her spoken intentions, has never actually fired anyone (322). Thomas, I suggest, successfully inverts The Misfit's strategy; instead of turning actions into words, Thomas finally transforms his words into physical action. That Thomas be caught red-handed, that his lies become flesh, that his devotion to writing become a sexual hand in Sarah's bag are crucial.

In the end Thomas may appear possessed by the devilish father in his head; Thomas may indeed seem to become his father. Anthony Magistrale argues that Thomas finally achieves a "willingness to identify with and move toward his male parent" that produces a sort of "resolution" to his "Oedipal confusions" (59), while other critics tend to regard Thomas as primarily a victim (Asals 111; Feeley 35; Muller 89). I prefer the view that Thomas exorcises his "father devil," that he becomes more like his virtuous mother and sexual Sarah, and less like his incorporeal, Manichean father or the sheriff, his father's double. After all, the father's voice, simply explained, is the expression of thoughts that Thomas longs to transcend even as he indulges them; I believe Thomas has wished to dismiss his father, the squatter, all along.

In his embarrassment at being caught red-handed, Thomas experiences a moment of spiritual progress. Indeed, Thomas becomes like St.

---

[6] Miles Orvell has also suggested that Thomas may want to be caught (165).

Thomas, nicknamed "doubting Thomas," the disciple who refuses to believe in the resurrection until he examines the hand of Jesus and places his own hand in the wounded side of Christ.[7] When hard physical evidence of the resurrection is presented to him, doubting Thomas strongly affirms the divinity of Jesus, calling Him "[m]y Lord, and my God" (John 20:28). The disciple transforms doubt into faith just as Thomas transforms error into virtue, and both transformations are triggered by encounters with the physical body. Recalling that the name Thomas means "twin," readers may also compare the various indications that Thomas becomes the twin of Sarah (and others) to the legendary identification of St. Thomas as the twin brother of Jesus.[8] The legend suggests that St. Thomas discovers himself by touching the wound in the side of Jesus; in similar fashion, readers may also conclude that Thomas discovers his essentially irrational, sexual nature when he places his hand in Sarah's bag. For that matter, they may also conclude that Thomas's shooting his mother is a symbolic embodiment of St. Thomas's encounter with Christ. David Eggenschwiler suggests that the mother symbolizes Christ (83); and O'Connor herself, in a letter dated 3 Mar. 1961, called the mother "the character whose position is right" (*HB* 434). On a symbolic level, the climax of the story is simultaneously a sexual encounter and a parallel to the hand's being placed in the Lord's side.

Even in the opening sentence of the story, when he moves "to the side" to verify the return of one he thought might be gone forever (*CW* 573), Thomas is implicitly compared to St. Thomas. In addition, apocryphal texts attributed to St. Thomas, most notably the Gospel of Thomas (discovered in the mid-1940s) and the Acts of Thomas, make the saint as much of a historian, and as questionable a historian, as O'Connor's character. Also interesting to note is that the Acts of Thomas and Gospel of Thomas have been described as the two key Christian texts known to Mani, founder of Manicheism, who also believed in the twin self and called Christ "the right hand" (Quispel 1721). Readers may, furthermore, consider Thomas's attempt to transform himself as a way of exorcising his conscious attraction to an anti-physical, Manichean per-

---

[7] M. Bernetta Quinn has noted the parallel between Thomas and St. Thomas (162).

[8] See Chapter 39 of the Acts of Thomas, where "a she ass's colt" addresses St. Thomas as "[t]hou twin of Christ" (383).

spective. I believe that Thomas listens to his father not in order to destroy women so much as to force himself to confront the virtues associated with androgyny.

Several factors point to the possibility that "The Comforts of Home" is about the blending of genders. If readers accept the notion that the story alludes to the Gospel of Thomas, they may note that this biblical text ends with the implication that Jesus considered it necessary for a woman to become a man in order to be saved, a concept that might explain some of the gender-confusion in the story. The last paragraph of the Gospel of Thomas reads as follows:

> Simon Peter says to them "Let Mary go out from our midst, for women are not worthy of life!" Jesus says "See, I will draw her so as to make her male so that she also may become a living spirit like you males. For every woman who has become male will enter the Kingdom of heaven." (qtd. in Doresse 370)[9]

Perhaps this passage is tied to Thomas's tenuous masculinity and to linking Sarah with the masculine. Thomas's inability to act at the beginning of the story, readers may note, is related to the fact that, at that moment, Sarah may be in possession of his phallic gun. Moreover, the wealth of phallic imagery in the story is accompanied by considerable ambiguity about the value of what one is "born with" or "without." Helen S. Garson points out that the word *drake* in Sarah Ham's other name suggests "masculine force" because it is "a term for an eighteenth century cannon" (120), and Josephine Hendin (132) and Miles Orvell (164) suggest that Star Drake is a variant of Temple Drake, the character in Faulkner's *Sanctuary* who imagines she is turning into a boy. I would like to suggest that the traditional symbolism of the drake is also relevant to

---

[9] Compare the translation in the Gospel According to Thomas as translated by David R. Cartridge (qtd. in Davies 171). The passage is labeled as "A Saying Added Later to the Basic Text":

> Simon Peter said to them, "Let Mary leave us, because women are not worthy of the Life." Jesus said, "Look, I shall guide her so that I will make her male, in order that she also may become a living spirit, being like you males. For every woman who makes herself male will enter the Kingdom of Heaven."

the gender-blending in the story. In *Birds with Human Souls: A Guide to Bird Symbolism*, Beryl Rowland reports that

> Vincent of Beauvais said that drakes sometimes kill the female in the enthusiasm of their mating, and presumably Chaucer was alluding to this trait when in the *Parliament of Fowls* he described the drake as "strayer of his owene kynde." Whether Chaucer was also using natural history in *The Miller's Tale* when he pictured the old husband merrily pursuing his young wife like a white duck swimming after her drake is hard to determine. The sexual differentiation is curious, but the allusion may have an ironic appropriateness. According to ornithologists, "the female is not purely passive but will follow the male about, assuming coition posture, calling and pushing against him...." (49)[10]

One interesting implication here is that both Sarah and Thomas are destructive and direct their destructiveness not only at others but perhaps at themselves as well. The primary point I want to suggest, however, is that, rather than dismissing the female, the story unifies the genders. As Thomas's experience parodies the apocryphal Gospel of Thomas, it also improves upon its treatment of gender.

Critical estimates of the end of "The Comforts of Home" vary from "merely a bizarre melodrama" (Walters 146) to "a disappointing resolution" (Muller 89); and interpretations of the ending range from the opinion that it dramatizes "the pathetic abortion of the process of [psychological] integration" (Murphy and Cherry 92) to the view—one that I am currently more disposed to accept—that Thomas may experience (as Joseph R. Millichap, following another line of argument, suggests) a sort of "fortunate fall" (99). Indeed, as Thomas and Sarah look with horror on the dead body of Thomas's mother, the point of view shifts to the perspective of Sheriff Farebrother, who observes them without their knowledge. Most readers are understandably puzzled by Farebrother's theory about the scene: "...the fellow had intended all along to kill his mother and pin it on the girl," and "[o]ver her body, the killer and the slut were about to collapse into each other's arms" (*CW* 594). As soon as readers discover Farebrother's theory, they may wonder how well this

---

[10] Rowland does not specifically identify the source of the final quotation in the passage quoted here.

theory will go over in court; they may well wonder whether Thomas will discover that he cannot pin (pen?) the murder on Sarah. Could he not come up with an explanation to match Farebrother's? My resolution to this problem is that Thomas will value Farebrother's reading because he wants to be caught in his errors as thoroughly as possible. The story encourages readers to regard the spying sheriff as the twin of both Thomas, who spied in similar fashion at the beginning of the story, and the cop in the crime movie Sarah describes, the one "[t]hey were always putting something over on" (579). Farebrother translates the scene into a sensational news report or perhaps one of Sarah's bad movie scripts; he tells himself that "[h]e saw the facts as if they were already in print," and readers also learn that "[h]e was accustomed to enter upon scenes that were not as bad as he had hoped to find them, but this one met his expectations" (594).[11] Understanding his expectations, readers are justified in saying that Farebrother produces yet another lie. Noteworthy, however, is the fact that, at the same time, Farebrother does not realize his interpretation of the final scene is a lie, and, more importantly, that even though Thomas *will* see Farebrother's interpretation as a lie, Thomas may also discover a more valuable truth. Thus readers can interpret the ending as an expression of what Thomas has desired and finally accomplished. Thomas, in other words, manages to transform Farebrother's lie into the truth he desires. Thomas has entered, and can believe in, a world in which good as well as evil is found in excess and in which he shares the physicality of his mother and Sarah Ham.

Frederick Crews suggests that O'Connor is overrated as a writer. Describing her as a writer who never departs from "the regnant Creative Writing mode," and adding that "[e]ven the most impressive and original of her stories adhere to the classroom formula of her day" (49), Crews suggests that the author is guilty of being too consciously in control of her fiction, too much the "good girl" intent on giving male authority what it wants. Although an answer to Crews's entire argument will require further analysis, I propose that the reading presented here provides the beginning of a rejoinder. In "The Comforts of Home," O'Connor would seem to agree with Crews's belief that writing is most powerful when it involves complexities deeply challenging to the author's sense of

---

[11] Asals suggests that Farebrother's "tabloid language" is responsible for the equation of Thomas and Sarah (115).

selfhood; and if "The Comforts of Home" is read as a story that raises, in the writer's mind, issues of the author's gender identity or allegiance to male authority figures, perhaps O'Connor is, after all, the kind of writer that Crews would like her to be.

WORKS CITED

Acts of Thomas. *The Apocryphal New Testament*. 1924. Translated by Montague Rhodes James. Oxford, Clarendon, 1950, pp. 365–438.

Asals, Frederick. *Flannery O'Connor: The Imagination of Extremity*. Athens, University of Georgia Press, 1982.

Burns, Marian. "O'Connor's Unfinished Novel." *The Flannery O'Connor Bulletin*, vol. 11, 1982, pp. 76–93.

Crews, Frederick. "The Power of Flannery O'Connor." *New York Review of Books*, 26 Apr. 1990, pp. 49–55. This essay reappeared as "The Critics Bear It Away" in Crews's *The Critics Bear It Away: American Fiction and the Academy*, New York, Random, 1992, pp. 143–67.

Davies, Stevan L. *The Gospel of Thomas and Christian Wisdom*. New York, Seabury, 1983. Contains translation of the Gospel of Thomas by David R. Cartlidge in an appendix, pp. 157–71.

Doresse, Jean. *The Secret Books of the Egyptian Gnostics*. Translated by Philip Mairet. New York, Viking, 1960. Contains translation of the Gospel of Thomas by Leonard Johnston and Jean Doresse in an appendix, pp. 355–70.

Eggenschwiler, David. *The Christian Humanism of Flannery O'Connor*. Detroit, Wayne State University Press, 1972.

Feeley, Kathleen. *Flannery O'Connor: Voice of the Peacock*. 2nd ed., New York, Fordham University Press, 1982.

Garson, Helen S. "Cold Comfort: Parents and Children in the Work of Flannery O'Connor." *Realist of Distances: Flannery O'Connor Revisited*, edited by Karl-Heinz Westarp and Jan Nordby Gretlund. Aarhus, Den., Aarhus University Press, 1987, pp. 113–22.

Hendin, Josephine. *The World of Flannery O'Connor*. Bloomington, Indiana University Press, 1970.

Magistrale, Anthony. "O'Connor's 'The Comforts of Home.'" *The Explicator*, vol. 43, no. 1, 1984, pp. 57–60.

May, John R. *The Pruning Word: The Parables of Flannery O'Connor*. Notre Dame, IN, University of Notre Dame Press, 1976.

Meyer, R. T. "Anthony of Egypt, St." *New Catholic Encyclopedia*. New York, McGraw, 1967. 16 vols.

[Meyers], Sister Bertrande. "Four Stories of Flannery O'Connor." *Thought*, vol. 37, 1962, pp. 410–26.

Millichap, Joseph R. "The Pauline 'Old Man' in Flannery O'Connor's 'The Comforts of Home.'" *Studies in Short Fiction*, vol. 11, 1974, pp. 96–99.

Muller, Gilbert H. *Nightmares and Visions: Flannery O'Connor and the Catholic Grotesque*. Athens, University of Georgia Press, 1972.

Murphy, George D., and Caroline L. Cherry. "Flannery O'Connor and the Integration of Personality." *The Flannery O'Connor Bulletin*, vol. 7, 1978, pp. 85–100.

O'Connor, Flannery. *Flannery O'Connor: Collected Works*, edited by Sally Fitzgerald. New York, Library of America, 1988.

———. *The Habit of Being: Letters*, edited by Sally Fitzgerald. New York, Farrar, 1979.

———. *Mystery and Manners: Occasional Prose*, edited by Sally Fitzgerald and Robert Fitzgerald. New York, Farrar, 1969.

Orvell, Miles. *Invisible Parade. The Fiction of Flannery O'Connor*. 1972. Reprinted as *Flannery O'Connor: An Introduction*, Jackson, University Press of Mississippi, 1991.

Quinn, M. Bernetta. "Flannery O'Connor, a Realist of Distances." *The Added Dimension: The Art and Mind of Flannery O'Connor*, edited by Melvin J. Friedman and Lewis A. Lawson, 2nd ed. New York, Fordham University Press, 1977, pp. 157–83.

Quispel, G. "Manicheans." *Man, Myth and Magic: An Illustrated Encyclopedia of the Supernatural*, edited by Richard Cavendish. New York, Cavendish, 1970. 24 vols.

Rowland, Beryl. *Birds with Human Souls: A Guide to Bird Symbolism*. Knoxville, U of Tennessee P, 1978.

"Saints." *Man, Myth and Magic: An Illustrated Encyclopedia of the Supernatural*, edited by Richard Cavendish. New York, Cavendish, 1970. 24 vols.

Walters, Dorothy. *Flannery O'Connor*. Boston, Twayne-Hall, 1973.

Becoming a Middle Georgia Writer: Rethinking the Influence of Carson McCullers and Erskine Caldwell on Flannery O'Connor

I have not been influenced by the best people.
(28 Aug. 1955, *HB* 98)

I relish the idea of being read by scholars.
(9 July 1955, *HB* 89)

In *Creating Flannery O'Connor*, Daniel Moran explains that when Flannery O'Connor's early books were published, it was quite common for reviews to compare O'Connor to Carson McCullers and Erskine Caldwell. Now things have changed: As Moran notes, "Readers who find O'Connor's work important and relevant may be irked by…finding O'Connor lumped together with Erskine Caldwell and Carson McCullers as a niche writer who specialized in southern curiosities" (7–8). Nevertheless, this essay's purpose is to persuade you that O'Connor was deeply influenced, throughout her career, by these two writers whom she also regularly condemned. The influence is greater than has been acknowledged by the vast majority of O'Connor critics, and it lingers in O'Connor's character, style, and themes. I rather agree with McCullers, who considered O'Connor, according to Virginia Spencer Carr, to be "a deft imitator" of McCullers (Carr 433). I shall address McCullers first, then Caldwell. While I suspect that in reading McCullers and Caldwell, O'Connor was on the lookout for technique, she also found increasingly valuable their commentary on the lives of Blacks and poor Whites. McCullers and Caldwell provided valuable sociological and cultural perspectives that the quite-sheltered-and-protected O'Connor needed. The extent of McCullers's influence has been obscured by critics' inclination to emphasize O'Connor's Catholicism as the crucial element missing from McCullers. Jean Cash explains, for example, that O'Connor disliked writers like McCullers (she could have included Caldwell, though Cash did not.) because O'Connor thought their works "so mired…in the secular world that they displayed no transcendent vision" (xvi). While I agree that O'Connor found ways to make her Catholicism compatible with a sort of universality in literature, I also believe she learned a great deal from these two Georgia writers who are now generally considered quite different from O'Connor.

Nowadays Carson McCullers and Erskine Caldwell, both natives of Middle Georgia, have quite different positions in the literary stock market we call the canon. McCullers is holding her own quite well,[1] but Caldwell's reputation is low and dropping. In purchasing books for this project, I found that many of the Caldwell books I was receiving had been removed from the shelves of university libraries around the country. So it may come as some surprise that O'Connor was quite unkind to both these writers. O'Connor wrote in a 28 Nov. 1963 letter, for example, "I dislike intensely the work of Carson McCullars..." (*CW* 1195). (O'Connor misspelled the name McCullers here and elsewhere.) O'Connor's response to Erskine Caldwell, who was basically the reality-television writer of his time, is similar to her response to McCullers. O'Connor expressed dismay over the fact that the French respected Caldwell's novels, and she feared that book reviewers would consider her an "unhappy combination...of Poe and Erskine Caldwell" (*MM* 28). Surely she thought Caldwell—and perhaps McCullers too—was part of "The School of Southern Degeneracy" that she so disdained (*MM* 38). When Harvey Breit on the interview show *Galley Proof* asked O'Connor about other southern writers, including Caldwell and McCullers by name, O'Connor's potentially condescending response was that "...it's *easier* for a Southerner to *begin* writing than for anyone from almost any other section of the country..." (*Conversations* 7—emphasis added).

McCullers's early novels, published as O'Connor was starting to think of herself as a writer, provided a sort of guidebook: How to Become a Famous Georgia Writer and Escape Georgia. Surely O'Connor was aware of McCullers throughout the time she was starting to think of herself as a serious artist. When O'Connor went to Georgia State College for Women as an undergraduate contributing creative writing and artwork to student publications (as she was taking lots of English classes and completing a major in sociology), she had to have been aware of McCullers. Only eight years O'Connor's senior, McCullers was famous

---

[1] For a discussion of ways in which McCullers has been received more positively than O'Connor has in Europe, see Zacharasiewicz, esp. 123–26.

already as the author of *The Heart Is a Lonely Hunter* and *Reflections in a Golden Eye*, which had been published while O'Connor was in high school. Coincidentally, *Reflections* and its attendant publicity appeared during what was probably the crucial month of O'Connor's young life, February 1941, when her father died of lupus. *The Ballad of the Sad Café* appeared in print while O'Connor was in college,[2] and by the time O'Connor's first published story, "The Geranium," appeared in 1946, McCullers had also published *The Member of the Wedding*. By then, O'Connor was already out of Georgia—she was studying at the Writers' Workshop at Iowa—but perhaps it was McCullers who demonstrated to O'Connor that it was indeed possible for a Georgia girl to live in New York City, to be accepted into Yaddo, and to become famous, all while writing about the lives of ordinary people in Middle Georgia. There are more parallels between the lives—studying music and journalism, puzzling over gender identity (their own as well as their characters'), working while seriously ill—but the point is made: McCullers was a role model. When *Clock Without Hands* appeared, while O'Connor called it "the worst book I have ever read," she also conceded that earlier novels by McCullers "were at least respectable from the writing standpoint" (22 July 1961, *HB* 446).

One sort of influence involves McCullers's use of Milledgeville—which we usually think of as O'Connor's town—in *The Heart Is a Lonely Hunter*, as the place where Antonopoulos is sent to Central State Hospital, where Antonopoulos dies, and where Singer, after learning of the death of Antonopoulos, goes into the town to a poolroom. Surely McCullers helped show O'Connor how very much could be done with local materials. Of course, it is not that unusual for critics to point out that McCullers was significant for O'Connor, but the influence is usually seen as coming through McCullers's treatment of young women. Characters like Mick Kelly in *Heart* or Frankie Addams in *The Member of the Wedding* (a novel in which O'Connor's town, Milledgeville, is mentioned explicitly—*CN* 488, 710) are source material for similarly rebellious female protagonists in early O'Connor stories—the protagonist of "A

---

[2] Thomson suggests some similarity between O'Connor's Tom T. Shiftlet in "The Life You Save May Be Your Own" and McCullers's Cousin Lymon Willis in *The Ballad of the Sad Café* (36).

Temple of the Holy Ghost" and the cross-dressing Sally Virginia Cope of "A Circle in the Fire." Consider this, for example, from "Temple":

> Her mother had arranged for them [cousins visiting the protagonist] to have supper in the back yard and she had a table laid out there under some Japanese lanterns that she pulled out for garden parties. "I ain't eating with them," the child said and snatched her plate off the table and carried it into the kitchen and sat down with the blue-gummed cook and ate her supper.
> "Howcome you be so ugly sometime?" the cook asked.
> "Those stupid idiots," the child said. (*CW* 202-03)

As in McCullers, the character's resentment is accompanied by a lyrically expressed longing that she tries to repress:

> The lanterns gilded the leaves of the trees orange on the level where they hung and above them was black-green and below them were different dim muted colors that made the girls sitting at the table look prettier than they were. From time to time, the child turned her head and glared out the kitchen window at the scene below.
> "God could strike you deaf dumb and blind," the cook said, "and then you wouldn't be as smart as you is."
> "I would still be smarter than some." (203)

This sort of borrowing of the attitude of Mick Kelly or Frankie Addams is the kind of McCullers influence I see most readily noted by O'Connor critics, as in Louise Westling's *Sacred Groves and Ravaged Gardens* (138) and in Brad Gooch's biography, *Flannery* (249-50). O'Connor's use of an intersex character in "A Temple of the Holy Ghost" might also have been inspired by *The Member of the Wedding*.

O'Connor cartoons produced while she was a student at Georgia State College for Women (now Georgia College) exhibit some of this same sort of influence. Sarah Gordon, in her introduction to a collection of O'Connor cartoons, points out that the cartoons show an O'Connor who was trying to fit in, who was trying to be a member of a group:

> In the cartoons, O'Connor sympathetically considers the needs and concerns of her audience: a good student herself, she nevertheless presents the persona of the slack, procrastinating one, ever complaining about assignments and seeking to escape them. She alludes to homesickness, a condition she would not have experi-

enced as a day student attending college one block from home. Yet her desire to relate to her readers was paramount—to be on their side, to be a part of the collegiate mix. ("Early Figures" 5)

The cartoon most relevant here is O'Connor's 26 Sept. 1944 cartoon for her student newspaper in which a suffering student—eyes crossed—is explained to be suffering from "homesickness" (73). Might we not speculate that O'Connor could have learned from Carson McCullers's works how to sympathize with the sadness of others?[3] It is worth pointing out that O'Connor's cartoons have none of the overt religiosity that later separated her from McCullers. Notice also that in 1944 O'Connor submitted some of her cartoons to *The New Yorker* (*CW* 1240), a magazine in which several of McCullers's stories had recently appeared.

It is possible to explain O'Connor's statements against McCullers as the result of their similarity. Ted Spivey suggests that O'Connor's overstatement of disdain for McCullers (and others) has to do with sex, and I agree with Spivey's suggestion that the strength of O'Connor's "denunciations" indicates that she was "caught up unconsciously in some of their views" (53). Spivey reports telling O'Connor in 1960 about a dream he had, in which "O'Connor kept part of herself locked in a closet; that side was Carson McCullers." O'Connor's reported response was as follows: "…she did not speak but smiled slightly as if in assent" (53). Biographer Jean Cash reports this scene in a slightly different form: she quotes Spivey as saying "I…dreamed that she had in her background—in the closet, another side to her. She was like Carson McCullers, dressed in blue jeans. I told her that dream and she didn't…dispute it. She smiled" (qtd. in Cash 251; ellipses are Cash's). Although O'Connor had little first-hand experience with sexual behavior, it should be added that McCullers and Caldwell both emboldened O'Connor to write sex scenes; I think she learned from them that she had to figure out some way to write about sex.

There is a famous tale about O'Connor's writing a sex scene at Iowa before she was completely ready, whereupon the program director, Paul Engle, took her out to the parking lot and to his car to explain, in pri-

---

[3] Rubin, for example, links O'Connor's *A Good Man Is Hard to Find* to McCullers's *Heart*, saying the two writers "share a strong artistic sympathy for the wretched, the deformed, the physical and mental misfits" ("Two Ladies" 27).

vate, "that sexual seduction didn't take place quite the way she had written it" (qtd. in Gooch 126). It can be argued that O'Connor's attempts—and struggles—to write about sex and romance throughout the rest of her career were motivated by a feeling that she was competing with McCullers.

The Heart Is a Lonely Hunter is important to O'Connor in ways beyond setting and the characterization of females. O'Connor's first published story, and the title story of her MFA thesis, "The Geranium," revises McCullers's staging of a frustrating confrontation on a stairway, between two men, Black and White, who ought to be able to communicate well but who simply cannot find friendship—Dr. Copeland and Jake Blount, who meet on the stairs as they successively visit Mr. Singer. Dr. Copeland (the character praised by Louis D. Rubin, Jr., as the most effective character McCullers ever created ["Carson McCullers" 119]) at one point in the novel feels considerably better after a visit with Singer, but then

> before he was out of the house this peace had left him. An accident occurred. As he started down the stairs he saw a white man carrying a large paper sack and he drew close to the banisters so that they could pass each other. But the white man was running up the steps two at a time, without looking, and they collided with such force that Doctor Copeland was left sick and helpless.
> "Christ! I didn't see you."
> Doctor Copeland looked at him closely but made no answer. (*CN* 127)

Blount then reports to Singer that he had "bumped into" Copeland "on the steps and he gave me this look—why, I never had anybody to look at me so dirty" (*CN* 127). When O'Connor creates a similar situation in her story "The Geranium," McCullers's Blount and Copeland become the less intellectual but equally pathetic White man Dudley and the middle-class Black man who lives in the same apartment house as Dudley's daughter. In O'Connor's story, both men are walking up the stairs, and they meet as Dudley falls on the stairs. The Black man, "clipping up the steps toward" Dudley with "an amused smile," addresses Dudley with what Dudley takes to be "a voice that sounded like a nigger's laugh and a white man's sneer" (*CW* 710). The Black man helps the White man Dudley up the steps and makes pleasant small talk, but Dudley is horrified: "He was walking with the nigger up the stairs. The nigger was waiting for him on each step" (*CW* 710). Dudley can perceive only condescension from the Black man who politely "patted him on the back and called him 'old timer'" (*CW* 711). In O'Connor's story, as in McCullers's novel, the meeting between Black and White unnecessarily ends in misery. Thus we see that O'Connor did take seriously McCullers's ideas about race in Middle Georgia.

Another intriguing detail about "The Geranium" is that when O'Connor first submitted it for publication, she sent it along with another story, "The Crop," a story about what is wrong with some female writers. (See *CS* 551.) The protagonist of "The Crop," Miss Willerton, wants to write about poor people and their passions, even though she does not know them well. One could take "The Crop" to be a story in which O'Connor is trying to prove she is not Carson McCullers. The irony is that "The Crop" also demonstrates a similarity between O'Connor and McCullers. For Miss Willerton, as for O'Connor and for McCullers, the best writing occurs when the writer gets sufficiently involved emotionally to identify with her characters, perhaps especially with characters of a social class lower than her own.

Another connection between McCullers's *Heart* and O'Connor's early work lies in a similarity between Jake Blount and O'Connor's Hazel Motes in *Wise Blood*. It is easy to imagine that O'Connor had a strong reaction to Blount's tortuous confrontations with a preacher named Simms, who says to Blount, "Child of Adversity, I smell the sinful stink of beer on thy breath....The mark of Satan is on thy brow. I see it. Repent. Let me show you the light" (*CN* 241). Such a scene provides a version of what O'Connor, in *Wise Blood*, would turn into confrontations between Hazel Motes and such preachers as Asa Hawks, Onnie Jay Holy, and Solace Layfield. The closest parallel to the McCullers passage just quoted is Hazel Motes's meeting with Asa Hawks, who says that "I can smell the sin on your breath" (*CW* 27) and later that "Some preacher has left his mark on you....Did you follow for me to take it off or give you another one?" (28). Passages in O'Connor's manuscripts of *Wise Blood* suggest that she considered additional connections to *Heart*. O'Connor tries out a character who, like McCullers's Antonopoulos, is insane and Greek (file 85a, p. 3; file 88, p. 96). Characters with qualities similar to those of Blount and Copeland appear (file 113, pp. 7–8, 10). There are instances in which McCullers's Singer seems to provide a model for the way a character is admired by others (file 113, p. 5), and in one sequence it is Hazel who is treated like a version of Singer (file 128c, p. 1; file 129, p. 4).

O'Connor's works also respond to the McCullers novel with the peacock reference in the title, *Reflections in a Golden Eye*. O'Connor knew something about military culture because of the presence in Milledgeville of Georgia Military College and the presence of WAVES on her college campus during World War II, as well as because of O'Connor's acquaintance with veterans attending the Iowa Writers' Workshop via the GI Bill. Still, McCullers's military-base setting in *Reflections* may also have had something to do with O'Connor's confidence that she could handle a veteran as protagonist. More significantly, the psychology of male sexuality is explored by McCullers in ways that O'Connor probably used, and McCullers's clinically cold narration in this novel probably also appealed to O'Connor. Capt. Penderton and Ellgee Williams have plenty in common with O'Connor's Hazel Motes and Enoch Emery in terms of repressed desire, actions taken unconsciously, and gender ambiguity. Ellgee Williams's similarities to Enoch Emery are especially intriguing. Both seem rather mindless men, at times close to animals. Both are without close friends. Both have plunged into religiosity and then, supposedly, gotten over it (*CN* 325; *CW* 28). And both are discovered to be major voyeurs—Williams spying on the Pendertons from among trees, Enoch hiding in the bushes at the swimming pool to peek at female bathers (*CW* 44).

To some extent, O'Connor did move away from passages in McCullers that she found inspirational: Alison Langdon's horror over childbirth in *Reflections* is echoed in O'Connor's "A Stroke of Good Fortune," the story she created from a chapter of *Wise Blood* that O'Connor decided was taking her novel in the wrong direction, and the implications of homosexual desire in *Reflections* are explored in manuscripts of *Wise Blood* that surprise most readers who know only the finished novel. See O'Connor's unpublished manuscripts at Georgia College, where Hazel is approached by characters who are probably homosexual, Mercy Weaver [file 108c-f] and Dufonce Jerger [file 113a], and where Hazel recalls having sex with a boy named Ford Tester [file 106b]. Enoch Emery, in another file, is kissed enthusiastically by the man dressed as Gonga the gorilla [file 134a]. (See Driggers et al. for descriptions of these manuscripts.)

While the usual understanding of O'Connor's reaction to McCullers is that O'Connor grew away from the early (and supposedly slight) influence of McCullers, the elder writer's influence appears in late works by O'Connor as well. O'Connor's investigations of sex between men, begun in *Wise Blood* manuscripts, reappear in manuscripts of later works and are explicit when Tarwater is raped by a man in her second novel, *The Violent Bear It Away*. The late story "The Comforts of Home," with its aggressively sexual female character Sarah Ham and its passive intellectual male protagonist Thomas, bears a number of resemblances to the relationship in *Reflections* between Leonora Penderton and Capt. Penderton. Finally, the stories O'Connor polished as she was near death, two of her finest works, the stories with which O'Connor concluded her final story collection, are also reflections of O'Connor's reactions to McCullers: O. E. Parker of "Parker's Back," the soldier with an obsession for a woman who does not clearly return the favor, the soldier saddled with embarrassing initials for a name, a man whose unconscious mind rules, a character less able to talk than to express himself through his body, is yet another version of McCullers's L. G. Williams. O'Connor's story "Judgment Day" is a final attempt to perfect her first published story, "The Geranium," that rewrite of McCullers's racial confrontation between Jake Blount and Dr. Copeland in *Heart*. The last two pages of O'Connor's final story show a Black man and White man encountering each other on the stairs once again, each locked in his private world, still, though O'Connor's White character now has his spiritual judgment day—and dies—during this climactic meeting (*CW* 694–95).

Why might O'Connor also look to another author with Middle Georgia roots, Erskine Caldwell? The Caldwell-O'Connor connection I am proposing here is even more surprising than the McCullers-O'Connor connection; he was less of a contemporary role model for O'Connor. However, there was his fame, starting in the early 1930s, as a successful writer from Georgia. He did sell 80 million books over the course of his career, based on materials from the rural part of the state not far from O'Connor's territory. *Tobacco Road*, *God's Little Acre*, and *Journeyman*, the three novels to be discussed here—came out from 1932 to 1935. Caldwell also on occasion received serious respect as a writer: When Lewis Nordan wrote a Foreword to the University of Georgia Press reprint of *Tobacco Road*, he reminded us that Saul Bellow thought "...Caldwell should have won the Nobel Prize" and that William Faulkner once referred to Caldwell as "one of the five best contemporary American writers," as were Dos Passos, Fitzgerald, Hemingway, and of course, Faulkner (Nordan vi). While Caldwell could satirize his grotesque characters mercilessly, he could also assert his sympathy for their plight in the oppressive culture of Middle Georgia.

While there is little clear evidence that O'Connor read much of Caldwell, there are significant hints. Arthur Kinney says she checked off, in an advertisement at the back of her copy of Porter's *Flowering Judas*, a series of titles O'Connor presumably had read, and on that list is *God's Little Acre* (Kinney 160, item 585). Also, O'Connor does report in a letter that new workers have arrived at Andalusia who look to her mother, Regina Cline O'Connor, as if they are from *Tobacco Road*, and O'Connor shifts into dialect as she adds that "...I am enjoying it while it lasts, and I aim to give my gret reading audiance a shot of some of the details sometime" (*HB* 41, Summer 1952). However O'Connor learned about Caldwell, the connections between Caldwell's fiction and O'Connor's—in terms of characters, style, and themes—are considerable. O'Connor surely learned a great deal from mealtime discussions with her mother about the lives of workers at Andalusia, the family farm, and about the lives of people in Milledgeville. As O'Connor used her mother's anecdotes, she shifted her treatment of race and poverty toward the more progressive views that she had seen expressed sometimes in Caldwell (and always in McCullers).

There is possibly a rather specific explanation for why O'Connor would find Caldwell useful. Katherine Hemple Prown argues persuasively that when O'Connor was working on her MFA at Iowa, she received and took seriously the clear message from her mentors that she should learn to write the way men write (37–38). It is easy to imagine that O'Connor learned that her fellow students also considered manly writing the standard. She was surrounded by men attending Iowa through the GI Bill, veterans planning war novels. And would it not be likely that the guys attending the workshop would bring up Caldwell as *the* famous male writer from Georgia? The men could easily ask her if she was going to write another *God's Little Acre*. And of course, O'Connor succeeded in leaving an impression of manliness: Louis D. Rubin, Jr., is not the only critic to have found O'Connor's style to be "masculine" ("Flannery O'Connor: A Note" 14).

"The Crop," the thesis story mentioned earlier, is about a woman writer, Miss Willerton, who rather explicitly thinks she should write like Erskine Caldwell, since she tries out the topic of sharecroppers, a topic that Erskine Caldwell basically owned at that time. One critic suggests that *Tobacco Road* is the book that Miss Willerton was reading until one of her relatives burned it (Whitt 213; *CW* 734–35). Things do not work out for Miss Willerton's short story about sharecroppers, but Miss Willerton does discover that she can love and hate such characters—and, in fantasy, even become one of them. "The Crop" has at times been interpreted as O'Connor's proof, to herself and her reader, that she is not Erskine Caldwell (Gordon, *Flannery* 4). I think the story is more interesting when we see in it O'Connor's struggle to figure out how she, perhaps like Miss Willerton, can someday make use of the strong emotions that Caldwellian characters provoke and of the serious social issues that Miss Willerton only begins to investigate. There are manuscripts of "The Crop," by the way, in which, like O'Connor, Miss Willerton has studied the psychology of children (file 15b) and in which—rather like O'Connor with her decision to drop the name Mary, thus impressing editors as perhaps a man named Flannery—Miss Willerton passes as male by using a male penname (file 15a).

Of course, O'Connor could have picked up some of the qualities that she and Caldwell share from a common ancestor. Sarah Gordon has argued that O'Connor was significantly influenced by the author Johnson Jones Hooper with his character Simon Suggs ("Not Such" 76–77). It is not unusual to see it claimed that O'Connor was influenced by others of the group called the Southwestern humorists, such as Augustus Baldwin Longstreet of Milledgeville (Pearson 53), author of *Georgia Scenes*, and of course, Mark Twain. Caldwell was certainly part of this tradition, even if he did not realize it.

Evidence that O'Connor specifically borrowed from Caldwell is a stylistic inclination toward repetition, which Caldwell loved and which O'Connor tried out. Readers of *Tobacco Road* will recall Jeeter Lester's obsession with "damn-blasted green-gutted turnip worms" (10) and readers of *God's Little Acre* will recall Ty Ty Walden's frequent use of the phrase "pluperfect hell" (1). Caldwell's repetition is so extreme that his characters seem almost incapable of thought, producing what C. Hugh Holman calls a "drab world" (36) and causing Kenneth Burke to say of Caldwell that the repetition makes Burke feel, when he reads Caldwell works, as if he were "playing with [his] toes" (360).

O'Connor's published works contain some Caldwellian characters who are significantly repetitious. There is Mrs. Freeman in "Good Country People" who reports every morning "how many times" her daughter Carramae "had vomited since the last report" (*CW* 264) and who is compared to a truck in her stubborn attempts always to stick to one statement about any topic (263). And there's the mother of Hazel Motes in *Wise Blood*, constantly asking her son what he has seen (35–36),

Solace Layfield asking Hazel "What you want?" (113–14), and Old Tarwater in *The Violent Bear It Away*, always calling people an "ass" or a "whore" (355). However, the truly impressive evidence of Caldwell's repetitions as an influence on O'Connor is in her manuscripts. In the drafts of *Wise Blood* at Georgia College, one of the most striking things is the characters' repetitiousness, which often suggests an inability to think. There are eighteen major instances of Caldwellian repetition in *Wise Blood* manuscripts—a clause repeated three or more times in short order, clauses or phrases or key words repeated from three to as many as eleven times in a short span. These are all unpublished passages and may not be quoted, of course; the reader will have to trust me about their existence. The key point is that O'Connor severely downplayed characters' repetitiousness as she finalized her novel, as she made her characters' obsessions and thoughts more interesting, their minds more complex. It seems clear, however, that the young O'Connor learned from Caldwell this satirical stylistic gimmick and then, to a large extent, unlearned it—because it is such a limited device, and because it understates the significance of the inner lives of the people of Middle Georgia.

It is worth noting that O'Connor and Caldwell might share some opinions about religion. There is a case to be made that Caldwell respects the religious impulses felt by his characters. In *You Have Seen Their Faces*, Caldwell writes, despite all his cynicism toward the reactionary aspects of southern churches and their preachers, that for "[t]he backland, pine-barren church-goer," religion is good because it "fits his needs and fulfills his desires" (38). Critic James Korges sees Caldwell and O'Connor as sharing an inclination to write about the physical in order to investigate "spiritual conditions" (24). Harvey Lee Klevar says Caldwell "sympathetically portrayed those driven by spiritual desires" and that O'Connor "shared Caldwell's sympathy" (18).

One Caldwell character that I think significantly influenced O'Connor is Sister Bessie Rice in *Tobacco Road*. Bessie is a preacher in her own made-up church, and she dislikes the preachers of established religion (aka "Hard-shell Baptists," *TR* 44). She decides an automobile is essential to her eccentric preaching and praying. Her inescapable feature is her deformed nose. Dude Lester says that looking at it is "like looking down the end of a double-barrell shotgun" because her "nose had failed to develop properly. There was no bone in it, and there was no top to it" (45). Nevertheless, Dude Lester marries her at the courthouse (93) in order to get the car that comes with the wife.

There are two major texts in which Bessie's influence is apparent. One is the story "The Life You Save May Be Your Own," the O'Connor story in which a man marries, in a civil ceremony, a woman he does not love so that he can get a car. The other major text Bessie influences is *Wise Blood*, in which a car is a necessity for the preaching career of a character who belongs to a personal, one-person church. And, like Bessie, who runs over and kills her potential double, the Lester grandmother (*TR* 164), Hazel runs over and kills his double Solace Layfield (*CW* 115). Bessie, in her insistence that God told her to marry Dude Lester (*TR* 81), is also like Sabbath Lily Hawks of *Wise Blood*, who tries to seduce Hazel Motes with talk about a "church in her heart" (*CW* 68). It may be more than a coincidence that when Onnie Jay Holy and Solace Layfield name their church, it is the "*Holy* Church of Christ without Christ" (*CW* 94, emphasis added). While Onnie Jay may feel he owns his church and therefore should put his surname on it, it could also be that they are following Bessie Rice, who says the name of her personal, made-up church is simply "Holy" (*TR* 97).

The most impressive pattern of similarities between Bessie Rice and *Wise Blood* has to do with versions of Sabbath in the manuscripts of the novel, not the published version. In early versions, Sabbath is a grown woman with serious (though eccentric) religious commitments. She belongs to a sect called David's Aspirants, she has visions of God (file 22a; file 71a, p. 3) and, like Bessie in her prayers (*TR* 92), the manuscript Sabbath speaks very familiarly with Divinity (file 137a, p. 10). Another similarity is physical ugliness: Sabbath has feet deformities that cause her to hide her feet (file 136, pp. 5–6) just as Bessie tries to hide her nose. There are numerous reminders in manuscript of how plain Sabbath is, both in the face (file 116f, p. 5; file 119b, p. 2) and generally (file 73, pp. 11, 14; file 75a, p. 2). The punch line for all this horrible ridicule is a bit that Caldwell would surely have used if he had thought of it: one of the messages that the Sabbath of the manuscripts receives from God is that He too is impressed by how very ugly she is (file 144a, p. 1).

Of course, O'Connor revised Sabbath considerably by the time she published *Wise Blood*, but I suspect that O'Connor continued to be intrigued by the idea of redeeming Caldwell's Bessie Rice, of creating a complex female religious figure who can be taken more seriously. Not that Bessie is always considered a joke; O'Connor scholar Robert H. Brinkmeyer, Jr., considers Bessie a basically sympathetic character (374). I nominate Mrs. Greenleaf in the story "Greenleaf," Lucette Carmody (the disabled child evangelist in *The Violent Bear It Away*),[4] and perhaps even Sarah Ruth Cates in "Parker's Back" as O'Connor's attempts to revise Bessie Rice into various independent women who could be more easily taken seriously as potential religious leaders as they practice various forms of do-it-yourself religion.

Caldwell's novel *God's Little Acre*, his biggest best-seller, centers around Ty Ty Walden's attempts to keep his family together. Unfortunately, his central strategy is to dig holes, hoping and failing to find gold on the land he perhaps should be trying to farm. His children are generally drawn toward South Carolina and its jobs for millworkers. Another major aspect of *God's Little Acre* is its beautiful women and the constant promise of the sexual act. The characters Darling Jill and Griselda and Rosamond are prime examples of female loveliness—as is a speechless character named Pearl in *Tobacco Road*, who interestingly refuses to have sex. Toward the end of all the violent and sexual shenanigans in *God's Little Acre*, Ty Ty Walden turns philosophical in ways that do not quite match the novel he is in as well as they fit some works by O'Connor:

> The trouble with people is that they try to fool themselves into believing that they're different from the way God made them. You go to church and a preacher tells you things that deep down in your heart you know ain't so. But most people are so dead inside that they believe it and try to make everybody else live that way. People ought to live like God made us to live. When you sit down by yourself and feel what's in you, that's the real way to live. It's feeling. Some people talk about your head being the thing to go by, but it ain't so. (*GLA* 183)

I think the influence of *God's Little Acre* on O'Connor appears significant in several spots: the extreme beauty of women in Caldwell could have prompted O'Connor to give daughter Lucynell Crater of "The Life You Save May Be Your Own" such attributes as "long pink-gold hair and eyes as blue as a peacock's neck" (*CW* 173). The sexual eagerness of Caldwell's women may be reflected in Lucynell's eagerness to leave her mother and her "pulling the cherries off [her] hat one by one and throw-

---

[4] File 172 in the O'Connor Collection at Georgia College contains a version of Lucette who is inclined to give up her religious career in order to escape her mother.

ing them out the [car] window" after her wedding (181). There may also be an echo of Caldwell's beauties in Sarah Ham of O'Connor's late story "The Comforts of Home," who exudes sexual invitation and who, like Rosamond in *God's Little Acre*, uses a "pearl-handled" gun (*CW* 587; *GLA* 60).

Ty Ty's philosophizing about the importance of the heart over the head, as I suggested before, could be applied to many situations in O'Connor's works, not just to her thorough chastening of a character named "Mr. Head" in the story "The Artificial Nigger." But what seems to me to have intrigued O'Connor most about Ty Ty is the down-into-the-earth symbol of the holes Ty Ty digs, even as he claims to be "scientific" (*GLA* 2), always careful not to find gold on the one little acre he has set aside for God's benefit. There are echoes of Ty Ty's ridiculous pits in the worse-than-useless pits of O'Connor's late story "A View of the Woods." More significant perhaps, once again, are O'Connor's manuscripts. Several times in the *Wise Blood* manuscripts, we are presented with a character who lives near, and stares into, large holes in the ground (file 25c; file 63, p. 53; file 74a, p. 2), and in one draft of "The Life You Save May Be Your Own," we are told that the basic motive of a character who is digging in his yard is that he, like Caldwell's Ty Ty, is scientifically minded (file 153c).

One often wonders how Mrs. Shortley in O'Connor's "The Displaced Person" could believe that "...the devil [is] the head of [religion] and God the hanger-on" (*CW* 294), but now I have read Erskine Caldwell's *Journeyman*, his novel published just after his great success with *God's Little Acre*, so now I better understand Mrs. Shortley's attitude.[5] The main character of *Journeyman* is the phony, corrupt preacher Semon Dye. The novel opens rather like the opening of "The Life You Save May Be Your Own," with other, somewhat less corrupt characters watching from their front porch as a God-talking stranger arrives with great drama. Semon Dye, even more than O'Connor's Mr. Shiftlet, robs the other characters blind with scheme after scheme, taking a car, more than one woman, etc. And like Mr. Shiftlet, Semon Dye abandons his women.

For this essay, the most interesting passage in *Journeyman* is a sur-

---

[5] See Coles (esp. 14–32) for a reading of "The Displaced Person" in which O'Connor's sympathy for the lives of Blacks and poor Whites is examined.

prising twist in the novel's climactic revival scene. Determined to rake in a lot of money, Semon Dye whips up his audience into religious ecstasy that is manipulative and blatantly sexual. He even, repeatedly, calls the moment of conversion "coming through" (*J* 179). Determined to reach one last reluctant woman named Lorene, Semon Dye starts acting out what it looks like to get religion. At first he seems to be mocking religiosity even as he sells it. He shouts "Unga-unga! Praise God!" (*J* 180) repeatedly. But as he repeats the silly "unga" sound, there is a reversal. His moment of recognition, which he interprets as complete failure, occurs as he realizes that "...he had come through himself" (*J* 183) in his attempt to reach Lorene. When the revival meeting ends, Semon Dye suddenly realizes "that he had forgotten to take up the collection" (*J* 187). The novel ends, rather like "The Life You Save," with a protagonist who takes what he can but who may have learned something also on a spiritual level, against what he would consider his better judgment.

There is debate among Caldwell critics about whether anything good could happen to Semon Dye as this "trickster has tricked himself" (Sexton 297) and "sees the light of God" (Cook, "Erskine" 366), but it is easy to see how O'Connor could have found in Semon Dye an example of an anti-religious character who could transform himself (or herself) into the opposite. It is also easy for me to agree with Edwin T. Arnold that the other characters in *Journeyman* manage to benefit from Semon Dye's actions, ill-intended though they are (xiii). In *Journeyman*, O'Connor could easily have found a precedent for her theme that good can come from even the most ridiculously extreme evil.

Ben B. Alexander has recently published a letter in which O'Connor tells the translator Maurice-Edgar Coindreau, on 18 Jan. 1959, that she has not (yet) read *Journeyman*. Just before this admission, O'Connor explains that "Being a Catholic I have never heard an itinerant preacher myself but the atmosphere in the South is permeated with their effects. One doesn't have to attend camp meetings to get the general idea" (*GT* 266). While I cannot claim that *Journeyman* directly influenced O'Connor, I am still inclined to suggest that Caldwell's satire helped shape "the atmosphere in the South" when it comes to popular notions about "itinerant preachers." O'Connor lived among people who had, often in secret, been "permeated" with notions from Caldwell. I conclude that O'Connor was probably more influenced by Caldwell than she realized.

Harold Bloom, who has spent his career pondering the nature of literary influence, decided a few years ago "to revisit [his] previous account of influence," to "define influence simply as *literary love, tempered by defense*" (*Anatomy* 8; emphasis in original). While it may seem that O'Connor did not go so far as to love McCullers or Caldwell, much of Bloom's theorizing about influence is applicable to O'Connor's relationship to both these writers. O'Connor could be influenced by McCullers and Caldwell without choosing them as influences. O'Connor probably learned more from them about writing and about her own culture than she wanted to admit. According to Bloom, the influenced writer may feel that she is completing what is missing in the earlier writers or may consciously reject what she sees as the essence of those writers (*Anxiety* 13–14). Surely O'Connor, embarrassed by her admission that Poe was important to her, ought to agree with Bloom that "…influence cannot be willed" (*Anxiety* 11). While I still assume that it is *something* of a tribute to McCullers and Caldwell that O'Connor was influenced by them, it certainly need not be taken as an insult to O'Connor that she was influenced. As Bloom suggests, "…influence need not make [writers] less original; as often it makes them more original…" (*Anxiety* 7).

A final thought: I want to revisit the famous passage in which O'Connor says she avoids "the Dixie Limited," also known as William Faulkner. The passage is usually taken as simply a statement about avoiding influence. But listen again to the lines that come just before that train reference, and I think we can hear O'Connor indirectly giving herself permission to be influenced, to pay attention to other writers, to pick up and develop what writers like McCullers and Caldwell have started:

> I think the writer is initially set going by literature more than by life. When there are many writers all employing the same idiom, all looking out on more or less the same social scene, the individual writer will have to be more than ever careful that he isn't just doing badly what has already been done to completion. The presence alone of Faulkner in our midst makes a great difference in what the writer *can* and cannot permit himself to do. (*MM* 45, emphasis added)

O'Connor permitted herself to use McCullers and Caldwell liberally, to take toward completion what she thought they had started. Although O'Connor became a universal writer, her literary roots in Middle Georgia mattered a great deal as she created her canonical art.

WORKS CITED AND CONSULTED

Arnold, Edwin T. Foreword. *Journeyman,* by Erskine Caldwell. Athens, University of Georgia Press, 1996, pp. vii–xv.

Bloom, Harold. *The Anatomy of Influence: Literature as a Way of Life.* New Haven, Yale University Press, 2011.

_____. *The Anxiety of Influence: A Theory of Poetry.* 2nd ed., New York, Oxford University Press, 1997.

Brinkmeyer, Robert H., Jr. "Is That You in the Mirror, Jeeter?: The Reader and *Tobacco Road.*" *Pembroke,* vol. 11, 1979, pp. 47–50. Reprinted in *Critical Essays on Erskine Caldwell,* edited by Scott MacDonald. Boston, G. K. Hall, 1981, pp. 370–74. Critical Essays on American Literature.

Burke, Kenneth. "Caldwell: Maker of Grotesques." *The Philosophy of Literary Form: Studies in Symbolic Action.* 2nd ed., Baton Rouge, Louisiana State University Press, 1967, pp. 350–60.

Caldwell, Erskine. *God's Little Acre.* 1933. Athens, University of Georgia Press, 1995.

_____. *Journeyman.* 1935. Athens, University of Georgia Press, 1996.

_____. *Tobacco Road.* 1932. Athens, University of Georgia Press, 1995.

Caldwell, Erskine, and Margaret Bourke-White. *You Have Seen Their Faces.* 1937. Athens, University of Georgia Press, 1995.

Carr, Virginia Spencer. *The Lonely Hunter: A Biography of Carson McCullers.* New York, Doubleday, 1975.

Cash, Jean W. *Flannery O'Connor: A Life.* Knoxville, University of Tennessee Press, 2002.

Coles, Robert. *Flannery O'Connor's South.* Baton Rouge, Louisiana State University Press, 1980.

Cook, Sylvia J[enkins]. "Camp Meetings, Comedy, and Erskine Caldwell: From the Preposterous to the Absurd." *The Enduring Legacy of Old Southwest Humor,* edited by Ed Piacentino. Baton Rouge, Louisiana State University Press, 2006, pp. 52–72.

_____. "Erskine Caldwell and the Literary Left Wing." *Pembroke,* vol. 11, 1979, pp. 132–39. Reprinted in *Critical Essays on Erskine Caldwell,* edited by Scott MacDonald. Boston, G. K. Hall, 1981, pp. 361–69. Critical Essays on American Literature.

Driggers, Stephen G., and Robert J. Dunn, with Sarah Gordon. *The Manuscripts of Flannery O'Connor at Georgia College.* Athens, University of Georgia Press, 1989.

Gooch, Brad. *Flannery: A Life of Flannery O'Connor.* New York, Little, 2009.

Gordon, Sarah. "Early Figures of Fun: Flannery O'Connor as Cartoonist." *The Cartoons of Flannery O'Connor at Georgia College* by Flannery O'Connor, edited by Marshall Bruce Gentry. Milledgeville, Georgia College, 2010, pp. 4–6.

_____. *Flannery O'Connor: The Obedient Imagination.* Athens, University of Georgia Press, 2000.

_____. "Not Such High-Falutin' Company: Flannery O'Connor's Southern Folk." *The Enduring Legacy of Old Southwest Humor,* edited by Ed Piacentino. Baton Rouge, Louisiana State University Press, 2006, pp.73–85.

Holman, C. Hugh. "Detached Laughter in the South." *Windows on the World: Essays on American Social Fiction,* Knoxville, University of Tennessee Press, 1979, pp. 27–47.

Kinney, Arthur F. *Flannery O'Connor's Library: Resources of Being.* Athens, University of Georgia Press, 1985.

Klevar, Harvey Lee. *The Sacredly Profane and the Profanely Sacred: Flannery O'Connor and Erskine Caldwell as Interpreters of Southern Cultural and Religious Traditions.* 1970.

University of Minnesota, PhD dissertation. Ann Arbor, MI, University Microfilms International, 1990.

Korges, James. *Erskine Caldwell*. Minneapolis, University of Minnesota Press, 1969. University of Minnesota Pamphlets on American Writers 78.

MacDonald, Scott, editor. *Critical Essays on Erskine Caldwell*. Boston, G. K. Hall, 1981. Critical Essays on American Literature.

McCullers, Carson. *Carson McCullers: Complete Novels*, edited by Carlos L. Dews. New York, Library of America, 2001. [*CN*]

Moran, Daniel. *Creating Flannery O'Connor: Her Critics, Her Publishers, Her Readers*. Athens, University of Georgia Press, 2016.

Nordan, Lewis. Foreword. *Tobacco Road*, by Erskine Caldwell. Athens, University of Georgia Press, 1995, pp. v–ix.

O'Connor, Flannery. *The Cartoons of Flannery O'Connor at Georgia College*, edited by Marshall Bruce Gentry. Milledgeville, Georgia College, 2010.

———. *The Complete Stories*. New York, Farrar, 1971. Notes about the publication of individual stories are found on pp. 551–55.

———. *Conversations with Flannery O'Connor*, edited by Rosemary M. Magee. Jackson, University Press of Mississippi, 1987.

———. *Flannery O'Connor: Collected Works*, edited by Sally Fitzgerald. New York, Library of America, 1998.

———. *The Habit of Being: Letters*, edited by Sally Fitzgerald. New York, Farrar, 1979.

———. Letter to Maurice-Edgar Coindreau. 18 Jan. 1959. *Good Things out of Nazareth: The Uncollected Letters of Flannery O'Connor and Friends*, edited by Benjamin B. Alexander. New York, Convergent Books-Random House, 2019, pp. 265–66.

———. *Mystery and Manners: Occasional Prose*, edited by Sally Fitzgerald and Robert Fitzgerald. New York, Farrar, 1969.

———. Unpublished manuscripts. Flannery O'Connor Collection, Special Collections, Georgia College Library and Instructional Technology Center, Milledgeville.

Pearson, Michael. "Rude Beginnings of the Comic Tradition in Georgia Literature." *Journal of American Culture*, vol. 11, no. 3, 1988, pp. 51–54.

Piacentino, Ed, editor. *The Enduring Legacy of Old Southwest Humor*. Baton Rouge, Louisiana State University Press, 2006.

Prown, Katherine Hemple. *Revising Flannery O'Connor: Southern Literary Culture and the Problem of Female Authorship*. Charlottesville, University Press of Virginia, 2001.

Rubin, Louis D., Jr. "Carson McCullers: The Aesthetic of Pain." *Critical Essays on Carson McCullers*, edited by Beverly Lyon Clark and Melvin J. Friedman. New York, G. K. Hall, 1996, pp. 111–23.

———. "Flannery O'Connor: A Note on Literary Fashions." *Critique: Studies in Modern Fiction*, vol. 2, no. 2, 1958, pp. 11–18.

———. "Two Ladies of the South." *Critical Essays on Flannery O'Connor*, edited by Melvin J. Friedman and Beverly Lyon Clark. Boston, G. K. Hall, 1985, pp. 25–28.

Sexton, Mark S. *Vernacular Religious Figures in Nineteenth-Century Southern Fiction: A Study in Literary Tradition*. 1987. University of North Carolina, Chapel Hill, PhD dissertation. Ann Arbor, MI, University Microfilms International, 1987.

Spivey, Ted R. *Flannery O'Connor: The Woman, the Thinker, the Visionary*. Macon, Mercer University Press, 1995.

Thomson, Rosemarie Garland. *Extraordinary Bodies: Figuring Physical Disability in American Culture and Literature.* New York, Columbia University Press, 1997.
Westling, Louise. *Sacred Groves and Ravaged Gardens: The Fiction of Eudora Welty, Carson McCullers, and Flannery O'Connor.* Athens, University of Georgia Press, 1985.
Whitt, Margaret Earley. *Understanding Flannery O'Connor.* Columbia, University of South Carolina Press, 1997. Understanding Contemporary American Literature.
Zacharasiewicz, Waldemar. "Antecedents and Trajectories of Two Twentieth-Century Writers from Georgia in Europe." *Transatlantic Exchanges: The American South in Europe—Europe in the American South*, edited by Richard Gray and Waldemar Zacharasiewicz. Vienna, Aus., Österreichische Akademie der Wissenschaften, 2007, pp. 115–34.

An Interview with Ashley Brown

Conducted 26 Jan. 2006 inside the English Department at the University of South Carolina, Columbia.

Samuel Ashley Brown (1923–2011) taught at Washington & Lee University (where he was one of the founders of the literary magazine *Shenandoah* and served for a time as Editor), at the University of California, Santa Barbara, and for many years, starting in 1959, at the University of South Carolina. He was also a two-time Fulbright Lecturer at the Federal University of Rio de Janeiro. Among the volumes he co-edited are *The Achievement of Wallace Stevens*, *Satire: An Anthology*, *The World of Tragedy*, and *The Poetry Reviews of Allen Tate, 1924–1944*. He published essays and translations in such journals as *The Southern Review*, *Ploughshares*, *The Sewanee Review*, *Poetry*, *The Virginia Quarterly Review*, and *Southern Humanities Review*. His papers are at Emory University.

Marshall Bruce Gentry: What was your relationship with Flannery O'Connor?
Ashley Brown: I met Flannery O'Connor for the first time in 1953. I'd known her before that through correspondence. I think she had a great deal of literary company through correspondence. But then, I say, that's the American way—I corresponded for years with people whom I met only once.

I first met her actually in Tennessee, at the home of Brainard and Frances Cheney, who had been friends of mine for several years. Mrs. Cheney, I might add, was a professional librarian. At one time, she was the president of the American Library Association. She had been, until recently, the chief records librarian at Vanderbilt. Her husband, Brainard Cheney, had been a novelist for several years, and he had three novels by that time. Also, increasingly, he was interested in rather serious philosophical and theological matters, and he had recently, as had his wife, become a Roman Catholic convert.

MBG: And your impression of Flannery when you first met her?

AB: Well, I was partly prepared for it, because I had seen a couple of photographs of her. And I knew how old she was. And she was very easy to get along with, had a kind of a soft way of speaking. But at the same time, she could be very funny about things, very quickly.

Later I remember seeing her at a conference, along with Caroline Gordon Tate and Katherine Anne Porter and Madison Jones and Louis Rubin. I found it rather amusing. The two older ladies that were there completely dominated the proceedings. (This was the occasion I believe, when Regina might actually have provided supper for a number of people.) Anyway, Flannery was rather subdued, I think.

MBG: Was she normally subdued when she was around other people?

AB: Well, no. It was that the other people were speaking. Caroline Gordon and Katherine Anne Porter, they had been acquainted a little bit. These two ladies were very experienced hams at conversation in all kinds of social occasions. Very much so. They were almost used to dominating the conversation. They were like two elderly actresses who haven't met for years, and they had much to talk about. Pretty fun to be around people like that.

MBG: When you were meeting Flannery O'Connor for the first time, where were you in your own life journey?

AB: In 1953, I was 29 years old. And I had been an instructor in English at Washington and Lee, in Virginia. I started there when I was quite young; I was only 22 and was taking my master's degree at Vanderbilt. The Cheneys were quite wonderful about introducing me to various people. I hadn't been at Vanderbilt more than a month, and I was introduced to Allen Tate and Andrew Lytle because of Cheney. I might also add, by the way, that I'd been a student of John Crowe Ransom at Kenyon College in Ohio. I took courses with him where I studied philosophy, not literature. I was rather vain in those days. I thought I could read everything myself. I studied philosophy and a great deal of history as well. And I eventually studied history very extensively at Yale graduate school.

I wanted to see the world. So what I was doing was having a kind of a *wanderjahr*. And specifically, I was going to go to Ireland. I wanted to see Ireland. And especially in a literary way, I was just looking forward to being physically in Ireland, at the places like the Martello Tower, where Joyce lived alone, other things of that kind. There is Yeats's castle, Thorballalee, other things like that. I even had notes of introduction to several different people that I could talk about with Flannery during the first meeting there, in a way, since I was going to be going to Ireland.

MBG: So you were talking to Flannery about going to Ireland?

AB: To my amazement, Flannery had a rather low opinion of Ireland. She called Blarney Castle "Baloney Castle." That was worthy of *Finnegans Wake*.

MBG: What do you think you understand about Flannery O'Connor that you think most people do not understand sufficiently?

AB: People who never met her, as I have, carry ideas about her, you know, some of them of a personal, intimate nature. Living in a remote place, on a farm, without any kind of literary company around her—people think it was like being condemned to purgatory or something. There were people who took some such attitude about her.

MBG: And so you would say that your friendship with Flannery was basically a literary friendship?

AB: I would say I would be just a kind of a part of a lending library after a while. Once I came here to Columbia, I was so close, you know. And I moved here in 1959.

MBG: You're an authority on poetry. Do you ever recall having conversations with Flannery about poetry?

AB: I think she was very sensitive to language. I remember something in one of her essays, like the tight organization of poetry is something that people who write short stories must pay attention to. Faulkner said that, too, that poetry is perhaps the greatest art; next to that comes short stories.

MBG: You've mentioned that you lent Flannery O'Connor a copy of *Lolita*. What else can you tell me about your lending of reading materials to Flannery O'Connor? And what else do you know about her reading?

AB: Oh, well, she read a great deal, of course. She seemed to read rather more rapidly than I do, but she knew how to do that, too. People should learn to read more rapidly, or at least learn how to skim. But for example, Evelyn Waugh is a writer she would talk about a great deal in those days. Waugh was central in the 1950s. And Flannery was interested in Nabokov before *Lolita* came along. His little novel, which was published serially in *The New Yorker*, which is called *Pnin*—that was something Flannery loved. I know she thought very highly of *Dead Souls* by Gogol, too.

MBG: What can you tell me about O'Connor's relationship with Caroline Gordon? What do you know about the back and forth between O'Connor and Gordon regarding O'Connor's manuscripts? Did either of them ever talk to you about what was going on between them, as Gordon was giving her advice?

AB: I thought I really should stay out of the picture. Flannery, almost from the beginning, depended on Caroline, sometimes just maybe to correct something—like her English, maybe. Flannery trusted Caroline. When Flannery died, she was almost 40, and she was a highly developed writer. But to become one in the few years she had, she always had Caroline as the recipient of the manuscripts, all the way to the end, in the hospitals in Atlanta and Milledgeville. So this relationship was actually quite important.

Caroline, by the way, was also a mentor for a number of other writers. Walker Percy was another one during that time. You can see the connection among the three of them. Caroline always had young people she encouraged, and sometimes she probably regretted it. She knew many people over the years. She'd know them and encourage their work and so forth.

Sometimes she might have been disappointed, for example, long ago, around 1930, when *Flowering Judas* was first out. Katherine Anne Porter was 40 years old, though she didn't present herself as that age at the time. But anyway, Caroline, and Allen, and Yvor Winters too, had an extremely high opinion of Katherine Anne Porter who, in 1930, I think, was known to very few people. She often depended on people.

But anyway, Yvor Winters and Caroline really thought they ought to put Katherine Anne Porter on the map, literally. And they did. And they made sure other people read the book, and they, in some cases, wrote reviews of Katherine Anne Porter's works to make them known. And in a few years, she got to be very well known, and she found friends who had money.

MBG: You think Caroline Gordon was disappointed in Porter?

AB: In some ways, I think. In other ways, not. But she was always glad to see her successful.

Caroline herself was mentored. I happen to know Caroline was a protégé of Ford Madox Ford. Back then, her whole fictional technique was borrowed from Ford as much as anything else. They knew each other in the old days, in Paris and in New York. Caroline was his part-time secretary. And that was rather the kind of relationship that even had overtones of, shall we say, romantic attachment about it. I have reason to think that Caroline once burned some letters from Ford Madox Ford that were written to her. And she said, "Well, you know, he's suffered enough out of romantic attachments." She almost thought she was doing him a favor, doing that.

MBG: Do you have any sense of how Caroline Gordon regarded Flannery differently than she regarded these other writers that she would mentor?

AB: Well, she got time. She obviously thought that Flannery was a kind of a saint. She thought Flannery had a God-given talent. If you were to read all of Caroline's correspondence, you'd think that Caroline had discovered another genius.

"Our Conversations Were in Script":
Miller Williams on Visiting Flannery O'Connor at Andalusia

with Alice Friman

This interview was conducted 23 June 2006 at the home of Miller Williams in Fayetteville, Arkansas.

Stanley Miller Williams (1930–2015) wrote many books, including such poetry collections as *Some Jazz a While: Collected Poems* (University of Illinois Press) and *Time and the Tilting Earth* (LSU Press). Williams also published with LSU *Making a Poem: Some Thoughts about Poetry and the People Who Write It*. The University of Missouri Press published Michael Burns's edited collection of thirteen essays by scholars and poets, entitled *Miller Williams and the Poetry of the Particular*. He taught for years at the University of Arkansas, where in 1980 he helped found the University of Arkansas Press, which he served as director for many years. In 1997, Williams read his poem "Of History and Hope" at Bill Clinton's second inauguration.

Marshall Bruce Gentry: What was the nature of your relationship with Flannery O'Connor?

Miller Williams: Well, I met her in 1957 when I was living in Macon, Georgia. I was at the time a field representative for Harcourt Brace Publishing Company, but I attended a number of functions at Wesleyan College in Macon. And Flannery spoke there that year. I went to hear her, and then went with a small group backstage, got to say hello to her, and we began to chat a bit and hit it off. She asked me if I was ever in Milledgeville, and I hadn't been, but I said, "Well, yes, I plan to be soon," and, she said, "Well, stop by."

I gave her a call a couple of weekends later and said, "I'm going to be in Milledgeville next weekend," and she said, "Well, come on by after lunch," and I did. And we simply sat on the porch, watched the peacocks, and talked. I took my daughter, my four-year-old daughter, Lucinda, with me, and Flannery let her chase the peacocks. She couldn't catch one, but she loved to chase them.

We visited often until 1961, when I moved away from Macon after I had left Harcourt Brace and began to teach biology at Wesleyan. We just talked. We enjoyed talking to one another, telling each other what we were working on, reading each other something of what we'd written, and watching Lucinda chase the peacocks. That was our relationship.

MBG: What did you read to each other? She was reading you stories?

MW: She would read a part of a story to me. And I would read a poem or so to her. And, "What do you think about this?" Then something would be read by one of us. And in the beginning, we always would say, "That's fine." And then after a while, one of us might say, "I don't quite understand this turn here." It took a couple of years to get to that. But we got there.

MBG: Do you remember specific things you told her about her stories?

MW: Once in a while, I would not understand something because she began in the middle, and I didn't have the context. But it was virtually, almost always, simply because I didn't have the context. But I was pleased that she allowed me to question what she had written, in the most gracious way.

MBG: What other conversations, what other things do you remember saying to each other?

MW: I know that we talked about the fact that I was not comfortable teaching science, that I was much more comfortable talking about English, and I had been asked to address the English classes at Wesleyan, though I was a biology teacher. And she shared that concern, and we never really talked about the possibility of that changing. Though it did change, and much to her credit, several years later.

MBG: So she is the one who made you give up biology?

MW: Made me, yes.

MBG: How about her sense of humor? What do you remember about the conversations and how she would engage in conversation?

MW: She said one time—I don't remember the character—but she said, "I had to let this person in the story, but I wouldn't let him in my house." That was something that brought a grin to my face. And whenever I said something about Lucinda that I thought was funny, she thought it was funny too, and enjoyed hearing about it. We laughed a lot.

MBG: What do you think that you know about Flannery O'Connor that other people do not understand or appreciate, do not give her enough credit for?

MW: I know how ordinary she liked to be, and how she enjoyed my talking to her as if she were my sister. She was uncomfortable around people who revered her. That was not her nature, and it was important to her that we just be a couple of writers, talking about what we'd written. And she said that she had written some poetry, but she didn't want to show it to me. She said, "I'll show you a poem when you show me a short story." But again, you see, all of this, she had a sense of humor about it.

MBG: Why did you dedicate your collected poems, *Some Jazz a While*, to O'Connor?

MW: Because while I'd learned a lot from a lot of people, she taught me *first* some things that I had to know. She taught me not only by saying so as a teacher would, but she taught me by example.

One was to try not to have a word in a written work of art that could be taken out without damaging the other words. I don't know of any fiction that is so pure in those terms. It would be hard to take anything out of one of her short stories without somebody missing it. The way that she put it, "Every word has to earn its place." And more than a couple of critics have said of my poetry that there's not a wasted word. I like to take credit for that, but it's not to my credit; it's to Flannery's. And she would say to me, "I don't see why you need that," or, "You've already said that."

MBG: She would say that about individual words?

MW: Yes. And phrases. "I knew that already," she said one time. When I'd say something unimportant, she'd say, "I knew that already." And I said, "But I didn't say that." "No," she said, "but you made me know it." And so if the reader knows it, it's done. And she was very strong about that.

Probably of the three most important things she taught me, that was one. The second was, "When the last line is at the bottom of the page, the reader shouldn't turn the page to see what's next." The last line should be so clearly the resolution that the reader knows it's over. And I have tried very hard to shape the poem in such a way that when one reads the last line, one knows the poem is over.

"A Poem for Emily," my most anthologized poem, in more textbooks than any other poem I've written, is spoken as if I'm standing at the crib of my granddaughter. And the last line ends—and you know it's the last line when I say it, even though I haven't read the poem—"...I stood and loved you while you slept." No one's going to turn the page to see what comes next. Flannery would have liked that. And her stories end that way. So you know they're over, and she was pleased when one of my poems ended so that it said, "That's it."

Another thing that she impressed upon me is the presence of the reader's involvement as a character in what is written. When the poem or the story begins, it's about the writer. But when it's over, you want the reader to say, "She wrote that about me," or, "He wrote that about me." Because you have thrown the reader into the story or poem so that the reader almost feels like a character in the story or poem. And that last line is the last line that the reader could have said, could have spoken, as if it were the reader talking. Flannery made a great point of the importance of this.

So the reader's involvement, the sense of resolution, and the economy of language: those three things, more than any others, she laid down for me, gently but firmly, and she made me feel very good in the concern that she showed in talking about my work. It made me think that she thought it mattered. She wasn't flippant. She wouldn't just toss it off. And I thought, "If Flannery O'Connor thinks it's worth putting this much into it, maybe I've got something here. Maybe there's a possibility."

Also, apart from her particularities of writing, she told me that one can come to one's own education. See, I only had three hours of freshman English. You know that story, don't you?

I was at Hendrix College, in Conway, in 1947. I was born in Hoxie, and my father was a Methodist minister, and generally we did not live in a town where there was a college. Methodist ministers are itinerant. They move every three or four years. So he was in Russellville at the time, and I went to Hendrix. Anyway, I recorded a double major in English and foreign languages.

Near the end of the first semester, I was called into the office of the head of the Psychology Department. In those days, aptitude tests were given to all incoming freshmen. And he said to me, "Mr. Williams"—in those days, freshmen were addressed that way—"Mr. Williams, your tests show that you have no aptitude, no verbal aptitude whatsoever. And

"Our Conversations Were in Script"

if you don't want to embarrass your parents, you must change your major to the hard sciences immediately."

I was taught to respect authority—my father was a liberal Democrat; he believed in respecting authority—and to trust my elders. And so I changed my major to biology, with a minor in chemistry. And I had not taken any foreign languages yet. So that three hours in freshman English was all I had, because in those days, no more was required.

And after my second year there, my father was moved to Jonesboro, where Arkansas State is, so I went up there to graduate, and then came to the University of Arkansas to get my Master's. And I taught first at McNeese State College in Lake Charles, Louisiana, where I met Hank Williams and where Lucinda was born. And we moved around—I also taught at Millsaps—until Wesleyan in Macon in 1957.

I had read everything I could get my hands on in literature. I am surprised that I managed to stay behind a teacher's desk in biology and biochemistry. When I was at Millsaps in Jackson, I attended the first two years of Ole Miss med school, because in the preclinical years of med school, you are always assigned PhD candidates. And I am what my father called ABD: All But Dissertation.

Now that I have Jordan, a woman of words who sent me to Chile for a year, one who sent me to the University of Mexico for a year, and two to Rome, I'm very comfortable with Spanish and Italian, although I never took languages in a classroom. And I directed a translation program and taught English graduate school students, and I published books in all these areas. I just did it outside the classroom.

But I'm saying all this now because Flannery felt that the classroom was almost incidental to her development. And it was by looking back at Flannery, as I was going through all of this, that I said, "I can do it. Flannery did it; I can do it." And I wasn't just rambling there. That's something else that I learned from Flannery. And that's why she has more credit for my being who I am than anybody else.

MBG: Let me go back to what you were saying earlier about Flannery and poetry. You said she didn't want to show you any of her poems. Tell us about how you told her that her stories were similar in character to poems.

MW: I said, "Flannery, you know, you call them short stories, but I call them long poems." And she'd grin, and her eyeballs would kind of roll back, and she'd say, "Miller, you call them long poems, but I call them short stories." I'll never forget her saying this: She said, "You know,

I could take a number of your poems and write them in prose, and they would make short stories." And she looked at me with a questioning look on her face, and I said, "Yes, Flannery, I could take some of your stories and turn them into poems, if I could compress them enough." And she said, "Well, you know, a lot of times your poems are that long." But that's the kind of conversation we had.

MBG: Did you see much of Flannery's mother on your visits to Andalusia?

MW: I didn't see much of her mother at all there. She would be out on the front porch to greet me, and then she would go back. Flannery would step in to say something to her or do something and come back out again, but we both knew who sat on that porch. Sometimes in the morning, over a cup of tea, almost always on the porch. And her mother was very gracious to me. Except, you know, "This is not the world I live in," she'd typically say. "I have my own."

MBG: What else can you tell us about her living on the farm? Did you just see her on the porch?

MW: That's the only way I know her. She was never in Macon that I knew of, except to give that talk. I know she would shop there sometimes. But not that I knew of. That porch essentially was her own room all that time.

MBG: Did she ever talk about being outside the house, around the farm? Did you have any notion about how she would move around during the day?

MW: She said that she liked to walk and that she felt she knew some of the animals. However, I think almost anyone would have felt that way.

She did like to walk. But the kind of conversations we had one couldn't have while strolling. They were too concentrated.

One time she was behind the house doing something when I got there, and her mother called her. But that's the only time that she didn't greet me at the front door.

MBG: So she would be in the house, and you would come knock on the door, and then she would—

MW: Yes. She knew I was coming, but she was in the house.

MBG: What else can you say about her self-confidence, as a writer and not as a writer? Did Flannery ever seem unsure of herself?

MW: She would, every once in a while, verbalize the frustrations she would have in particular stories she was working on. One time, she

"Our Conversations Were in Script"

said, "I really never felt I was just going to give up on one until now," but she didn't give up on it. But it was important that she said that after all she'd written. "I never really thought I was just going to give up on one until now." But I think, you know, she may have said that for every story. I can hear someone say it to another, "I've never been so..." and you may say that fifty times. But obviously the second time it is not true anymore, because you already have been the way you say you have never been. But that's the kind of statement that one might just use to pull out of the ditch. So I don't know if it was really true, but she did say that.

MBG: What other words would you use to describe her personality?

MW: Open, gracious, inviting, and confident. By open, I mean she wasn't shy. Gracious and inviting: inviting, I mean that one was not likely to be shy around her. She'd welcome one in. And not to the house—to her. And I think that would sum up what I feel about her, if you put those words together, the four of them. That would do it.

MBG: When you read the stories, does it seem as if you are reading the voice of Flannery, or does that seem like a different voice to you?

MW: It seems like the voice of Flannery to me. But I have to say that maybe because I heard her read the stories. She could tell me about having met someone in town or at a speaking engagement, and if she told me about an hour and a half with this person, I'd feel I was hearing a short story. She had a sense of quiet and leanness. Usually when someone is telling a story, a whole lot of fruit and flowers are going to be on the limb. But when she told the story, it was as if she had already gone through four or five drafts, and it just went right to the point. And that's it. It made her a very interesting person to talk to.

MBG: People talk about there being a lot of tension between Flannery and her mother. Did you ever see it?

MW: I wondered if they ever had easy conversations. I would attribute to her the qualities that I attribute to Flannery, except for inviting. She didn't seem to say, "Talk to me," to me or to Flannery. As I said, she was always very nice to me. But it was as if they had a contract. And they were fulfilling it as nicely as they could. You've known marriages like that, haven't you?

MBG: Sure. Lots of marriages that are distant—

MW: They know they're married, and they're going to behave as if they're married. But you don't attribute it back to either of them.

MBG: What do you think Flannery valued most about her friendship with you? What do you think you offered her? What do you think she valued about you?

MW: Honestly, maybe I should begin by saying that living where she did, it got lonely, artistically and intellectually. I think I was somebody to talk to about literature, about life, about art. And I didn't have to be as good as Flannery; it was sufficient that I knew the rules of the game. I knew what we were about. And I had read almost everybody who came up in conversation.

But I think it's also important that we were not writing in the same genre. I think it would not have been nearly as comfortable for her to talk to me as a fiction writer. Because then you've got to compare in a way that we did not have to compare. In fact, if I had been a fiction writer then, she would not have wanted to say, "You know, our work has a lot more in common than you think." But when we're different, when we're fiction writer and poet, then she could say, "Our work is not as different as you think," because it makes it all the more interesting to find similarities.

And we talked about something else that you bring up. All of art takes its life from that which is different but the same at the same time. In fact, let's put it this way: suppose someone says, "I love her," or someone says, "I don't like her." Do you want to go on with that conversation in either case?

But suppose someone says, "You know, I love her because I don't like her." And you want to say, "Tell me more about this." It's when a statement or a situation contradicts itself: "The more clothes she has on, the nakeder she seems." Wow, I want to know more about this woman. "It felt so good, I couldn't stand any more." That contradicts itself, but we want to know more. And if you read her stories, you'll see that in every one of them, there's something like that, something that says, "The slowest guy in town is going to win this race." It's that sort of thing. And we were both fascinated by that, because we kept discovering it.

And I would be writing a poem or she'd be writing a story, and we hadn't been able to make it work out. And then we would say to each other, "You know, I was being consistent. I was being logical. It all made sense." And the sense it makes has got to be a sense that's off the page. And that's another term that we used for our objective: "off the page." Because, in fact, she would say that what she really wants you to know about her characters is off the page. You come to know the characters, but you can't find anywhere where you actually learn that. It came to you off the page, from the sum total of the action and dialogue. This is awfully close to the mind of a poet.

MBG: Do you remember informing her about anything?

MW: I had been to Breadloaf Writers' Conference for three or four years, and Robert Frost was involved in that. And he was also very good to me. And he remarked on the attention I brought to my work. I would be with him in the summertime, at the Breadloaf Writers' Conference, at which I was in the classroom, raising my hand—and that was what she was truly interested in: what went on, whom I'd met (like Howard Nemerov and John Ciardi), how I liked it, what was said. That was comfortably in the format we followed.

MBG: What specific connections do you see between O'Connor's life at Andalusia and her fiction? Are you aware of bits and pieces of her life that found their way into stories?

MW: One thing in her stories, consistently, is the saving moment of solitude. You have to get away from it all. And being alone was one of the terrible things in her life and one of the salvations of her work. That gets back to what we were talking about, the contradiction. It contradicts itself. She was very, very tired of being alone. And yet she believed if you do not have that particular moment alone, you're lost. And she would isolate her character, and in that moment of isolation, as it were at Andalusia, comes self-recognition and survival.

She also was awfully good at allowing a person to be alone in a crowd. You've probably been there yourself. People think that you're there with them, but they're not.

MBG: You said earlier that Flannery made you give up biology.

MW: When LSU advertised for a poet to teach in the writing program in 1961, I mentioned it to Flannery. I told her I would like to do that, except that I wouldn't want to leave or move away. And she wrote to the English Department at LSU, and said, "The person you want teaches biology at Wesleyan College in Macon." And they couldn't believe that. But they couldn't ignore it.

So they called me and asked me for some poems. And I sent them some poems and a couple of essays, and they wrote back and said, "You're hired." And I didn't want to believe it. And I was truly distressed at having to leave Flannery, and I never saw her again.

I'm not being flippant when I say that I am where I am because of Flannery O'Connor.

MBG: Did you correspond after 1961?

MW: Yes.

MBG: And was the friendship different after you moved?

MW: No, but it wasn't nearly as good as being there. I mean, we ourselves don't write as we do when we speak. And the letters were a bit more formal than our conversations. And her letters were type-written. And that has an aspect of metaphor about it, that they were type-written, as opposed to being in script. Because our conversations were in script. They were not type-written.

Alice Friman: The feeling that I get is that there was a warmth, an openness about her. And you also said that what you talked about mostly was about art, which of course is an intellectual intimacy. But did she ever—perhaps not in words, even—admit her feelings about her illness, her feelings about being at Andalusia, and even her feelings toward her work?

MW: So far as Andalusia is concerned, when I asked her if it would be easier to populate her story if she lived in New Orleans or Chicago, she said, "There are more people here at Andalusia than in either one of those cities." She knew the way. And I knew what she meant; she didn't go on with it.

As for her illness, she told me about her illness and that she would not live a lot longer—as a matter of fact, and dry-eyed, as if she were describing the situation of a character in one of her stories—and made it clear that this was not to be a topic of conversation.

I'm very glad for that last question. I'm glad you asked it. Because it does say something otherwise unsayable, I think, about her character and her relationship to herself.

AF: What?

MW: I only knew the Flannery O'Connor that she wanted me to know. But isn't that true of anyone? You're not just the woman I see sitting there.

AF: I hope not. I used to look much better.

MW: I mean, you're another woman, too. I wish that, going on 77, I understood the human mind better than I do. It continues to please and amaze and confound me. And especially Flannery's.

I always thought a little bit that we were not just on a porch but on a stage, that there was a script there. I know that she was fond of me personally, and I was fond of her. She would not have continued to ask me back, otherwise. She didn't need me to tell her how to write. We both enjoyed the conversations, we enjoyed the visits. But there was a format to our meetings. Comfortable, and something I was grateful for.

AF: She set those parameters?

MW: I think that we established them together. We did, to some degree, tiptoe towards one another, and were comfortable with the format that we were following. And it wasn't something that I would…I got a divorce shortly after I moved from Macon. I never mentioned the failing marriage to her, just because that didn't belong to the world we created and lived in.

Prodigal Daughters:
Flannery O'Connor and Alice Walker

My starting point here is the idea that both Flannery O'Connor and Alice Walker took very seriously and very personally the biblical parable of the Prodigal Son. Let us review part of the parable, slightly revised from the second half of chapter 15 in Luke:

> And now she began to feel the pinch, so she hired herself out to one of the local inhabitants who put her on his farm to feed the pigs. And she would willingly have filled her belly with the husks the pigs were eating, but no man gave unto her. Then she came to her senses and said, "How many of my mother's paid servants have more food than they want, and here am I dying of hunger! I will leave this place and go to my mother and say: 'Mother, I have sinned against heaven and against you; I no longer deserve to be called your daughter; treat me as one of your paid servants.'" So she arose, and came back to her mother. While she was still a long way off, her mother saw her and was moved with pity. She ran to the girl, clasped her in her arms, and kissed her tenderly. Then her daughter said, "Mother, I have sinned against heaven and against you. I no longer deserve to be called your daughter." But the mother said to her servants, "Quick! Bring out the best robe and put it on her; put a ring on her finger and shoes on her feet. Bring the calf we have been fattening, and kill it; we are going to have a feast, a celebration, because this daughter of mine was dead and has come back to life; she was lost and is found." And they began to celebrate. Now the elder daughter was out in the fields, and on her way back, as she drew near the house, she could hear music and dancing. Calling one of the servants, she asked what it was all about. "Your sister has come," replied the servant, "and your mother has killed the calf we had fattened because she has got her back safe and sound." She was angry then and refused to go in, and her mother came out to plead with her; but she answered her mother, "Look, all these years I have slaved for you and never once disobeyed your orders, yet you never offered me so much as a goat

for me to celebrate with my friends. But, for this daughter of yours, when she comes back after swallowing up your property—she and her men—you kill the calf we had been fattening." The mother said, "My daughter, you are with me always and all I have is yours. But it was only right we should celebrate and rejoice, because your sister here was dead and has come to life; she was lost and is found."

My minor revision of the parable suggests the issues I want to address. What do I mean by a Prodigal Daughter? One who wants to get away from, but who comes back to, the mother, one who goes off with an inappropriate man, one who struggles to accept or reject parental authority. One could also, I suppose, use the term to refer to a repentant daughter. How then might we apply the term Prodigal Daughter (hereafter PD) to Alice Walker and Flannery O'Connor? One way is that we might see some of their characters as PD's and discuss how their authors regard that prodigality. I think that Walker and O'Connor were more generously disposed toward PD's, at least in the stories I am discussing here, than they are generally considered to be. I can never forget Frederick Crews's putdown of O'Connor as an overly obedient writer, so it pleases me to argue for O'Connor's endorsement of disobedience in her characters. Both authors are critical, furthermore, of mothers who fail their daughters, who do not live up to the high standard the parable sets for the behavior of parents.

Another way we might apply the term PD to Alice Walker and Flannery O'Connor is to think about the authors themselves. We might see Walker as the unrepentant prodigal, the daughter who left Georgia and is reluctant to come back, the daughter who was once arrested in Washington while protesting the war in Iraq. (I should acknowledge here that when Walker returned to Eatonton, Georgia, in 2019 for a celebration of her birthday, she said she could imagine returning to Eatonton to live.) We might even think of Walker as O'Connor's literary daughter and conclude that Walker became an author too radical—say, on religion—for O'Connor to approve of her. And Walker, in writing about coming back to Georgia to visit Andalusia once with her biological mother, has said that she (Walker) was capable of hating O'Connor's "guts" ("Beyond" 57). Much of O'Connor's fiction can be read in terms of the parable. My student Scott Daniel once suggested to me that the parable of the Prodigal Son is also behind "The Comforts of Home," and I think one could say the same thing about "The Enduring Chill." One can also read O'Connor's life story in relation to a Prodigal Daughter. Surely O'Connor herself must have thought of her life this way. She took off for graduate school and life in the North, only to return to her mother and live out her life at Andalusia, supposedly repenting that she ever left Milledgeville, pleased as punch to be back.

Now that I have spelled out several possibilities, let me make my stance clear: I think both writers are in favor of the daughters' prodigality, very much on the side of those who reject the parent. I think O'Connor does a good job as a literary mother to Walker, and Walker does a good job as a literary daughter. I am not sure it would have occurred to me to apply the term PD to such O'Connor characters as daughter Lucynell Crater in "The Life You Save May Be Your Own" or Hulga/Joy Hopewell in "Good Country People" but for the insights provided by Walker's "Everyday Use," the story, Sarah Gordon has reported, that Walker read in 1977 at O'Connor's alma mater (73). In Walker's story we can imagine that we have rewrites of both these O'Connor characters in a story narrated by their mother. Lucynell in a sense becomes Maggie in Walker's story, and Hulga/Joy becomes Dee/Wangero.[1]

To analyze the individual stories, I might as well start with the toughest task, that of defending Hulga. I will not waste your time with any claim that O'Connor accepted Hulga's conscious philosophical or religious principles. But I do believe that when we focus on Hulga's prodigality of a less intellectual sort, she becomes a sympathetic figure. Hulga's prodigality is found not only in her rejection of her totally banal and judgmental mother, but also in her falling for a man. As I have argued in my book on O'Connor, Hulga's unconscious wish about what should happen to her with Manley Pointer is that she should become his captured goddess, an Aphrodite fit to compare favorably to the neighbor's daughters, Glynese and Carramae Freeman. When Hulga courageously goes to the barn with Manley the Bible salesman and climbs the ladder up into the loft, she thinks she intends to control herself and Manley with her mind, but instead she falls, however momentarily, in love. O'Connor's narrator lists all of Hulga's attempts to maintain her

---

[1] I think it is safe to generalize that Walker's first story collection, *In Love and Trouble*, responds in several ways to O'Connor's early works. Read the stories "Entertaining God" and "The Welcome Table" and "The Diary of an African Nun" and you will likely sense connections.

control, but finally, Hulga loses it. If one wishes for more evidence that there was personal emotional experience behind this story, see Mark Bosco's articles on Flannery and the Danish textbook salesman Erik Langkjaer.

Once Hulga confesses to Manley—she says "I have a number of degrees" as if she were confessing to a sexual history—and once he forgives her as if he thought she were confessing to a sexual history—"I don't care a thing about what all you done"—he gets to a key point: the issue of "if you love me or don'tcher" (*CW* 280). The narrator may have been on the lookout for a way to undercut the remainder of the paragraph, but, I think, the narrator is not successful. The end of the paragraph is the following: "...and he caught her to him and wildly planted her face with kisses until she said, 'Yes, yes'" (280).

Why the double "yes"? I think it suggests a change from the beginning of the preceding paragraph when she answered the same question singly and in qualified form: "Yes...in a sense" (*CW* 280). And certainly we have here a major shift away from Hulga's single yes in answer to Manley's riddle when they first meet. The narrator ridicules that single yes by reporting that she "replied as if she had considered [his question] from all angles," as if Manley had "put [a] question up for consideration at the meeting of a philosophical association" (275). When Hulga's "Yes, yes" leads to Manley's demand that she show him where her wooden leg attaches, she again is up to the challenge. We are told that Hulga "felt as if her heart had stopped" (281), but surely what is really happening is that her heart is courageously starting to work. When Manley tells her that the wooden leg, which "[s]he took care of...as someone else would his soul" (281), is "what makes you different" (281), she deserves credit for having the feeling that "This boy, with an instinct that came from beyond wisdom, had touched the truth about her" (281). Her agreeing to take off her leg is "like surrendering to him completely," like "losing her own life and finding it again, miraculously, in his" (281).

The philosophical satire that also appears in this passage does not undercut the truth of a prodigal heart. Hulga's *true* personality is in the trip to the barn, not in her trip to college. There is even a sort of repentance in Hulga, I think, for we see her regretting her dependence on her brain as she courageously tries to use her heart. And thus I believe she deserves better than she gets at the end of the story. Applying the concept of the PD to "Good Country People" ultimately leads me to conclude that Hulga's true act of leaving home was in falling for Manley, and when she emerges from the barn and crawls home after the story ends, she deserves a caring reception by her mother. Does the story imply that Hulga will get "the best robe" along with "a ring on her finger and shoes on her feet"? Hardly. Hulga will be grilled mercilessly by the good country person Mrs. Freeman, and Hulga's mother will stand by and listen, occasionally offering more of her maddening advice. If we focus on Hulga's real prodigality, I think we can say O'Connor feels with her and for her.

It may seem difficult to regard Lucynell Crater as a PD, but as with Hulga, probably, her prodigality is in her present and future more than in her past. The daughter Lucynell may seem the totally obedient daughter, so limited in mental capacity that she couldn't conceive of rebellion against the mother who has the same name. And yet a case can be made that from the moment Tom T. Shiftlet appears at her house, Lucynell falls for him, jumping and stamping and pointing and making her "excited speechless sounds" (*CW* 172). Lucynell studies Mr. Shiftlet "with a cautious sly look as if he were a bird" (173), we are told, and therefore when she follows him around and starts learning her first word— "Burrttddt ddbirrrttdt" (177)—we may suspect she wants him. Of course, the mother Crater considers Shiftlet an appropriate match for her daughter, but she thinks that daughter Lucynell's marriage will result in their living together—all three of them. Mother expects—and probably perceives—no rebellion in her daughter's cooperation with the marriage plot, and mother Crater tells Shiftlet that Lucynell is perfect in her obedience. Mother Crater is also confident that "Lucynell don't even know what a hotel is" (179) so that marrying her is cheap. If a PD is one who takes and squanders her inheritance, Lucynell may not qualify; it is Shiftlet who receives the $17.50 from mother Crater. But if a PD is one who wants to run away, Lucynell qualifies. Dressed for her wedding and honeymoon in an old "white dress" topped off by "a Panama hat...with a bunch of red wooden cherries on the brim" (180), Lucynell has a "placid expression," but it is occasionally "changed by a sly isolated little thought like a shoot of green in the desert" (180). And what is that green thought but a desire to run away with Shiftlet, get away from her mother? The mother cries as the couple leaves, but the daughter "looked straight at her and didn't seem to see her there at all" (181). Lucynell is eager to go. After the couple hit the road, Lucynell may not be fully aware of the meaning of her next gesture, but it is surely a signal to us readers: "[S]he was pulling the cherries off the hat one by one and throwing them out the window" (181). Are we to retain any doubt that Lucynell is immensely pleased by the prospect of losing her innocence?

Since I have suggested what will become of Hulga, perhaps I should also suggest that after Lucynell wakes up in the roadside stand where Shiftlet has abandoned her and the awe-struck waiter who called her "an angel of Gawd" (*CW* 181) helps her to find her way home, Lucynell will continue her somewhat confused quest. This is not a PD who will be content back home with mama. Alice Friman tells me she thinks it is Andre Gide who wrote that after the parable of the Prodigal Son ends, the son will eventually recall why he left home the first time and he will decide to leave again. Surely the same is true of Lucynell; nothing has happened to make her understand why she should not try again to escape. The story demonstrates that one can be both "an angel of Gawd" and a PD. Mother Crater might welcome her daughter home in a fashion almost as expressive as that found in the parable, but the mother will become even more controlling, more fearful and thus more fearsome, and Lucynell's urge to leave will grow and grow.

Alice Walker's story "Everyday Use," collected within Walker's *In Love and Trouble*, is simultaneously an homage to O'Connor and, to some extent, an extension and explication of O'Connor's stories as they relate to the parable of prodigality. There are two daughters in Walker's story, one who has never left—Maggie—and Dee, the one who has left home and is now back for a visit. Dee, like Joy Hopewell, has gotten educated notions of her superiority to her relatives, has rejected her mother's ways, and has given herself a new name. When Dee-become-Wangero arrives, she brings along her new man. Maggie is as controlled, though not nearly as challenged mentally, as Lucynell. Actually, Maggie is even less rebellious than Lucynell, so it may make sense to think of Maggie as the other daughter in the parable, the non-prodigal one. What happens in Walker's story is that Dee/Wangero, the PD, comes back in order to ask for more of her inheritance, because she has learned to appreciate the family's possessions, especially their two oldest quilts. At the climax of the story, the mother of Maggie and Dee/Wangero decides that the stay-at-home daughter should have both quilts. The daughter who went away goes away again, disappointed again, while Maggie sits, apparently happy and also astonished with her mother, the recipient of a rare hug and of two quilts that had already been promised to her as wedding presents. The narrating mother assures us that Maggie eventually "will marry John Thomas (who has mossy teeth in an earnest face)" and leave the mother "free" (50), but like the daughter in "The Life You Save May Be Your Own," she probably expects to have a daughter close by.

The critical consensus on "Everyday Use" seems to be that the mother makes a wise choice, that the stay-at-home daughter has an appreciation of family values and family history that is more valuable than the more prodigal daughter's appreciation of quilts as art objects. A number of years ago I taught an introductory course on literary theory, using as one of my textbooks *A Handbook of Critical Approaches to Literature* (Guerin et al.), in which various schools of criticism are illustrated, frequently using "Everyday Use" as an example. And every single theoretical school seemed to take Maggie's side, and the mother's side, over Dee's. I thoroughly disagree.[2]

I do not actually recall reading the assertion in criticism that I keep expecting to read somewhere and that *A Handbook of Critical Approaches to Literature* seems to invite: that Walker treats Maggie as an angel of God because Walker is imitating O'Connor, agreeing with O'Connor that PD's with new names are bad, that daughters who stay home and are more obedient to the mother are good. I also expect to read that when the mother in Walker's story presents two old quilts to Maggie, the mother is the perfectly accepting parent of the biblical parable. I should also mention that "Everyday Use" is justly famous as a commentary on the artistry of women and the significance and complexity of quilt culture. As Walker's characters debate quilts, we can find an allegory, in which Dee as Feminism needs to learn about the artistry of Non-Feminists like her mother and sister. See Susan Benwick for a fascinating explanation of quilt politics. Bernick makes a key point that seems to me to be forgotten in most discussions about the quilts in "Everyday Use"—that quilting is essentially about expressing "love" (141). So it matters how much the mother loves her daughters.

---

[2] In the years since the original version of this article was published, I have become aware of other critics who happen to have reached conclusions about "Everyday Use" that are similar to mine. See Susan Farrell's 1998 article "Fight vs. Flight" and Nagueyalti Warren's *Alice Walker's Metaphysics* (48–52). Carol M. Andrews has published an article on "Good Country People" and "Everyday Use" that differs from mine in emphasis and nuance, but I find Andrews's readings basically compatible with mine.

I reject the critical consensus about Walker's story—so strongly that at times the story has been difficult for me to teach—because "Everyday Use" seems to me to be primarily about the everyday uses to which the mother puts both of her daughters, neither of whom is treated justly. First, let me show you why I do not think the mother is good to the stay-at-home daughter. Nothing ever happens in the story to suggest that the mother stops believing in this description of Maggie that her mother provides: "Have you ever seen a lame animal, perhaps a dog run over by some careless person rich enough to own a car, sidle up to someone who is ignorant enough to be kind to him? That is the way my Maggie walks" (*In Love* 49). Nor does the mother repent for this statement about Maggie: "She knows she is not bright. Like good looks and money, quickness passed her by" (50). And does the mother ever accept responsibility for limiting Maggie's life? I do not think so. Actually, I suspect the mother of blaming Dee for Maggie's problems. Why that crack about a dog run over by a rich person's car, when she knows Dee is about to arrive in a car? The mother suggests only Dee was worth sending to school, but she never mentions that she tried to think of something to do to give Maggie equal treatment; it is as if the mother thinks Dee personally stole her education from Maggie. The mother also seems to blame Dee by implying illogically that since Dee was glad when their old house burned (49–50), and the burning of the house was the start of some of Maggie's problems (49), Dee must be the cause of whatever went wrong for Maggie.

Dee, clearly a prodigal, rarely gets a break. She is criticized as selfish for wanting new shoes to match the dress that Dee had "made from an old suit somebody gave" the mother (*In Love* 50). Dee is criticized for showing off her education by reading to her mother and sister (50). She is criticized for losing a boyfriend (51) and for having a new one (52). She is criticized for the act that starts the parable: wanting some of her family's things. (Of course, in the parable, the parent gives such things willingly.) Dee is even criticized, I think, for enjoying the meal the family shares. When the mother reports "Everything delighted her" (55), I detect sarcasm. The mother's ultimate injustice, I believe, occurs before the prodigal's return. The mother imagines the perfect reunion, a reunion we might compare to the parable's reunion, in which everything is happy, in which love takes charge, in which past errors are forgotten. But the mother cannot sustain the thought. She compares the reunion scene to a TV show, emceed by a White host "like Johnny Carson," in which the participants are forced to pretend to love. As soon as the mother refers to her "quick and witty tongue" (48) that she uses to chat with her Johnny Carson, the mother kills the dream of the happy reunion. "Who ever knew a Johnson with a quick tongue?" (49), she asks. Well, the answer, she (perhaps inadvertently) reveals, is Dee. It is as if the mother denies that the prodigal is indeed her daughter.

I do not mean to suggest that I am disappointed to see Maggie get the quilts at the end of the story. But look at how the mother presents the climax:

> [S]omething hit me in the top of my head and ran down to the soles of my feet. Just like when I'm in church and the spirit of God touches me and I get happy and shout. I did something I never had done before: hugged Maggie to me, then dragged her on into the room, snatched the quilts out of Miss Wangero's hands and dumped them into Maggie's lap. (*In Love* 58)

Is hugging Maggie something the mother has never done? Who's the star of this show? I think Walker here may have learned from O'Connor that when the mother pats herself on the back as God's favorite, she deserves another kind of touch: a hit on the head. I think that "Everyday Use" is an excellent story that ought to be read as a study of prodigality and of how difficult and unlikely it is for the PD to receive a genuine welcome home. The fact that Walker uses the oppressive mother's voice to tell her story leads most readers to accept the mother's oppressiveness as correct, but I think Walker learned from O'Connor how oppressive and tricky and wrong a narrator who sounds like a parent can be. If we value the mother's final action, we should notice, as Marianne Hirsch does (189), that the mother may be starting to act *like* Dee.

A final point worth making is that Alice Walker is, to some extent, Flannery O'Connor's Prodigal Daughter. In a literary sense, I think we can reasonably imagine that these two authors repeat some of the good behavior found in the parable. Let us see O'Connor as giving Alice Walker her inheritance, through O'Connor's works. Let us say Walker was a bit of the prodigal, as when she said that visiting Andalusia made her, however momentarily, despise O'Connor ("Beyond" 57). But as Walker struggled with O'Connor, she also took inspiration from her. Louise Westling has suggested that O'Connor taught Walker and others in the sense that "[h]er hilarious rage blasted the doors open for a host of younger writers who are creating possibilities for women's subjectivity and agency that O'Connor could never have imagined" (131). Some people see O'Connor and Walker as irreconcilable, as Sarah Gordon notes (73; see also J. O. Tate's comments in "From the Panel" 63–64), and it could be that Alice Walker has dreams of the sort Mary Gordon says she has, in which O'Connor disapproves of everything she does (329–30). But like a character in one of O'Connor's own stories, Flannery died before she did anything to spoil her goodness, in this case the inheritance she gave to Walker. And Walker used her inheritance both prodigally and wisely, *making* O'Connor into a good mother.

Let me end by repeating and seconding some of what Walker says in an essay about O'Connor, that "…truth about any subject only comes when all sides of the story are put together" ("Beyond" 49) and that "[e]ach writer writes the missing parts of the other writer's story" (49). A recent illustration of this "all sides" notion came to light when Walker's late-1960s story "Convergence: The Duped Shall Enter Last: But They Shall Enter" was rediscovered in the Walker archive at Emory University. Walker's story is a response to O'Connor's "Everything That Rises Must Converge." Walker's story and Nagueyalti Warren's article on teaching these two stories together are found in a collection edited by Robert Donahoo and me. Walker says, "[i]t was for [O'Connor's] description of Southern white women that I appreciated her work first, because when she set her pen to them not a whiff of magnolia hovered in the air (and the tree itself might never have been planted)" ("Beyond" 52). I hope I have suggested persuasively that O'Connor was a good-enough literary mother to Walker, in part because she helped as Walker figured out how to write about the lives of Black women.

WORKS CITED

Andrews, Carol M. "Hyphenated Identity in 'Good Country People' and 'Everyday Use.'" *Shenandoah*, vol. 60, no. 1–2, Spring/Fall 2010, pp. 133–41.

Bernick, Susan E. "A Quilt Is an Art Object When It Stands Up like a Man." *Quilt Culture: Tracing the Pattern*, edited by Cheryl B. Torsney and Judy Elsley. Columbia, University of Missouri Press, 1994, pp. 134–50.

Bosco, Mark, S.J. "Consenting to Love": Autobiographical Roots of 'Good Country People.'" *The Southern Review*, vol. 41, 2005, pp. 283–95.

———. "Erik Langkjaer: The One Flannery 'Used to Go With.'" *Flannery O'Connor Review*, vol. 5, 2007, pp. 44–55.

Crews, Frederick. "The Power of Flannery O'Connor." *The New York Review of Books*, 26 Apr. 1990, pp. 49–55. This essay appeared as "The Critics Bear It Away" in Crews's *The Critics Bear It Away: American Fiction and the Academy*, New York, Random, 1992, pp. 143–67.

Farrell, Susan. "Fight vs. Flight: A Re-evaluation of Dee in Alice Walker's 'Everyday Use.'" *Studies in Short Fiction*, vol. 35, no. 2, 1998, pp. 179–86.

"From the Panel Discussion." "Of Time and Place and Eternity" O'Connor Symposium, 14–15 Apr. 1984, Georgia College, Milledgeville, *The Flannery O'Connor Bulletin*, vol. 13, 1984, pp. 59–72.

Gentry, Marshall Bruce. *Flannery O'Connor's Religion of the Grotesque.* Jackson, University Press of Mississippi, 1986.

Gordon, Mary. "Flannery's Kiss." *Michigan Quarterly Review*, vol. 43, 2004, pp. 329–49.

Gordon, Sarah. "Milledgeville: The Perils of Place as Text." *The Flannery O'Connor Bulletin*, vol. 20, 1991, pp. 73–87.

Guerin, Wilfred L., et al. *A Handbook of Critical Approaches to Literature.* 4th ed., New York, Oxford University Press, 1999.

Hirsch, Marianne. *The Mother/Daughter Plot: Narrative, Psychoanalysis, Feminism.* Bloomington, Indiana University Press, 1989.

O'Connor, Flannery. *Flannery O'Connor: Collected Works*, edited by Sally Fitzgerald. New York, Library of America, 1988.

Walker, Alice. "Beyond the Peacock: The Reconstruction of Flannery O'Connor." In *Search of Our Mothers' Gardens: Womanist Prose.* San Diego, Harcourt Brace, 1983, pp. 42–59.

———. "Convergence: The Duped Shall Enter Last: But They Shall Enter." *Approaches to Teaching the Works of Flannery O'Connor*, edited by Robert Donahoo and Marshall Bruce Gentry. New York, Modern Language Association, 2019, pp. 212–23.

———. *In Love and Trouble: Stories of Black Women.* San Diego, Harcourt Brace, 1973. "Everyday Use" appears on pp. 47–59.

Warren, Nagueyalti. *Alice Walker's Metaphysics: Literature of Spirit.* Lanham, MD, Rowman and Littlefield, 2019.

———. "Teaching O'Connor's 'Everything That Rises Must Converge' and Alice Walker's 'Convergence' in the Twenty-First-Century South." *Approaches to Teaching the Works of Flannery O'Connor*, edited by Robert Donahoo and Marshall Bruce Gentry. New York, Modern Language Association, 2019, pp. 150–58.

He Would Have Been a Good Man: Compassion and Meanness in Truman Capote and Flannery O'Connor

Flannery O'Connor critics have occasionally noted similarities between O'Connor and Truman Capote. Usually they contrast them in terms of their writing styles and theological assumptions and then, as a rule, find Capote lacking in the comparison. I think the connections are so numerous and interesting that we may learn about O'Connor through Capote. Both writers were capable of impressive meanness and compassion toward both literary characters and real people. Moreover, there are important similarities between O'Connor's "A Good Man Is Hard to Find" and Capote's 1965 nonfiction novel, *In Cold Blood* (a study of Perry Smith and Dick Hickock's murder of the Clutter family in Kansas in 1959), and between Capote's "Handcarved Coffins" and O'Connor's "The River." Capote's novel about a mass murder is, among other things, a tribute to O'Connor; I say that despite the extent to which "Handcarved Coffins" may seem to recant part of that tribute. An examination of Capote's borrowings from O'Connor's fiction indicates his sometimes grudging respect for the power of her work, from which he probably acquired increased compassion toward the meanness in criminals, as shown through *In Cold Blood*. Capote seems unsure at times of what to do with his own meanness, for he directs some of it at O'Connor in "Handcarved Coffins." This analysis also suggests we should reconsider O'Connor's treatment of criminality and the extent to which O'Connor may have meant it when she said she admired her Misfit. O'Connor's compassion for criminals is greater than Capote's, in part because O'Connor has a better understanding of how the expression of meanness is an essential element of compassion. I believe that O'Connor's fascinating struggle with how to treat The Misfit leaves open the possibility of his goodness and the possibility that O'Connor is ultimately compassionate toward him.

The relationship between Truman Capote and Flannery O'Connor was strained, and if one judges by their published comments, one concludes that the strain existed primarily because of O'Connor. Capote, famous for his sarcastic comments, apparently had a high opinion of O'Connor. He told Pati Hill in an interview that O'Connor was one "of the younger writers who seem to know that style exists," adding, somewhat patronizingly, that O'Connor "has some fine moments, that girl" (Capote, "Art" 29). He has also been quoted as saying "Flannery O'Connor had a certain genius" (qtd. in Grobel 36). O'Connor's level of enthusiasm for Capote was considerably lower. In a letter to Betty Hester dated 8 Dec. 1955, O'Connor wrote, "Mr. Truman Capote makes me plumb sick" (*HB* 121). Why would O'Connor react with such meanness toward Capote? Ted R. Spivey argues that O'Connor's distaste for Capote has to do with "her revulsion at the frankly sexual in literature" (31). Spivey believes that O'Connor also envied Capote's success (82). After all, Capote was only about six months older than O'Connor, and perhaps O'Connor was troubled to see another southerner so readily accepted by a northern literary establishment. Spivey suggests that her "fanatical denunciations" actually show she was "caught up unconsciously in some of [his] views" (53).

Capote himself discouraged investigations of his connections to other writers. Peter G. Christensen complains that "Capote pretended to be above questions of literary influence." Christensen adds that Capote "bristled when it was suggested that he borrowed" (221–22). Nevertheless, Capote did borrow from O'Connor. Helen Garson suggests Capote takes from O'Connor the name Hulga for a character in his last, unfinished novel, *Answered Prayers* (70), and she sees connections between Capote's "Handcarved Coffins" and two O'Connor stories, "Greenleaf" and "The River" (26). His most significant borrowings appear in a work Capote claimed was nonfiction, *In Cold Blood: A True Account of a Multiple Murder and Its Consequences*. Why would Capote borrow from O'Connor for this book? A practical connection, though perhaps Capote did not know it at the time, is that both writers were inspired by newspaper crime reports, but more significantly, he knew O'Connor's fiction had the psychological and mythic depth his work needed. Capote was insecure about needing to be inspired by another writer, but I believe his goal was to learn from O'Connor, not to plagiarize her.

O'Connor might have been on Capote's mind because they each had a story in the second edition of an important textbook, *The House of Fiction*, edited by Caroline Gordon and Allen Tate, which was published in 1960 as Capote was starting work on *In Cold Blood*. O'Connor's "A

Good Man Is Hard to Find" appears next to Capote's "Headless Hawk" in the anthology, and the two stories undergo comparison by the editors. "Commentary on Capote and O'Connor" ends with the significant observation that Capote's stories lack "the theological framework" of O'Connor's, in part because Capote's works include "no one like 'The Misfit,' with his crisp, dogmatic explanation of why he is compelled to commit murder" (Gordon 386). I know of no reason to believe Capote was reading O'Connor's works while he worked on *In Cold Blood* (from 1959 to 1965), but Capote would surely have been reminded of O'Connor's works when she died eight months before the executions of Hickock and Smith in 1965. Many of the final pages of Capote's book were written following the executions.[1]

Several critics have noted significant borrowings from "A Good Man" for *In Cold Blood*. Jon Tuttle has noted two. First, citing the similarities between O'Connor's grandmother and Mrs. Bonnie Clutter, who both suffer moments of mental instability and who both are the last members of their families to be shot, Tuttle suggests Capote borrowed a speech O'Connor gives the grandmother as she is about to be killed (Tuttle 193–94). The grandmother insists, "I know you're a good man. You don't look a bit like you have common blood. I know you must come from nice people!" Then she adds, "I know you're a good man at heart. I can just look at you and tell" (*CW* 147). With *In Cold Blood*, words similar to the grandmother's are reported by Perry Smith as having come from Mrs. Clutter: "...she felt I was a decent young man, I'm *sure* you are, she says, and made me promise I wouldn't let Dick hurt anybody" (Capote, *In Cold Blood* 242). The second borrowing Tuttle sees is

---

[1] Not all of the O'Connor connections in *In Cold Blood* have to do with intentional borrowing or with borrowing specifically from "A Good Man." Melvin J. Friedman notes that Capote's Kansas "is not significantly different from Flannery O'Connor country" (168). Friedman sees an "O'Connor reminder in *In Cold Blood*...when we are told...that Perry Smith's sister Fern changed her name to Joy" (Capote, *In Cold Blood* 185). This sounds like an inversion of the name change in O'Connor's "Good Country People." Friedman also suggests that "Willie-Jay, of *In Cold Blood*, whose name Capote admits he has invented, resembles in many ways O'Connor's 'Bible Belt' preachers, both in name (think of Onnie Jay Holy in *Wise Blood*) and in evangelical manner." Still, Friedman concludes "that the connections which involve *In Cold Blood* are largely fortuitous" (167–68).

of The Misfit's words about how one ought to live if Jesus did not do what he said he did: "...it's nothing for you to do but enjoy the few minutes you got left the best way you can—by killing somebody or burning down his house or doing some other meanness to him. No pleasure but meanness" (*CW* 152).[2] *In Cold Blood* attributes similar sentiments to York and Latham, two killers on death row with Hickock and Smith: "They shared at least one firm opinion: the world was hateful, and everybody in it would be better off dead. 'It's a rotten world,' Latham said. 'There's no answer to it but meanness. That's all anybody understands—meanness. Burn down the man's barn—he'll understand that. Poison his dog. Kill him'" (Capote, *In Cold Blood* 323). Tuttle believes that Capote ignores the religious significance of The Misfit's speeches (Tuttle 194), though there is certainly plenty of talk about religion within *In Cold Blood*.[3] Another significant borrowing, noted by David Guest, has to do with passages in which The Misfit and Dick Hickock describe their varied experiences. Here is The Misfit:

> "I was a gospel singer for a while," The Misfit said. "I been most everything. Been in the arm service, both land and sea, at home and abroad, been twict married, been an undertaker, been with the railroads, plowed Mother Earth, been in a tornado, seen a man burnt alive oncet," and he looked up at the children's mother and the little girl who were sitting close together, their faces white and their eyes glassy; "I even seen a woman flogged." (*CW* 149)

And here is the passage from *In Cold Blood* in which Capote uses The Misfit's syntax and rhythm as Dick Hickock demonstrates he is more experienced than another killer:

> I've walked a lot of mean streets. I've seen a white man flogged. I've watched babies born. I've seen a girl, and her no more than fourteen, take on three guys at the same time and give them all

---

[2] One might also compare this speech by The Misfit, about there being only two paths from which to choose, to Perry Smith's thoughts about his situation as *In Cold Blood* opens: either he will meet up with his religious friend, Willie-Jay, or he will join Dick Hickock's plan to commit a crime (Capote, *In Cold Blood* 45).

[3] Capote once opined about mass murderers, "They all believe in God" (qtd. in Grobel 126).

their money's worth. Fell off a ship once five miles out to sea. Swam five miles with my life passing before me with every stroke. Once I shook hands with President Truman in the lobby of the Hotel Muehleback. Harry S. Truman. When I was working for the hospital, driving an ambulance, I saw every side of life there is—things that would make a dog vomit. (Capote, *In Cold Blood* 333).

Among the many other similarities between O'Connor's "A Good Man" and Capote's *In Cold Blood* are the extreme foreshadowing, the premise of an Edenic American landscape violated by an invader, the similarities between the murdered families, the similarities between the killers, revelations of mistrust among members of an apparently normal and complacent American community, the satirizing of average Americans, skepticism about the ability of the legal and penal systems to understand the mysteries of the human heart, the suggestion of a motive for murder in a dysfunctional child-parent relationship, the significance of religion to criminals who consciously deny its relevance, killers who wander the countryside aimlessly but who know there are only two paths one can take, and heavy use of animal imagery—especially in the form of cats, parrots, and snakes. Perry Smith's fantasy of a parrot that defeats a snake (Capote, *In Cold Blood* 92–93) is uncannily similar to the ending of "A Good Man," where The Misfit, wearing a parrot shirt, shoots the grandmother at the moment when she appears snakelike (*CW* 152). One sometimes wonders whether Capote's killers patterned their lives after the fiction of Flannery O'Connor.[4]

The most interesting similarity between *In Cold Blood* and "A Good Man Is Hard to Find," the one that brings up fresh questions about

---

[4] One also wonders what Capote might have said if confronted with all these similarities and the specific borrowings. I suspect he would reply that what he did is far from plagiarism, and that in two places, *In Cold Blood* presents critiques of those who commit plagiarism. When Perry Smith learns that a copycat killer in Florida has duplicated the Clutter murders, he says he "wouldn't be surprised" to learn the killer was "a lunatic" (Capote, *In Cold Blood* 200). And late within *In Cold Blood*, we learn that the poem handed to Dick Hickock by the unredeemable Lowell Lee Andrews on his way to being executed is actually a plagiarism of Gray's "Elegy" (Capote, *In Cold Blood* 332). It is this passage that precedes Hickock's borrowed speech about his varied experiences.

O'Connor, is that surrounding both works we find instances of the authors' admiration for their murderous characters. Just as O'Connor tried to discover ways in which her Misfit could in a profound sense be a good man, throughout *In Cold Blood* Capote searches for the soul of a poet within Perry Smith. In real life Capote was helpful to both Dick Hickock and Perry Smith, assisting them with their appeals and stays of execution and eventually even buying their tombstones. And he befriended the murderers as he interviewed them for his book. Alvin Dewey—the primary detective in the Clutter case and a major character in *In Cold Blood*—told George Plimpton that Capote "saw himself in Perry Smith...in their childhood." Joe Fox went further: "He adored Perry" (quoted in Plimpton 173–74). Harold Nye went furthest, speculating that Capote and Perry Smith "had become lovers in the penitentiary" (quoted in Plimpton 188). And yet, when the time came to turn all his work into a book, Capote refused to let his emotional involvement get in the way of his art. Ned Rorem reports that Capote was finally eager to see Hickock and Smith die, and Rorem quotes Capote as once saying that *In Cold Blood* "can't be published until they're executed, so I can hardly wait" (quoted in Plimpton 300). It is the nature of Plimpton's work that things are sometimes reported fourthhand: Kathleen Tynan told Plimpton that Capote, upon hearing that Hickock and Smith would be executed, said to Kenneth Tynan, "I'm beside myself! Beside myself! Beside myself with joy! (quoted in Plimpton 215–16). Of course, Capote could be hiding his true feelings, but clearly there is a limit to Capote's friendship.

The most significant debate has to do with whether *In Cold Blood* is sufficiently fair to Perry Smith. The book does claim to be fair, even compassionate. The book's epigraph, from François Villon's "Ballade des pendus" (Ballad of the Hanged), surely works to emphasize the similarities between Capote and the two murderers. Villon's poem was written while the fifteenth-century French criminal and poet was himself in danger of being hanged (Bonner xxii–xxiii), and the speaker in Villon's poem is one of the criminals already hanged. Surely Capote could see himself in Villon, an outsider who desired a general amnesty.[5]

---

[5] Here is Anthony Bonner's translation of the beginning of the first stanza of Villon's poem, also called "XIV—Villon's Epitaph":
Brother men who after us live on,

One could defend *In Cold Blood* as being fair to Perry even while it labels him as unlike other humans. The primary theme of all of Capote's work up to and including *In Cold Blood* has been described by William L. Nance as "acceptance of the unconventional, of the misfit in others and in oneself," an interpretation Nance says Capote personally endorsed (Nance 220–21). Or one could argue that Capote is fair because he tries to prove that Smith is actually like everyone else, including his victims. This may be Capote's goal in pointing out that, when the surrounding community learns that the Clutter family has been killed, some at first consider Mrs. Clutter responsible (Capote, *In Cold Blood* 61, 70). According to George R. Creeger's study of animal imagery in *In Cold Blood*, Capote shows that conventional people label criminals as animals rather than as humans in order to hide from themselves their own capacity for violence against fellow humans (Creeger 6). This argument implies that *In Cold Blood* actually shows everyone to be essentially the same in that we are all capable of violence. As Nance points out, the fictional final scene in *In Cold Blood* equates all of the book's "dreamer[s] of unfulfilled dreams," all of the book's "victims" (210), so it is no stretch to say the ending compares Perry Smith and the murdered daughter, Nancy Clutter. It is also easy to compare Smith with Mrs. Clutter in their habits of collecting things, for they both have sentimental attachments to possessions that others see as having little value. Another version of this defense of Capote is that he proves that average Americans made Smith a killer; David Galloway claims that what happens within *In Cold Blood* is "not so much murder as suicide: in a real sense America was both killer and victim, turning the deferred-payment shotgun against herself" (161).

>   harden not your hearts against us,
>   for if you have some pity on us poor men,
>   the sooner God will show you mercy.

That is the end of the epigraph for *In Cold Blood*; here is the rest of the first stanza:
>   You see us, five, six, strung up here:
>   as for our flesh, which we have fed too well,
>   already it has been devoured and is rotten,
>   and we, the bones, now turn to dust and ashes.
>   Let no one laugh at all our miseries,
>   but pray to God that He absolve us all. (Villon 163)

An opposing argument is that *In Cold Blood* proves that Smith and Hickock really are different from the rest of us and are undeserving of our sympathy. The insanity defense that Capote promotes for pages could be a concession of this major point. Even Capote's title, which could be a nod to O'Connor's *Wise Blood*, may constitute a betrayal of Hickock and Smith, since most readers will think the title refers to the killers' being cold-blooded rather than to, say, a cold-blooded American legal system. David Guest makes the amazing argument that O'Connor's Misfit is Capote's "model psychopath" and that Capote was not therefore as inclined to defend Smith and Hickock as he claimed to be (Guest 129–30). Another interesting charge against Capote is that, within the book, he never takes an explicit stand on Smith's behalf. The peculiar insistence on objectivity and near invisibility in the narration of *In Cold Blood*, a stylistic choice Capote often insisted was crucial to his book's success, can be considered a cop-out. As Guest claims, "Capote's narrator is both omniscient and impotent" (109). I can agree with Guest that Capote's choice of narrator forced him into a weaker presentation of a case on the murderers' behalf, but at the same time, I can testify, based on years of teaching *In Cold Blood*, that the book does open many students' eyes to the case against capital punishment. Here, however, it is not necessary to reach a conclusion about whether Capote did the right thing. What is clear is that O'Connor helped Capote write a great book in that he took from her lessons in seeing the potential good in a bad person, in putting aside meanness for the sake of compassion.

I hope it is already apparent that the issues raised by Capote's book are issues worth raising in O'Connor's works. But before I shift from Capote, it is worth noting that he wrote another "nonfiction" piece about murder, "Handcarved Coffins," which clearly alludes to O'Connor's "The River," a story that combines drowning and baptism. While Jack De Bellis speculates that *In Cold Blood* was Capote's revenge on the South and "a way of release from his psychological bondage to the South" (535), a better case can be made that it is in "Handcarved Coffins," published in 1980, that Capote most forcefully pushes O'Connor away. I should begin by clarifying that I do not consider "Handcarved Coffins" to be nonfiction; even Gerald Clarke, who generously accepts most of *In Cold Blood* as "uncompromising realism" of a basically accurate sort, sees "Handcarved Coffins" as "mostly fictional" (359). Clarke says, "The idea for *Handcarved Coffins* came from Al Dewey" (516), but most of the crimes in "Handcarved Coffins" are so cartoonish as to be almost beside the point.[6]

Although he clearly considered "Handcarved Coffins" similar to *In Cold Blood*, Capote directed his focus in the story—in contrast to his nearly invisible presence within *In Cold Blood*—on himself, as an active character and narrator imagining the criminal's motives. Capote becomes aware that Robert Hawley Quinn is killing people because his friend Jake Pepper, a detective, introduces Capote to the case. When Jake's fiancée, Adelaide Mason, drowns or is drowned, Capote becomes the superior detective, probably because he bears none of Pepper's guilt over failing to save Adelaide. Robert Siegle is correct in suggesting that in "Handcarved Coffins" Capote discovers the truth about the killer "by identifying him with a character in his own private psychodrama" and thus the process of creating fiction is demonstrated to be the way to produce nonfiction (445–46).

The central symbol in "Handcarved Coffins" is the Blue River, which probably provides the motive for the murders. Capote's story equates the killer Quinn with the Reverend Bobby Joe Snow, who forcibly baptized the young Truman. It is no secret that Capote hates the reverend. The most important O'Connor connection here, which Helen Garson has noted but which nobody has analyzed, is the character Marylee Connor. (Flannery O'Connor's first name, of course, was Mary, and note that "Marylee" rhymes with "Flannery"!) The sister of Adelaide, Connor seems unable to stomach discussions of murder when she first appears, but she is the one able to figure out that her sister's life is being threatened (Capote, "Handcarved" 89), and we later realize that Connor denies that Quinn is a murderer. Detective Jake Pepper, perhaps unfairly, explains that she is "sweet but not too bright" (102). She is with Adelaide at the Blue River, reading as Adelaide drowns, and she is sure Quinn was not involved (124–25). She finally moves to Florida, mails Capote a picture of Adelaide holding a cat (136), and gets a job as a receptionist for a circus. This character in a story with a baptism scene reminiscent of "The River" is surely meant to comment on O'Connor. Jake Pepper takes a

---

[6] John Hersey considers "Handcarved Coffins" to be "a gobbet of commercial trash" and uses a quotation from Flannery O'Connor to argue that one must not mix fiction and nonfiction (1–3). Several other critics have been more positively disposed toward "Handcarved Coffins."

swipe at all "female literature" (94), but Capote knows better than to endorse Pepper on that point. If he is rejecting O'Connor here, it is because Capote objects to her writing about baptism in a way that simply strikes too close to home for him.[7] The major accusation that "Handcarved Coffins" makes against O'Connor is that she seems too comfortable around a murderer—too inclined to see a good man in one. It is as if Capote were complaining that O'Connor made him too compassionate toward Perry Smith.

According to Jack Hicks, the river in "Handcarved Coffins" carries significant symbolism for Capote's career: "The Blue River is a metaphor for the author's desire for historical/mythic continuity, his hope for a revivified narrative flow. It is first a source of life....But it is soon treacherous...and finally demonic and death-dealing, a mirror in which to see his own forced, infernal baptism forty years earlier. To be born ritually into this world, Capote implies, is to be dragged in unwillingly, to be ceremonially drowned, inundated first beneath the waters of a hell-on-earth" (Hicks 172-73). It is no stretch to apply Hicks's comment to Capote's true feelings about O'Connor. Perhaps he has to reject the inspiration he took from her in order to declare his personal and artistic independence. Hicks reads the final scene of "Handcarved Coffins" as showing that Capote refuses to join the probable murderer Quinn when invited into the middle of the Blue River, because Capote's "own sense of power grows, out of his knowledge that historical, literary, and literal rivers are all poisoned, and out of the desire not to be submerged" (176) by the man whom Capote imagines as a substitute for the preacher who baptized him. If the story is read this way, at the end of it Capote frees himself from several oppressive ghosts. If freedom is Capote's goal in this story, he may be thinking of O'Connor as another authority figure he is ready to rebel against. In other words, one might be tempted to say that in "Handcarved Coffins," Capote, as a sort of O'Connoresque Misfit, feels he is confronting the fact that he is one of O'Connor's own children, and

---

[7] John C. Waldmeir says the river in "Handcarved Coffins" contributes to "the theological complexity" of *Music for Chameleons*, the collection in which it appears, so it is probably not safe to conclude that Capote rejects religion in "Handcarved Coffins." Waldmeir sees the story "dramatizing all that is at stake in the ritual of baptism, the complex and dangerous exchange between life and death that Saint Paul described a[s] 'dying to Christ'" (165).

thus he must symbolically shoot her. And Capote as Misfit might even experience a bit of an O'Connoresque religious insight at the end of "Handcarved Coffins." Robert Siegle sees Capote becoming one with the murderer in the work's final reference to acts of God (449–50), in the claim that everything is ultimately mysterious: Quinn says, with intentionally ambiguous pronouns, "The way I look at it is: it was the hand of God" (Capote, "Handcarved" 146).

Of course, if Capote finally has some appreciation of Quinn, a man he hated, then the character Marylee Connor / O'Connor might be right after all in finding something of value in Quinn. And what Capote ends up demonstrating in "Handcarved Coffins" is that, as he pronounces his rejection of O'Connor, he seems closer to her spirit than he was while writing *In Cold Blood*. While *In Cold Blood* attempts an objective compassion that is ultimately fragile, "Handcarved Coffins," for all its possible artistic faults, bring Capote closer to his murderer (and to O'Connor) because Capote's meanness is not masked.

So what do all of these speculations about Capote's uses of and opinions about O'Connor teach us about her? I hope I have indicated enough of the wealth of connections between the two of them to suggest that we may learn something about O'Connor through Capote. The primary issue raised here is how well, how justly and compassionately, O'Connor treats her Misfit. I believe that O'Connor, fascinated as she had to be in order to create them, rarely went all the way in endorsing the voices of her misfit characters and misfit narrators. I have a renewed sense of her struggle to affirm her own "meanness"—her unswerving insistence on following her own path—and I have an increased appreciation for the times when her misfit voice is allowed to speak. O'Connor was finally able to endorse meanness, not as a place to stop, but as a stage in a process, a stage one might revisit repeatedly.

Of course, there are moments in real life when O'Connor identified with The Misfit. For example, writing to Betty Hester on 10 Nov. 1955, O'Connor reported that after a woman who saw her on crutches exclaimed, "Bless you, Darling!" and obliquely tried to remind O'Connor that "The lame shall enter first," O'Connor "felt exactly like the Misfit" (*CW* 969). But the primary issue is what she did in her fiction, and O'Connor seems to have been quite conflicted about her Misfit. In "On Her Own Work," O'Connor makes some comments about the grandmother and The Misfit that suggest the complexities in how she regards both of them. Many of O'Connor's comments here seem intended to prove that the grandmother's moment of grace is the key to the story. And yet notice how indirectly and tentatively

O'Connor can go about making claims for the grandmother: she says, "...I think the unprejudiced reader will feel that the Grandmother has a special kind of triumph in this story which instinctively we do not allow to someone altogether bad," but O'Connor makes this claim only after admitting "that the old lady is a hypocritical old soul; her wits are no match for the Misfit's, nor is her capacity for grace equal to his" (*MM* 111).

O'Connor could be quite harsh toward The Misfit; in a letter to Andrew Lytle dated 4 Feb. 1960, she seems to equate The Misfit and Satan, writing that the grandmother's "moment of grace excites the devil to frenzy" (*CW* 1121). On the other hand, in a letter dated 6 Oct. 1959, O'Connor told John Hawkes that "I can fancy a character like The Misfit being redeemable" (1108). And two pages after O'Connor calls The Misfit "altogether bad" in "On Her Own Work," she amazingly reverses herself: "I don't want to equate The Misfit with the devil." O'Connor tries to explain herself by adding, "I prefer to think that, however unlikely this may seem, the old lady's gesture, like the mustard-seed, will grow to be a great crow-filled tree in the Misfit's heart, and will be enough of a pain to him there to turn him into the prophet he was meant to become" (*MM* 112–13).[8] O'Connor immediately adds, "But that's another story." Of course one can conclude O'Connor is claiming that she did not really make The Misfit redeemable, but when one compares O'Connor with Capote, one is led to ask why O'Connor seems to have left The Misfit's potential only partially investigated. There is something about The Misfit that is crucial to the power of O'Connor's fiction. Did she abandon him in a manner at all comparable to what might be interpreted as Capote's abandonment of Perry Smith? Capote might reasonably have worked to get Smith a life in prison, where he might have developed some of his talents or might have rediscovered his affection for his religious friend Willie-Jay. What could O'Connor do (or what did she do) for her potential prophet, The Misfit, that would be the right thing? I will discuss five possible answers, some of which overlap.

First, O'Connor could prove that The Misfit is something other than human, that other rules apply to him. Josephine Hendin argues that The

---

[8] Capote described for Plimpton his goals while writing *In Cold Blood* in a manner reminiscent of O'Connor's statement about the grandmother's effect on The Misfit: "I've always thought of [*In Cold Blood*] as being like something reduced to a seed. Instead of presenting the reader with a full plant, with all the foliage, a seed is planted in the soil of his mind" (quoted in Plimpton 203).

Misfit is finally shown to be an animal like Pitty Sing, the cat he picks up at the story's end (Hendin 151), and although Hendin probably does not want The Misfit to be good, one could probably adapt her argument and argue that it is enough for O'Connor to show that The Misfit is a good, even prophetic animal. I do not think O'Connor did, and I do not think this is good strategy. The Misfit is altogether human.

Or, O'Connor could make The Misfit good in that he puts his independence first, totally rejecting the grandmother's attempted influence. Those who see The Misfit taking over the story through the force of his fascinating personality and having the final word, in a meaningful sense, may prefer this view. This strategy would also probably be the most straightforward one, but there is a reason to doubt whether O'Connor used it. I have argued elsewhere that The Misfit suffers a crucial failure of courage, hypocritically refusing to live up to his own principles (Gentry 108–12).

A third way that O'Connor could make The Misfit good is that we could see him starting to change into a good man. When The Misfit tells henchman Bobby Lee to "Shut up" after Bobby Lee says that killing is "fun," and when The Misfit adds, "It's no real pleasure in life" (*CW* 153), he may be starting to suffer the kind of "pain" that O'Connor said could change him. Laura Mandell Zaidman proposes another version of this argument; she claims that as O'Connor revised the story, she transformed the grandmother "from a woman desperately in need of God's grace to a medium of grace for The Misfit" (43) and that when The Misfit acceptingly touches Pitty Sing, one should be open to "the possibility, however remote, of The Misfit's becoming a good man by the end of his life" (50). I do not believe that this action makes it absolutely clear that The Misfit is on his way to a new life. Picking up a cat is the sort of false kindness he has exhibited throughout the story, and his final statement of his own misery can be read as a sign that he will become worse, not better, after the story ends. Furthermore, it may be a bad sign that he recommends silence to Bobby Lee—not to mention that he seems to lapse into silence himself—immediately after he has agreed that the reason the grandmother could "have been a good woman" was, as Bobby Lee says, that "She was a talker…" (*CW* 153).[9] As

---

[9] When one considers the extreme extent to which "absolute silence" was insisted upon in O'Connor's first Catholic elementary school, St. Vincent's in Savannah (Cash 14), the value for O'Connor of being able to be "a talker" becomes even more apparent.

much as O'Connor loved her Misfit, in the final version of the story, she identified more with the grandmother's normality than with The Misfit's profound meanness. I have argued elsewhere that the narrator of "A Good Man" becomes good by dropping a tone of meanness in the course of telling the story (Gentry 37–39), but perhaps giving up one's meanness causes the same problems that Capote encountered when he retreated into the narratorial objectivity of *In Cold Blood*.

Fourth, O'Connor could make The Misfit good by making him similar to everyone else in the story who exhibits some goodness. I am interested in the other ways the story breaks down distinctions between The Misfit and the grandmother, although I still see O'Connor as identifying with the more conventional and less interesting grandmother. Critics continue to uncover similarities between The Misfit and the grandmother. For example, J. Peter Dyson's study of "A Good Man Is Hard to Find" in relation to *The Mikado* emphasizes the sense in which The Misfit and the grandmother take on the paradoxically combined role of judge and executioner from the Gilbert and Sullivan operetta (144). Frederick Asals also suggests a way to see the grandmother as a bit of a Misfit. Asals perceptively notes that when the grandmother lets the cat loose, what we see is "her visceral acknowledgement of her *own* failure" (20), her rejection of herself before The Misfit gets around to rejecting her.

Finally, when O'Connor wrote that The Misfit could become a prophet, she added, "But that's another story." The best argument I can make that O'Connor granted The Misfit justice is that she wrote about him in other guises. But what is striking is the struggle she went through to endorse his potential. One could say that O'Connor finds value in a murderous protagonist in both of her novels or perhaps in Thomas in "The Comforts of Home," but all of these characters lose their personalities as they become good. The exception might be Enoch Emery, but O'Connor drops his story even more abruptly than she drops The Misfit. In reexamining "The River," the story that apparently bothered Capote so much, one could interpret Harry/Bevel Ashfield as a good little Misfit, rejecting his parents, rejecting Mrs. Connin, and rejecting Mr. Paradise, as he grabs what he wants. Perhaps it is significant that "The River" immediately follows "A Good Man Is Hard to Find" in O'Connor's first story collection. But Harry/Bevel cannot survive the experience, so he may fall short of being the model Misfit.

One can find spots in O'Connor's fiction where she did justice to the mean voice of The Misfit. One is the narrative voice of "The Lame Shall Enter First," the story that provoked O'Connor to write to John Hawkes on

6 Feb. 1962, "In this one, I'll admit that the devil's voice is my own" (*CW* 1157). I can easily imagine a version of The Misfit as the narrator of that story. There are other O'Connor stories in which the narrator's voice never drops its tone of satirical meanness, notably "A Late Encounter with the Enemy," in which the narrator rips apart Gen. George Poker Sash along with the Old South. Another spot is in a character that some critics equate with O'Connor herself: the unnamed little girl in "A Temple of the Holy Ghost," the mean child who, at the end of the story, starts to pray "Hep me not to be so mean" (208), but who then gets an answer to her prayer from the intersex sideshow performer, who tells her, using ambiguous pronouns, that her meanness is good, just as the sideshow performer's "freakishness" is good. The intersex character says "I don't dispute hit. This is the way He wanted me to be" (209). The little girl learns to affirm her own meanness, and at her best, O'Connor did too.

In Truman Capote, O'Connor had a disciple who, first, profitably misunderstood her. *In Cold Blood* is a compassionate book in which meanness has little value. In "Handcarved Coffins," as Capote expresses his anger toward his misfit and his resentment of O'Connor (in part for her being too compassionate), he revealed the value he found in his misfit, in O'Connor, and in meanness. Rereading "A Good Man Is Hard to Find" in the light of Capote, we see more of the value of meanness. In the passages cited earlier about The Misfit's varied experiences, which Capote transformed into the experiences of Dick Hickock, I think we can see Capote reversing O'Connor's effect. Dick Hickock is the ultimate loser, at a dead end no matter how much he brags. The Misfit, in contrast, shows us that he is fond of changing so that even his final change, his sudden claim that life offers "no real pleasure" (*CW* 153), can leave open the strong possibility that The Misfit will continue to change.

When I think of The Misfit's struggle toward goodness as an ongoing process with value assigned to various forms of his meanness, it is easier to conclude that O'Connor is compassionately searching to discover a way to find in him a good man. When O'Connor said "But that's another story" in discussing The Misfit's transformation into a prophet, I think she was referring to other stories she did write. In "A Good Man Is Hard to Find" she makes use of what may seem like meanness, the inclination to shoot The Misfit every minute of his life. Her compassion is evident in her refusal to excuse him as simply being crazy or an animal, in her analysis of his excuses, in her dramatizations of the opportunities for change that he lets slip by, and in her suggested denials of his pride in his uniqueness. O'Connor's most compassionate act toward The Misfit is to leave him alive and wandering, disgusted with himself, still "aloose from the...Pen" (*CW* 137), not yet forced or willing to shut up. The fact that O'Connor leaves us with the creepy image of The Misfit holding that cat indicates that O'Connor always saw a function for meanness.

WORKS CITED

Asals, Frederick. "Introduction." *A Good Man Is Hard to Find: Flannery O'Connor*, edited by Frederick Asals. New Brunswick, NJ, Rutgers University Press, 1993, pp. 3–25. Women Writers: Text and Contexts.

Bonner, Anthony. "A Short Biography." *The Complete Works of François Villon*, translated by Anthony Bonner. New York, McKay, 1960, pp. xvii–xxiii.

Capote, Truman. "The Art of Fiction XVII: Truman Capote." Interview by Pati Hill. *Paris Review*, vol. 16, Spring-Summer 1957, pp. 35–51. Reprinted in *Truman Capote: Conversations*, edited by M. Thomas Inge. Jackson, University Press of Mississippi, 1987, 20–32.

———. "Handcarved Coffins: A Nonfiction Account of an American Crime." *Music for Chameleons*. New York, Random, 1980, pp. 67–146.

———. *In Cold Blood: A True Account of a Multiple Murder and Its Consequences*. New York, Random, 1965.

Cash, Jean W. *Flannery O'Connor: A Life*. Knoxville, University of Tennessee Press, 2002.

Christensen, Peter G. "Major Works and Themes." *The Critical Response to Truman Capote*, edited by Waldmeir and Waldmeir, pp. 221–29.

Clarke, Gerald. *Capote: A Biography*. New York, Simon and Schuster, 1988.

Creeger, George R. *Animals in Exile: Imagery and Theme in Capote's* In Cold Blood. Middletown, CT, Center for Advanced Studies, Wesleyan University, 1967. Monday Evening Papers 12.

De Bellis, Jack. "Visions and Revisions: Truman Capote's In Cold Blood." *Journal of Modern Literature*, vol. 7, 1979, pp. 519–36.

Dyson, J. Peter. "Cats, Crime, and Punishment: The Mikado's Pitti-Sing in 'A Good Man Is Hard to Find.'" *English Studies in Canada*, vol. 14, 1988, pp. 436–52. Reprinted in *"A Good Man Is Hard to Find": Flannery O'Connor*, edited by Frederick Asals. New Brunswick, NJ, Rutgers University Press, 1993, pp. 139–63. Women Writers: Text and Contexts.

Friedman, Melvin J. "Towards an Aesthetic: Truman Capote's Other Voices." *Truman Capote's* In Cold Blood: *A Critical Handbook*, edited by Irving Malin. Belmont, CA, Wadsworth, 1968, pp. 164–76.

Galloway, David. "Why the Chickens Came Home to Roost in Holcomb, Kansas: Truman Capote's In Cold Blood." *Truman Capote's* In Cold Blood: *A Critical Handbook*, edited by Irving Malin. Belmont, CA, Wadsworth, 1968, pp. 154–76.

Garson, Helen S. *Truman Capote: A Study of the Short Fiction*. New York, Twayne, 1986. Twayne's Studies in Short Fiction 36.

Gentry, Marshall Bruce. *Flannery O'Connor's Religion of the Grotesque*. Jackson, University Press of Mississippi, 1986.

Gordon, Caroline, and Allen Tate. "Commentary on Capote and O'Connor." *The House of Fiction: An Anthology of the Short Story with Commentary*, edited by Caroline Gordon and Allen Tate. 2nd ed., New York, Scribner's, 1960, pp. 382–86.

Grobel, Lawrence. *Conversations with Capote*. New York, New American Library, 1985.

Guest, David. *Sentenced to Death: The American Novel and Capital Punishment*. Jackson, University Press of Mississippi, 1997.

Hendin, Josephine. *The World of Flannery O'Connor*. Bloomington, Indiana University Press, 1970.

Hersey, John. "The Legend of the License." *Yale Review*, vol. 70, 1980, pp. 1–25.

Hicks, Jack. "'Fire, Fire, Fire Flowing like a River, River, River': History and Postmodernism in Truman Capote's 'Handcarved Coffins'." *History and Post-War Writing*, edited by Theo D'haen and Hans Bertens. Atlanta, Rodopi, 1990, pp. 171–84. Reprinted in *The Critical Response to Truman Capote*, edited by Waldmeir and Waldmeir, pp. 167–77.

Malin, Irving, editor. *Truman Capote's* In Cold Blood*: A Critical Handbook*. Belmont, CA, Wadsworth, 1968.

Nance, William L. *The World of Truman Capote*. New York, Stein, 1970.

O'Connor, Flannery. *Flannery O'Connor: Collected Works*, edited by Sally Fitzgerald, New York, Library of America, 1988.

———. *The Habit of Being: Letters*, edited by Sally Fitzgerald, New York, Farrar, 1979.

———. *Mystery and Manners: Occasional Prose*, edited by Sally Fitzgerald and Robert Fitzgerald, New York, Farrar, 1969.

Plimpton, George. *Truman Capote: In Which Various Friends, Enemies, Acquaintances, and Detractors Recall His Turbulent Career*. New York, Talese-Doubleday, 1997.

Siegle, Robert. "Capote's 'Handcarved Coffins' and the Nonfiction Novel." *Contemporary Literature*, vol. 35, no. 3, 1984, pp. 437–51.

Spivey, Ted R. *Flannery O'Connor: The Woman, the Thinker, the Visionary*. Macon, Mercer University Press, 1995.

Tuttle, Jon. "Glimpses of 'A Good Man' in Capote's *In Cold Blood*." *ANQ*, vol. 1, Oct. 1988, pp. 144–46. Reprinted in *The Critical Response to Truman Capote*, edited by Waldmeir and Waldmeir, pp. 193–95.

Villon, François. *The Complete Works of François Villon*, translated by Anthony Bonner. New York, McKay, 1960.

Waldmeir, John C. "Religion and Style in *The Dogs Bark* and *Music for Chameleons*." *The Critical Response to Truman Capote*, edited by Waldmeir and Waldmeir, 1999, pp. 155–66.

Waldmeir, Joseph J., and John C. Waldmeir, editors. *The Critical Response to Truman Capote*. Westport, CT, Greenwood, 1999. Critical Responses to Arts and Letters 32.

Zaidman, Laura Mandell. "The Evolution of a Good Woman." *The Flannery O'Connor Bulletin*, vol. 26–27, 1998–2000, pp. 43–51.

O'Connor's Legacy in Stories by Joyce Carol Oates and Paula Sharp

Who can follow us into such meanness?
(Oates, "Firing a Field" 35)

When we read that a new writer writes just like Flannery O'Connor, don't we sometimes groan? I love O'Connor, but even today, her image in the popular imagination—or, at least, that part of the popular imagination that writes book blurbs and book reviews—strikes me too often as the image she had before very many people were reading her sensitively. When I read that a contemporary writer is compared to O'Connor, I fear that writer may merely describe the South using bizarre details or that the contemporary writer will only imitate O'Connor as grotesque satirist. Only occasionally do I conclude that such comparisons work to benefit O'Connor's reputation, even indirectly. O'Connor comes off looking like a clever caricaturist but not much more, a quirky regionalist for other regionalists to copy.

For the sake of avoiding a repetition of this troubling pattern, I would like to propose that two of the best writers to be inspired by O'Connor are sophisticated readers of her fiction, both of whom happen to be northerners. The first is Joyce Carol Oates, born in 1938 in Lockport, New York. This comparison probably comes as no surprise—Harold Bloom is one of many who consider O'Connor to be "Oates's inescapable precursor" (5). The other writer indebted to O'Connor is Paula Sharp, born in San Diego in 1957 and later a public defender in New York City. Sharp also teaches literature, including O'Connor's works. Specifically, I would like to discuss some of the similarities between several of O'Connor's works and stories by Oates and Sharp: the story that appears in anthologies almost as regularly as O'Connor's do, Oates's "Where Are You Going, Where Have You Been?" and stories from Sharp's collection *The Imposter: Stories About Netta and Stanley*. The two Sharp stories I will emphasize are "Joyriding," which is subtitled "An Introduction," and "A Meeting on the Highway," which is a story related to "Joyriding." In these stories, Oates and Sharp respond creatively to O'Connor's fascination with our secret desires for trespass and with the mysterious connections between danger and salvation. Furthermore, I believe that studying Oates and Sharp leads us to read again O'Connor's "A Good Man Is Hard to Find" with a new eye.

Both Oates and Sharp use what we might call O'Connoresque descriptions. I think of Arnold Friend's car, which so impresses the protagonist Connie in Oates's story, with his name "written in tarlike black letters on the side, with a drawing of a round, grinning face that remind[s] Connie of a pumpkin, except it [wears] sunglasses" (124)—or of Oates's description of Ellie Oscar, who wears "a bright orange shirt unbuttoned halfway to show his...pale, bluish chest" (128). In reading Sharp's "Joyriding," I think of O'Connor when a character apparently named Roxanne DuPont says, "My brother has a tumor in his stomach the size and shape of a monkey's head" (8). And this passage from "A Meeting on the Highway" seems to take off from *The Violent Bear It Away*:

> Grandpa Bubba was the only person Stanley had an affiliation with who was dead. In Stanley's mind, death and his grandfather were hence one and the same. He pictured death as a thin man wearing a short-brimmed straw hat who drove a pink car and smiled, friendly-like, exposing his bad, bluish teeth. Stanley distrusted him as he would a man who pulled up behind him on the road and offered him candy. (164)

Although many authors have imitated O'Connor's grotesque descriptions, Oates and Sharp take the O'Connor influence farther than the use of the grotesque. In the first place, Oates and Sharp do not confine their psychological landscape to the South. Connie and Arnold Friend could exist anywhere in America, and while Sharp's characters Netta and Stanley have lived in the South (with "A Meeting on the Highway" set in New Orleans), "Joyriding" is set in New York City, and its main character, Byron Coffin, lives in New Jersey.

The O'Connor character that I think most profoundly inspires Oates and Sharp to respond in their own fiction is what we might call the Philosophical Criminal with a Car. The primary examples of this character are The Misfit in "A Good Man Is Hard to Find," Tom T. Shiftlet in "The Life You Save May Be Your Own," and Hazel Motes in *Wise Blood*. What do they have in common? These criminals all feel a longing to investigate ultimate truths as they observe themselves being defined outside the boundaries of normal society by the falsehoods that constitute it. A corollary is that all three know the law to be profoundly imperfect. All three are themselves fakes, and they know it. All three are haunted by parents they hate and love. All three at least appear capable of murder. And, perhaps most importantly, all three are attracted to cars that simultaneously promise freedom and entrapment.

We should note that other characters typically find somewhat inappropriate significance in the Philosophical Criminal with a Car. Both characters named Lucyneil Crater in "The Life You Save May Be Your Own" consider Tom T. Shiftlet the man they desire in spite of all the evidence. And almost everyone in *Wise Blood* has a use for Hazel Motes: Sabbath Lily Hawks wants a man, Asa Hawks wants a disciple, Hoover Shoats wants a business partner. In many of these instances, characters who misinterpret O'Connor's Philosophical Criminals fail to get what they want.

Both Oates and Sharp create characters who resemble O'Connor's criminals. Arnold Friend sees himself as an outlaw, he knows he is faking it when he dresses up like a teenager, he seems not to worry about the law, he probably commits murder, and he is dependent upon his car. The plot of "Where Are You Going, Where Have You Been?" is initiated by Arnold's audacious arrival at the home of fifteen-year-old Connie, an average suburban girl who hates her life and is therefore easily seduced by a man who resembles the ideal teenage male of popular culture. Arnold Friend talks her into going for a ride that may result in her death.

Stanley Wilkes in Sharp's story collection is like O'Connor's criminals in that he is introspective, he realizes he is an imposter, he is skeptical of legal reasoning even when it would free him, he is haunted by his relatives, he is charged (at least) with murder, and in "Joyriding" he is trapped by the temptation to go for a joyride as soon as his cousin Antoinette (or Netta) points out to him the presence of the limousine. The plot of "Joyriding" is that after Stanley hijacks the car, he and Netta go ahead and pick up the man the limousine was scheduled to transport—Byron Coffin, a Wall Street lawyer who is completely tired. Stanley also picks up Roxanne Dupont simply because she "look[s] so worried" (7) standing on the street, and Stanley delivers her to the World Trade Center. Then Stanley heads into the Holland Tunnel, where "a prize Belgian gelding named Oglethorpe" (15), escaping from his horse trailer, causes an accident, whereupon Stanley is arrested and Byron Coffin suffers a heart attack. The charging of the horse toward Stanley's car brings up a time when "Stanley's grandmother had driven him and his cousin down the wrong side of a six-lane divided highway," an event which has "left Stanley with a permanent resistance to astonishment" (17). This event is basically what begins the plot of "A Meeting on the Highway," in which Stanley, on his eleventh birthday, watches his grandmother Arthurine break laws and cause a wreck, and then get away with her crimes. Later in life, Stanley

> would recall Arthurine smiling at the black road ahead of her, the wind in her hair, and ask himself not what drove people to break the law, but how it was possible that some human beings could pass an entire lifetime without ever committing a crime. (169)

I hope these summaries indicate the similarities among O'Connor's criminals and those of Oates and Sharp. Indeed, Paula Sharp accepts as reasonable the comparison of her Stanley to The Misfit and Arnold Friend.

> Both the Misfit and Friend have a similar charm and allure; like Stanley, they're beyond the pale—a misfit and a man who is everything a girl's parents have warned her against, and more. They are the Other, the embodiment of life's limitless possibilities, sociopaths who glitter with the brilliance of personal freedom. I suppose this is why they drive impressive cars, since a flashy automobile is the American emblem of liberty and escape. (Letter to the author, 28 Feb. 1994)

Nevertheless, I believe that Oates and Sharp significantly alter the O'Connor character type. Compared to O'Connor's characters, Oates's Arnold Friend has virtually no complexity of mental life. Arnold probably most resembles an O'Connor character when he tells Connie, "The place where you came from ain't there anymore, and where you had in mind to go is cancelled out. This place you are now—inside your daddy's house—is nothing but a cardboard box I can knock down any time" (134). The speech recalls one of Hazel Motes's sermons in *Wise Blood*: "Where you come from is gone, where you thought you were going to never was there, and where you are is no good unless you can get away from it. Where is there a place for you to be? No place" (93). One obvious difference between the two passages is that Arnold Friend apparently delivers his speech with full conviction—at least as a strategy of seduction—while half of Hazel Motes's mind rejects each word he says.

Sharp's Stanley, unlike O'Connor's characters, is clearly a very nice guy. When Roxanne DuPont describes her brother's tumor, Stanley thinks, "Thank God I stopped for you!" (8). While his politeness might seem to resemble that of The Misfit, Stanley's politeness is genuine. Sharp even shocks the reader with the assertion that Stanley has "a rich inner life never accurately reflected in his speech" (5), adding that "Stanley [thinks] to himself: On a clear night like this, Jersey City, the ugliest city in the world, glimmers like a diamond necklace stretched out on the banks of the black river" (5). Ultimately, Stanley means no real harm. When he philosophizes, he is less inclined than the reader to let himself off the hook:

> He had thought often about crime and believed that explanations based on an examination of the criminal's social background were always feeble. If you looked far enough inside a person, all you would find at the center was the plain and inexplicable thing he was as a child: *the Stanley in us* is what he thought to call it at that instant as he rounded the Quality Inn and raced down Manila Avenue. (19)

The most significant connection between these two contemporary writers and O'Connor has to do with the tendency of O'Connor's characters to project significance onto the Philosophical Criminal. Both Oates and Sharp, I believe, are deeply intrigued with this psychological pattern. Some evidence for the claim that Oates is primarily intrigued with the psychology in O'Connor's works is found in her writing about O'Connor. Oates, one of O'Connor's early critics (who published a critical essay on O'Connor the same year that "Where Are You Going, Where Have You Been?" appeared) locates O'Connor's originality in her "commitment to the divine origin of the unconscious" ("Visionary" 151) and speculates that O'Connor's "…'Christ' experience itself may well be interpreted as a psychological event that is received by the individual according to his private expectations" (170). Oates says that she rejects O'Connor's religious commitments (165), and this distinction between Oates's secularity and O'Connor's religiosity is often considered the crucial difference between them (Waller 70–71). However, that Oates can clearly identify with O'Connor's interest in breaking through what Oates calls "the cheap, flashy wasteland of modern America" (145) is a significant connection between these two authors.

If Oates is drawn to O'Connor's psychology rather than to her religiosity, the psychological flatness of Arnold Friend leads us to discover the most interesting influence of O'Connor on Oates's story: Connie's complicated reaction to Arnold Friend. Some critics have wondered whether O'Connor tells us enough about the minds of her characters—for example, the grandmother's psychology as she responds to The Misfit in "A Good Man Is Hard to Find." Perhaps Oates avoids this problem by emphasizing the workings of Connie's mind. We may feel led to ask whether Connie, like O'Connor's grandmother, is able to experience a psychological transformation—a sort of salvation—as she is threatened. Writing in 1993, Oates, for all her expressed doubts about O'Connor's religion, attributes to Connie an example of what she calls—using O'Connor's phrase—"moments of grace" (Afterword to *Where* 522).

There is also a possibility that Connie, unlike the grandmother, will wake up from the story's terrors. Perhaps "Where Are You Going, Where Have You Been?" is the story of a girl too fond of pop love lyrics who dreams of a psychopathic murderer because her unconscious knows the complexity of desire. It is increasingly common in Oates criticism to suggest that Connie may in some sense be dreaming the story's horrors. Larry Rubin presents the most thorough argument that Connie dreams Arnold Friend's visit, and several other critics agree (Gratz; Johnson 100–01; Winslow 267–68). The dream is usually considered to begin after Connie lies down on her bed to listen to the hypnotic pop music, as she is "bathed in a glow of slow-pulsed joy that seem[s] to rise mysteriously out of the music itself and [lie] languidly about the airless little room, breathed in and breathed out with each gentle rise and fall of her chest" (123). In the next paragraph of the story we are told that Arnold Friend drives up.

Critics have interpreted Arnold Friend in a multitude of ways: as Satan (Wegs 69, White 389); as a satyr (Easterly); as "an erotic transformation of Connie's father" (Schulz and Rockwood 162); as Bob Dylan in the role of a messiah (Tierce and Crafton 220); as "simply Connie's projected other self" (Weinberger 207). Some of these critics' readings note a dreaminess to the story, without accepting Arnold as part of the dream. Ellen G. Friedman sees Arnold as the "reality" Connie cannot resist because her dreams make her vulnerable (12).

The major argument against seeing Arnold Friend as a dream—or as a supernatural figure—is that the source for Arnold and for Oates's story is clearly the story of Charles Schmid, a real murderer (Quirk). In fact, the textual source for Oates's story is an article in *Life* magazine by Don Moser, who writes of Schmid's murders of teenaged girls in Tucson, Arizona, suggesting several of the details of "Where Are You Going, Where Have You Been?": the boots stuffed to make Arnold taller, his gold car, Connie's just-washed hair, etc. A. R. Coulthard has complained that "Where Are You Going, Where Have You Been?" can and should be taken as simple realism based on news accounts, that it is a mistake to allow Oates to trick us into the tendency "to 'mysticize' the story into a dream allegory" (505).

While I recommend D. F. Hurley's direct answer to Coulthard's article, my own inclination is to look for a middle ground between saying that Arnold Friend is only a psychopathic murderer based on real events and saying that Arnold is only a dream.

Critics of Oates at times seem determined to choose between possibilities they label incompatible, while O'Connor critics affirm and combine multiple readings. J. O. Tate and Victor Lasseter have identified sources for several parts of "A Good Man Is Hard to Find" from the Atlanta newspapers that O'Connor read, but that does not mean O'Connor scholars have refused to see The Misfit as more than a literal murderer. On the contrary, O'Connor critics often make claims that recall some of the symbolic readings of Arnold Friend. These critics are also often comfortable with the idea that the random arrival of a murderer in "A Good Man Is Hard to Find" is profoundly appropriate. Consider Suzanne Morrow Paulson's discussion of ways in which "A Good Man Is Hard to Find" resembles dreams experienced by the grandmother (88), or Madison Jones's labeling The Misfit as "the conclusion always implicit in the life of the family" (121). Josephine Hendin has called the grandmother and The Misfit "two Christs...crucifying *each other*" (150). Although no Oates critic has gone quite that far in comparing Connie and Arnold Friend, it still seems to me that there are interesting similarities between O'Connor and Oates suggested in these critical comments. I think it helps in this situation to apply Philip Roth's comments in his 1960 essay "Writing American Fiction" on the murders of two teenaged girls in Chicago by a thirty-five-year-old man. The circumstances of the murder and its aftermath are so bizarre that Roth concludes that American civilization "tosses up figures almost daily that are the envy of any novelist" (176). Roth's observation should remind us that, in contemporary writing, the realistic and the fantastic or dream-like often coincide.

If it is easy to conclude that Arnold Friend might be real and also might be a product of Connie's dream, Oates criticism remains tentative in exploring what the story means—if Arnold is a dream. Sometimes the story is taken as horrific, its ending implying Connie's death. Frank R. Cunningham sees the story as a warning, illustrating Oates's "frequent thesis that the death of the spirit begins very young in contemporary America" (19), a reading that holds whether Arnold is real or imagined. For Greg Johnson, the conclusion marks the beginning of Connie's "enslavement within a conventional, male-dominated sexual relationship" (102). In other readings, Connie is unharmed, and perhaps even benefits from her experience. Nancy Bishop Dessommes says, in a reading that compares Oates and O'Connor, that Connie is "saved by the force that conquers her" (440). David Gratz claims that the story's apparent horrors merely represent Connie's fear of maturation, and Larry Rubin proposes that Connie's dream "might improve the situation" (58). Similarly, treating Arnold as a "transgressive other" who is "useful, even appealing" in the story because Arnold "openly confronts the codes of the family" (256), Marilyn Wesley argues persuasively that Oates sees Connie's safe life at home as something she needs to transcend.

Oates herself has encouraged the multiplicity of symbolic readings of Arnold Friend; indeed one could argue that she has encouraged contradictory readings. In an essay in her *(Woman) Writer* that discusses the making of her story into the film *Smooth Talk*, Oates finds "no suggestion in the published story that 'Arnold Friend' has seduced and murdered other girls, or even that he necessarily intends to murder Connie" (318). And yet Oates has also written that "...presumably doomed Connie makes a decision to accept her fate with dignity, and to spare her family's involvement in this fate" (Afterword to *Where* 522), a line that suggests that Connie might be murdered.

I am reluctant to accept either of these statements by Oates as the key to "Where Are You Going, Where Have You Been?" It may not matter, finally, whether Arnold Friend is devil or cipher or god. Whether he is fantasy or reality, through him Connie experiences the revelation of a world beyond the life of her adolescence. Her going with Arnold at the end is her rejection of the family life she has always known was shallow. She refuses to become her sister June. On the other hand, as her name suggests, Connie has always been a bit of a *con*—"Everything about her had two sides to it, one for home and one for anywhere that was not home" (119)—and she is capable of recognizing others' trickery. Her noticing Arnold Friend's makeup, wig, and ridiculous boots signals her awakening to the fakery involved in the pop culture around which she has centered her life. She thus refuses, I believe, to become an Ellie Oscar, a forty-year-old baby in the back seat with nothing but the radio. Connie's awareness of the real threats posed by Arnold Friend stands for her awareness that her sexual maturation and sexual desires promise to endanger her, that love is not what is promised in songs. At the story's end, Connie even becomes aware that as a woman she is imagined to be a "sweet little blue-eyed girl" in spite of her "brown eyes" (136)—in other words, that she will become the object of oppressive fantasy. The story leaves uncertain what practical use Connie can make of these insights, but this confusion should not obscure the reader's realization that Connie might have been a good woman if somebody had been there to threaten her every minute of her life. I am open to the possibility that Connie profoundly misunderstands a murderer in her driveway; however, she does project on him a revelation. Projection in this story is complex, but the moral quality of Oates's criminal does not matter so much as what Connie makes of him.

In Paula Sharp's stories, the power of creative misreading—of creative projection—is pushed even farther. The results are not always affirmative: the police report on Stanley's crimes in "Joyriding" is a sad distortion, a projection of the expectations of the police (12–15). But the possibility for useful projection clearly exists. In one of the few reviews that qualifies its praise of *The Imposter*, Jack Butler, in *The New York Times Book Review*, writes that readers merely "glimpse Stanley and Netta" in "Joyriding" (22). What Butler sees as a failure to provide full characterization, I see as a result of Sharp's emphasis on projection. The fact that we do not get to know Stanley thoroughly in this first story in Sharp's collection alerts us to the fact that the meaning placed on him by a character in the story depends on that character's imagination.

In "Joyriding," the interpreter of the Philosophical Criminal is neither Roxanne Dupont nor Netta—it is a man, Byron Coffin. "Joyriding" is filled with examples of his misunderstandings of his situation and of Stanley—indeed, Byron realizes he has been kidnapped only on the story's penultimate page. And yet, in the course of the story, we see Byron Coffin projecting successfully on Stanley Wilkes the image of savior. In recalling the sequence of events, Byron thinks of many clues he should have been able to use to figure out his predicament; thus a plausible explanation for Byron's failure to catch on to the fact he is being kidnapped may be provided by Byron's own words about his work as a lawyer: "Perhaps some human beings just secretly [desire] to be taken in" (3). One sign that Byron longs for escape from his life is that when Roxanne Dupont needs advice about how to visit a hospitalized man with whom she is having an affair, Byron comes up with the best technique for deception.

> "Does he work at an office somewhere?" Byron heard himself say. "Could you pretend to be an emissary from his friends at work, perhaps deliver him a big flower arrangement with a note from the office?" Byron was surprised at himself, but he continued with some pleasure. "I am certain that is the procedure in my law firm under such circumstances." (11)

He may have as much of the heart of a criminal as Stanley does; certainly he shares with Stanley the feeling that the car is both his freedom and his coffin.

Part of the role of the misinterpreted criminal in "Joyriding" is played by Oglethorpe, a claustrophobic horse escaped from his trailer. When Byron Coffin sees the horse, he begins to have a heart attack, sure that he is seeing another car running wild. At the end of the story, the sum total of Byron's misinterpretations seems to lead to a salvation he has secretly desired, perhaps (but not necessarily) tied to Stanley:

> Stanley's face reappeared near the window. A thought surged in Byron's mind: he wished that he was this young man, tall and vigorous...and then finally he hoped simply to be Byron Coffin, or anyone at all. This was followed by a jumble of thoughts and desires before Byron sensed a sparkle of electricity, and a warmth that began in his toes. (20)

The story ends in "joy" for Byron as he re-enters "the world of the living" (20). One suspects that he may later recall the signs that Roxanne Dupont would be a better romantic partner for him than his wife is. Sharp appears to be so interested in the power of misinterpretation and projection that even a gelding in the Holland Tunnel can be taken seriously as Stanley's partner in provoking the heart attack that offers the occasion for Byron to free himself from the coffin of his routine life.

Other stories by Sharp tell us more about Stanley. I have insufficient space here to dwell on "The Golden Car," a story that may recall "Where Are You Going, Where Have You Been?" Suffice it to say that when Stanley's father appears by surprise one day driving a golden car and tries to abduct Stanley, Stanley's relatives attack the car and rescue him, perhaps leaving Stanley able to identify with the Connies of this world.

The more significant story for my purposes here is "A Meeting on the Highway," in which Stanley as a child gets to project significance on not one but two other Philosophical Criminals with Cars—his New Orleans grandmother Arthurine and a man whose car she hits. This story implies that Arthurine's bizarre behavior is motivated primarily by her preoccupation with her feelings for the dead husband who left her the car she recklessly drives and by her desire not to be charged with a repair bill after she has a wreck. Understanding none of this, Stanley watches his grandmother drive into an accident and then audaciously lie to avoid accepting blame; what Stanley sees is his grandmother's inspiring ability to outwit the man whose car she has hit, a man Stanley apparently associates with his grandfather and with death. No wonder Stanley associates cars with power and later cannot resist a joyride.

As pleasurable as it may be to review the signs of O'Connor's influence on contemporary writers, the ultimate reward of this investigation is allowing contemporary writers to show us another way to reread O'Connor. The emphasis I see in Oates and Sharp on the wonders of projection makes me wonder whether we should look for more signs of creative projection in O'Connor. I stated above that O'Connor's characters generally fail when they project, but there are exceptions. To my mind, the best example of an O'Connor character successfully projecting significance on another character is Mrs. Flood of *Wise Blood*, who, at the end of the novel, creates a guide to enlightenment out of an unwilling partner; Mrs. Flood can learn despite Hazel Motes's refusal to teach her about religious mystery and despite the evidence that she misinterprets him (Gentry 133–36).

Oates and Sharp use the psychology of projection to discuss love, a theme O'Connor is generally considered to have shortchanged. However, if we reread O'Connor with projection and love in mind, what do we discover? For one thing, I believe we find an insight into "A Good Man Is Hard to Find." As I stated above, some critics have said we do not know as much as we need to know to accept as the climax what O'Connor labeled the grandmother's moment of grace: her touching The Misfit and calling him "one of my babies" (*CW* 152). Stanley Renner balks at seeing the grandmother as redeemed, arguing that she "may be capable of some insight into her shortcomings, but she has not been presented as a person whose realization would take a religious form at all, certainly not one…devoutly pat" (130). O'Connor used this climactic passage to argue that her stories contain love. In a letter dated 5 Mar. 1960, O'Connor replied to her correspondent "A" (Betty Hester), who consistently noted the absence of romance in the stories: "You say there is love between man and God in the stories, but never between people—yet the grandmother is not in the least concerned with God but reaches out to touch the Misfit" (*HB* 379; *CW* 1124). If we consider the ending of "A Good Man Is Hard to Find" with Oates's and Sharp's stories in mind, I think we might conclude that the grandmother's moment of insight is believable precisely because she too is engaging in a projection about love—she mistakes The Misfit for her son Bailey and expresses a love she has been tragically unable (for years, at least) to express to her son.

I realize, of course, that Bailey is central to one of the most famous misreadings of O'Connor. On 28 Mar. 1961, O'Connor wrote an astonished letter in response to an English professor who had written her about the consensus reached by three professors and ninety students:

> In general we believe that the appearance of the Misfit is not "real" in the same sense that the incidents of the first half of the story are real. Bailey, we believe, imagines the appearance of the Misfit, whose activities have been called to his attention on the night before the trip and again during the stopover at the roadside restaurant. Bailey, we further believe, identifies himself with the Misfit and so plays two roles in the imaginary last half of the story. (qtd. in *HB* 436)

Part of O'Connor's reply is to insist that the "only importance" of Bailey "is as the Grandmother's boy and the driver of the car" (*HB* 437; *CW* 1148). I would suggest that critics of O'Connor have taken this dismissal of Bailey too seriously. I am not claiming that Bailey is dreaming; bringing up dreams does sometimes produce overly fanciful interpretation. But I do think that the grandmother—who starts the story wanting "connections" (*CW* 137)—has longed to connect with her son for quite some time and is in a state in which The Misfit can, for a moment, become Bailey, the son she wanted to dance with back in The Tower (141). The projection is plausible because at the crucial moment, The Misfit is wearing Bailey's shirt (150), and the look of pain on The Misfit's face (152) may remind the grandmother of Bailey's pained look as he went to his death. (If The Misfit realizes that he is not really the person the grandmother is seeing before her at the climax, he has another reason to shoot her. His primary motive is that he wants to kill his own parent, whom he imagines the grandmother to be.)

Surely is it easier to believe that the grandmother is capable of breaking through to her son than it is to believe she could love her murderer. As Thomas Hill Schaub reminds us, the name Bailey refers to a castle wall or the space inside the walls of a castle (132), and although things are consistently tense between mother and son, the grandmother could perceive the defensiveness in her son's meanness and continue to love him. Perhaps for the grandmother, the good man hard to find is her own son Bailey—and her tragedy is that she finds him only in another man, after Bailey is dead. I have argued elsewhere that the good man in this story is the narrator, whose treatment of the characters becomes significantly less harsh as the story proceeds (Gentry 37–39). The exception to that pattern is Bailey, who, for his failure to act, is ridiculed throughout the story. Perhaps the problem for some readers in accepting the grandmother's epiphany can be solved when we note that through a projection, she is able to find a good man where even the narrator cannot.

I hope that this discussion has suggested one or two interesting ways in which O'Connor influences other writers. I believe we do our best job of honoring Flannery O'Connor when we discover her followers to be reinterpreting her—even, perhaps, profitably distorting her—rather than making themselves carbon copies of her. O'Connor encourages us to view her as yet another Philosophical Criminal—dangerous but potentially transfiguring, perhaps because she too does not allow us to understand her perfectly.

WORKS CITED

Bloom, Harold. Introduction. *Joyce Carol Oates*, edited by Harold Bloom. New York, Chelsea, 1987, pp. 1–6. Modern Critical Views.

Butler, Jack. "Aimlessly Toward Wisconsin." Review of *The Imposter: Stories About Netta and Stanley*, by Paula Sharp. *The New York Times Book Review*, 15 Sept. 1991, p. 22.

Coulthard, A. R. "Joyce Carol Oates's 'Where Are You Going, Where Have You Been?' as Pure Realism." *Studies in Short Fiction*, vol. 26, 1989, pp. 505–10.

Cunningham, Frank R. "Joyce Carol Oates: The Enclosure of Identity in the Earlier Stories." *American Women Writing Fiction: Memory, Identity, Family, Space*, edited by Mickey Pearlman. Lexington, University Press of Kentucky, 1989, pp. 9–28.

Dessommes, Nancy Bishop. "O'Connor's Mrs. May and Oates's Connie: An Unlikely Pair of Religious Initiates." *Studies in Short Fiction*, vol. 31, 1994, pp. 433–40.

Easterly, Joan. "The Shadow of a Satyr in Oates's 'Where Are You Going, Where Have You Been?'" *Studies in Short Fiction*, vol. 27, 1990, pp. 537–43.

Friedman, Ellen G. *Joyce Carol Oates*. New York, Ungar, 1980. Modern Literature Monographs.

Gentry, Marshall Bruce. *Flannery O'Connor's Religion of the Grotesque*. Jackson, University Press of Mississippi, 1986.

Gratz, David K. "Oates's 'Where Are You Going, Where Have You Been?'" *The Explicator*, vol. 45, no. 3, 1987, pp. 55–56.

Hendin, Josephine. *The World of Flannery O'Connor*. Bloomington, Indiana University Press, 1970.

Hurley, D. F. "Impure Realism: Joyce Carol Oates's 'Where Are You Going, Where Have You Been?'" *Studies in Short Fiction*, vol. 28, 1991, pp. 371–75.

Johnson, Greg. *Understanding Joyce Carol Oates*. Columbia, University of South Carolina Press, 1987. Understanding Contemporary American Literature.

Jones, Madison. "A Good Man's Predicament." *The Southern Review*, vol. 20, 1984, pp. 836–41. Reprinted in *"A Good Man Is Hard to Find": Flannery O'Connor*, edited by Frederick Asals. New Brunswick, NJ, Rutgers University Press, 1993, pp. 119–26. Women Writers: Texts and Contexts.

Lasseter, Victor. "The Genesis of Flannery O'Connor's 'A Good Man Is Hard to Find.'" *Studies in American Fiction*, vol. 10, 1982, pp. 227–32.

Moser, Don. "The Pied Piper of Tucson." *Life*, 4 Mar. 1966, pp. 18–24A, 80C–D, 82, 84, 87–90.

Oates, Joyce Carol. "Firing a Field." *Angel Fire: Poems*. Baton Rouge, Louisiana State University Press, 1973, pp. 35–36.

———. "The Visionary Art of Flannery O'Connor." *New Heaven, New Earth: The Visionary Experience in Literature*. New York, Vanguard, 1974, pp. 141–76.

———. "'Where Are You Going, Where Have You Been?' and *Smooth Talk*: Short Story into Film." *(Woman) Writer: Occasions and Opportunities*. New York, Dutton, 1989, pp. 316–21.

———. *Where Are You Going, Where Have You Been?: Selected Early Stories*. Princeton, Ontario Review, 1993.

O'Connor, Flannery. *Flannery O'Connor: Collected Works*, edited by Sally Fitzgerald. New York, Library of America, 1988.

———. *The Habit of Being: Letters*, edited by Sally Fitzgerald. New York, Farrar, 1979.

Paulson, Suzanne Morrow. *Flannery O'Connor: A Study of the Short Fiction*. Boston, Twayne-Hall, 1988.

Quirk, Tom. "A Source for 'Where Are You Going, Where Have You Been?'" *Studies in Short Fiction*, vol. 18, 1981, pp. 413–19.

Renner, Stanley. "Secular Meaning in 'A Good Man Is Hard to Find.'" *College Literature*, vol. 9, 1982, pp. 123–32.

Roth, Philip. "Writing American Fiction." *Reading Myself and Others*. Enlarged ed., New York, Penguin, 1985, pp. 173–91.

Rubin, Larry. "Oates's 'Where Are You Going, Where Have You Been?'" *The Explicator*, vol. 42, no. 4, 1984, pp. 57–60.

Schaub, Thomas Hill. *American Fiction in the Cold War*. Madison, University of Wisconsin Press, 1991.

Schulz, Gretchen, and R. J. R. Rockwood. "In Fairyland, Without a Map: Connie's Exploration Inward in Joyce Carol Oates's 'Where Are You Going, Where Have You Been?'" *Literature and Psychology*, vol. 30, 1980, pp. 155–67.

Sharp, Paula. *The Imposter: Stories About Netta and Stanley*. New York, HarperCollins, 1991.

———. Letter to Marshall Bruce Gentry. 28 Feb. 1994.

Tate, J. O. "A Good Source Is Not So Hard to Find." *The Flannery O'Connor Bulletin*, vol. 9, 1980, pp. 98–103.

Tierce, Mike, and John Michael Crafton. "Connie's Tambourine Man: A New Reading of Arnold Friend." *Studies in Short Fiction*, vol. 22, 1985, pp. 219–24.

Waller, G. F. *Dreaming America: Obsession and Transcendence in the Fiction of Joyce Carol Oates*. Baton Rouge, Louisiana State University Press, 1979.

Wegs, Joyce M. "'Don't You Know Who I Am?': The Grotesque in Oates's 'Where Are You Going, Where Have You Been?'" *Journal of Narrative Technique*, vol. 5, 1975, pp. 66–72.

Weinberger, G. J. "Who Is Arnold Friend?: The Other Self in Joyce Carol Oates's 'Where Are You Going, Where Have You Been?'" *American Imago*, vol. 45, no. 2, 1988, pp. 205-15.

Wesley, Marilyn C. "The Transgressive Other of Joyce Carol Oates's Recent Fiction." *Critique*, vol. 33, no. 4, 1992, pp. 255–62.

White, Terry. "Allegorical Evil, Existentialist Choice in O'Connor, Oates, and Styron." *Midwest Quarterly*, vol. 34, 1993, pp. 383–97.

Winslow, Joan D. "The Stranger Within: Two Stories by Oates and Hawthorne." *Studies in Short Fiction*, vol. 17, 1980, pp. 263–68.

In Search of Vera—as Charlotte Hock and as Joy/Hulga Hopewell

with Charles Puckett

I.

Based on the family memories of Charles Puckett, on interviews with his sister Deborah Puckett Pennington, and with his uncle Mike Puckett—as well as some historical research—our argument is that a person named Vera F. Puckett of the Milledgeville area had so much in common with both the character Charlotte Hock in Pete Dexter's National Book Award-winning novel *Paris Trout* and with Flannery O'Connor's character Joy/Hulga Hopewell in the famous story "Good Country People" that Vera F. Puckett deserves to be considered a significant source for both these literary characters.

Charlotte Hock is the female character with an artificial leg who works for the character Paris Trout in his store. She is a person who consistently tolerates his grotesque eccentricities, and who owns the car that Paris Trout borrows when he goes to commit the murders that provide the climax for the novel *Paris Trout*, which is based on the murders committed by Marion Stembridge in Milledgeville in 1953. Charlotte Hock is *clearly* based on the life of Vera F. Puckett.

Joy/Hulga Hopewell is O'Connor's character who requires a wooden leg because of a shotgun blast. She seems unsure of how to behave like a woman, in part because she lives in rejection of her mother's ways. She changes her name from Joy to Hulga, apparently in identification with a male deity, Vulcan/Hephaestus. And she is famously taken advantage of by a phony Bible salesman, Manley Pointer. This article is about a bit of evidence that O'Connor used her local reality in the composition of her work. It suggests what O'Connor may have meant when she claimed that she was like Hulga but not *totally* like Hulga, when she talked about having created a character that she could control. Why is news of possible influence surprising? For one thing, Pete Dexter claims to have no memory at all of Vera Puckett; he believes he made up his character

Charlotte Hock from scratch. And as for O'Connor, the surprise is more complex. Most O'Connor fans knows O'Connor separated her fiction from the details of her own life, and we will remind you how forceful O'Connor could be about that separation, using some of her letters about "Good Country People." On 24 Sept. 1955, O'Connor wrote Betty Hester that Hester overestimates the extent to which O'Connor is Joy/Hulga Hopewell: "...to have sympathy for any character, you have to put a good deal of yourself in him. But to say that any complete denudation of the writer occurs in the successful work is, according to me, a romantic exaggeration. A great part of the art of it is precisely in seeing that this does not happen" (*HB* 105). The paragraph ends with a famous line, "Any story I reveal myself completely in will be a bad story." Six days later, again writing to Hester, O'Connor picks up the same train of thought, discussing Hulga as a sort of "projection of myself...—presumably only a projection, because if I could not stop short...I could not write it....You have to be able to dominate the existence that you characterize. That is why I write about people who are more or less primitive. I couldn't dominate [a figure like Simone Weil] because she is more intelligent and better than I am but I can project a Hulga" (106). O'Connor later admitted to "informing" Hester "that Hulga is like me" (24 Aug. 1955, *HB* 170). Biographer and scholar Jean Cash has been one of many who has described how much of Flannery O'Connor and her mother there is in the relationship between Hulga and Mrs. Hopewell in "Good Country People" (Cash 171–72), and over the years, O'Connor scholars have come to take it for granted that O'Connor put a great deal of herself into Hulga.

Another way to consider the significance of the discovery of source material, of course, is to compare the discovery to other similar discoveries. When Mark Bosco wrote his articles about Erik Langkjaer as the major source for Manley Pointer in "Good Country People," the world of O'Connor studies was shocked—and for the most part, somewhat *pleasantly* shocked. It is thrilling to see that while O'Connor was juggling her philosophical and religious thoughts, she was also talking about a boyfriend who had dumped her. Bosco persuaded us that Erik is Manley and that therefore Hulga is Flannery. Our suggestions here deepen the significance of Bosco's findings rather than denying them.

It is also interesting to reconsider Brad Gooch's take on Flannery and Erik. Gooch puzzles over the fact that O'Connor did not write about the Marion Stembridge murders when they occurred in 1953, that her letters from those days focus instead on Erik Langkjaer (Gooch 235).

O'Connor's story "The Partridge Festival," a story that, like Dexter's novel *Paris Trout*, is clearly about the murders, was not written until about four years after O'Connor wrote "Good Country People" and about seven years (Driggers et al. xx–xxi) after Marion Stembridge, who probably suffered from PTSD, committed the murders and committed suicide in downtown Milledgeville. But perhaps a solution to this puzzle is suggested by the possibility that the way O'Connor first reacted to the Stembridge murders was to see a connection between Stembridge's disabled and betrayed employee, the one-legged Vera, and Hulga, the disabled character O'Connor created to embody her own sense of betrayal by Erik Langkjaer.

Now for some of the life of Vera Puckett as we have been able to reconstruct it. We are discovering a large number of fascinating details. According to the 1930 Census, Vera, living near Milledgeville, was a five-year-old at the time, so we conclude she was born the same year as Flannery O'Connor. Vera attended Peabody High School, which O'Connor also attended.[1] Vera's leg was lost by the time she was in high school, and because of a gunshot blast—probably the result of an accident. Vera's artificial leg probably made noise. She had a very bad relationship with her mother. She changed her name, to "Pete," using it so consistently that some of her relatives did not know that her real name was Vera. In March 1954, at least, she had blonde hair, like Hulga. Vera dressed in pants and rather looked like a man. She had a car that was equipped with extra controls that allowed her to drive it. She worked for Marion Stembridge in his store in downtown Milledgeville on Wayne Street, at the time of his murders and suicide on 2 May 1953, and she was listed in his will as one of his beneficiaries. Stembridge left $1,000 to Vera, who had worked for him for at least two years.

Another fascinating portion of Vera's life is that she was convicted of crimes on more than one occasion: the *Georgia Central Register of Convicts, 1817–1976* lists Vera F. Puckett as being convicted of "Cheating & Swindling" on 22 May 1954 in Baldwin County, of which Milledgeville is the county seat. (This date is prior to O'Connor's composition of "Good Country People," but we have no evidence that O'Connor was

---

[1] Very few records of Peabody High in Milledgeville are available in Special Collections at the Georgia College Library. Anyone with records they are willing to share is encouraged to contact Special Collections.

aware of Vera's conviction.) Subsequent crimes were in the Atlanta area: On 23 Aug. 1955, Vera F. Puckett was convicted of "Common Cheating & Swindling" in DeKalb County, and on 26 Jan. 1956, "Vera Puckett" was convicted in Fulton County of "Worthless Checks." In her later years, we believe, Vera/Pete lived as a man, and Pete had a woman as a partner. There are family tales of the children being warned to avoid her. She moved to Florida, and we assume she died and is buried there.

What is the significance for Dexter's novel? Vera's backstory supports the explanation that one might reasonably make up for why she went to work for Marion Stembridge. Vera and her relatives, mostly farmers, lived in the same area, east of Milledgeville, where Stembridge's relatives lived. So Vera and Marion probably knew each other long before he hired her. And of course, she was probably, as a disabled woman, grateful for any job. She is part of a pattern in Dexter's novel of women intimidated and therefore extremely tolerant of oppressive men, and Charlotte even believes that she at one point allows Paris Trout to steal her car (Dexter 288). While Pete Dexter denies any memory of Vera Puckett, he may well have heard of Vera because he lived in Milledgeville at the time of the Stembridge murders. Dexter was only nine years old at the time of the killings (quoted in Robillard 22), but he did some historical research about the events for his novel, so critic Douglas Robillard, Jr., has concluded that in some significant ways, "It is likely that his work as a journalist predisposed Dexter to 'stick to the facts'" (76). We suggest that Vera Puckett's role in the novel is basically a matter of Dexter's inclination to stick to facts, and we think there is no doubt that Vera is *the* source for Charlotte Hock.

And what is the significance of Vera/Pete Puckett for O'Connor and her writing? There is much to speculate about. It seems reasonable to believe O'Connor would remember a classmate with an artificial leg, even if the two students were not acquainted with each other personally. Stembridge and several of his relatives attended Georgia Military College in Milledgeville at the same time as several of O'Connor's relatives—including her mother, Regina Cline O'Connor—so it is likely that the families knew of each other over many years. And O'Connor would probably be inclined to listen to any gossip about Vera, which was probably plentiful, especially after the murders. One way in which it is clear that O'Connor was paying attention to the Stembridge murders is that an early draft of "The Partridge Festival" (file 199a in the O'Connor Collection at Georgia College) accurately describes Stembridge's looks and uses the details of his business dealings, so we assume she would have noted Vera's connection to Stembridge. I should mention here that in a letter to Betty Hester on 10 Nov. 1955, O'Connor refers to having "a one-legged friend" (*HB* 117), and this friend supposedly reminded O'Connor about the saying that "The lame shall enter first." We are *not* inclined to think that this one-legged friend is Vera.

The speculation that Joy/Hulga is a combination of Flannery and Vera/Pete suggests that O'Connor may have seen Vera Puckett to some extent as an alter ego—a person who struggled mightily to fit in, a person who struggled with gender identity, a person whose disability controlled her life. If O'Connor thought of Hulga as a version of Vera, we are also left with the possibility that she saw her character Hulga as not just a victim of an evil man, but perhaps even as a character guilty of failing to stop an evil man's life of crime.[2]

We also think that as we contemplate how O'Connor used Vera, we are getting another glimpse, as paradoxical as this may sound, of how O'Connor believed that her unconscious could take control of a story. In *Mystery and Manners*, O'Connor discusses the creation of the symbol of the wooden leg in "Good Country People," but then she contradicts herself a bit, insisting that "...it is a wooden leg first" (99). It is easy to say that because O'Connor knew of women with wooden legs, she means what she says, but there is more complexity here. In O'Connor's following paragraphs, in a talk for a writers' conference, she uses the writing of "Good Country People" to illustrate what she means by "what Maritain calls 'the habit of art'" (101). O'Connor explains, "It is a fact that fiction writing is something in which the whole personality takes part—the unconscious as well as the conscious mind" (101). When she wrote "Good Country People," O'Connor could claim that "...it is a story that was under control throughout the writing of it..." (100), a claim that can be quite confusing, but in the context of seeing Vera as a source for Hulga, it is easier to take Flannery O'Connor at her word when she describes the process by which she composed the story. When the conscious mind re-

---

[2] If O'Connor understood the full extent of Vera's connection to Marion Stembridge—that not only did Vera get $1,000 in Stembridge's will, but also that Vera's father received from Stembridge's will the contents of Stembridge's store—there may be even more significance to the absence of Hulga's father from "Good Country People."

laxes, unconscious forces can take a sort of control.

> When I started writing that story, I didn't know there was going to be a Ph.D. with a wooden leg in it. I merely found myself one morning writing a description of two women..., and before I realized it, I had equipped one of them with a daughter with a wooden leg....I brought in the Bible salesman....I didn't know he was going to steal that wooden leg until ten or twelve lines before he did it....This is a story that produces a shock for the reader, and I think one reason for this is that it produced a shock for the writer. (100)

If Flannery is being fully honest with us here, it makes sense to see Vera Puckett as part of the unconscious reservoir of images that can rise to the surface during the composition of a work of art. If Hulga is partly Flannery, the addition of Vera may have made it easier for O'Connor to put into Hulga a significant portion of Flannery. Vera could be crucial to O'Connor's ability to write not only about having a shattered leg but also about having a broken heart.

While the emphasis here is on how our understanding of "Good Country People" might be changed, it seems also possible that we might come up with a new appreciation of "The Partridge Festival." Vera F. Puckett does not appear in O'Connor's story that most directly addresses the Stembridge murders, but we do have a character that, like Charlotte Hock and like Joy/Hulga Hopewell, struggles to understand a very dangerous man. Because of our speculations about Vera, we may find ourselves more interested in a character in "The Partridge Festival" named Mary Elizabeth—a character in some ways similar to O'Connor. Mary Elizabeth pushes more effectively than Hulga or Charlotte for the truth about her plot's villainous man, Singleton. It is probably Mary Elizabeth, in a story finished seven years after the Stembridge murders, who is able to achieve Flannery's intellectual insight into the significance of human villainy, an insight Hulga is not quite in a position to work out. While "The Partridge Festival" does not spell out Mary Elizabeth's insight, we would suggest that the insight is that extreme villainy—of the sort found in Manley Pointer or in Marion Stembridge or in Singleton—has its source in an extreme insanity that should not be romanticized and that is also beyond moral responsibility. The weight of moral responsibility is on those who have the ability to control such villainy, and women are typically prevented from exercising such power.

Vera "Pete" Puckett as Cowboy. This is Vera "Pete" Puckett in a souvenir photo from the 1950s, based on her apparent age and style of dress: note the rolled up denim pants and saddle-oxford shoes, common fashions of that era. Note also that her left leg is bent forward only, whereas her right leg is bent to the side. She is wearing what appears to be a man's short-sleeved shirt with rolled sleeves, which is in keeping with family memories of her at this time as well. *Courtesy Charles Puckett*

Vera "Pete" Puckett in skirt. This is Vera "Pete" Puckett as an older woman, judging by appearance. Unlike the other pictures, she is wearing more feminine apparel, as was out of character for her by all accounts. One might wonder if this is taken when she returned home to attend her father's funeral and wore a dress in accordance with his wishes. The scenery is reminiscent of what one might see in a cemetery. I also note that, again, her left leg is positioned pointing forward and her right leg to the side as seen in the "cowboy" photo. The dress ends below the knee: this could be in keeping with the fashion of the day or to better obscure her prosthesis—perhaps both. The collared shirt, however, and the hair color and side part match other photos. *Courtesy Charles Puckett*

Vera "Pete" Puckett with Stan Puckett. This is Vera "Pete" Puckett, 25-30 years old, with my oldest brother, Stan Puckett. Since he was born in May of 1947 and appears to be very young here, this picture was probably taken in the late 1940s or early 1950s in Milledgeville, Georgia. This photo would then predate the Marion Stembridge murders of 1953. From Stembridge's records, we know "Pete" worked at his store for at least two years; thus, it seems likely that she was in his employ at the time or soon to be. *Courtesy Charles Puckett*

II

Three years after the first version of this article was published, photographs of Vera/Pete Puckett were rediscovered by Charles Puckett and verified by his relatives. Charles Puckett published a short follow-up article about Vera/Pete Puckett and the photographs in the *Flannery O'Connor Review*, and he gave Gentry permission to reprint those photographs in this book. One of Charles Puckett's comments most relevant to appreciating the photographs has to do with what must have been the pressures on Vera:

> Vera was...fitted for what may have been the best prosthesis of the time, but for the remainder of her life she would have to make choices: wear pants, not a custom of the time and place for a young woman; wear a dress, which would only highlight her "otherness"; or work in an environment in which she stood visible only from the waist up. Counter work may have been what she experienced in her time as an employee of Marion Stembridge.... (145)

Charles Puckett also points out that "The pictures you see here show Vera "Pete" Puckett dressed in both female and male attire, the dress likely from her later years..." (146), worn perhaps for a visit back to the area where she once lived, for her father's funeral, for which "...she wore a dress, in accordance with his and her mother's wishes" (146). Chuck Puckett concludes concerning the family photos of Vera/Pete Puckett, "She is alone in most cases, which may reveal some subtle truths about how she lived most of her life, and there is one in which she is with my oldest brother, the first born of her nieces and nephews" (146).

AUTHOR NOTE: The authors wish to thank James Owens for assistance throughout their searching of the Internet and throughout their research in Georgia College's Special Collections.

WORKS CITED

Bosco, Mark, S.J. "Consenting to Love: Autobiographical Roots of 'Good Country People.'" *The Southern Review*, vol. 41, no. 2, 2005, pp. 283–95.

———. "Erik Langkjaer: The One Flannery 'Used to Go With.'" *Flannery O'Connor Review*, vol. 5, 2007, pp. 44–55.

Cash, Jean W. *Flannery O'Connor: A Life.* Knoxville, University of Tennessee Press, 2002.

Dexter, Pete. *Paris Trout.* New York, Random, 1988.

———. Interview. Conducted by Marshall Bruce Gentry, 24 Feb. 2017.

Driggers, Stephen G., and Robert J. Dunn, with Sarah Gordon. "Development of O'Connor's Fiction." *The Manuscripts of Flannery O'Connor at Georgia College.* Athens, University of Georgia Press, 1989, pp. xx–xxi.

Georgia Central Register of Convicts, 1817–1976. Available through Ancestry.com. Accessed 11 May 2017. Copies of the records relating to Vera F. Puckett are also found in the Marion Wesley Stembridge Vertical File, Box 1, Folder 1 of 2. Flannery O'Connor Collection, Special Collections, Georgia College Library and Instructional Technology Center, Milledgeville.

Gooch, Brad. *Flannery: A Life of Flannery O'Connor.* New York, Little, 2009.

O'Connor, Flannery. *Flannery O'Connor: Collected Works*, edited by Sally Fitzgerald. New York, Library of America, 1988.

———. *The Habit of Being: Letters*, edited by Sally Fitzgerald. New York, Farrar, 1979.

———. *Mystery and Manners: Occasional Prose*, edited by Sally Fitzgerald and Robert Fitzgerald. New York, Farrar, 1969.

———. Unpublished manuscript of "The Partridge Festival." Flannery O'Connor Collection, Special Collections, Georgia College Library and Instructional Technology Center, Milledgeville, File 199a.

Pennington, Deborah Puckett. Interview. Conducted by Charles Puckett and Marshall Bruce Gentry, 14 Jan. 2017.

Puckett, Charles. "The Story Behind the Story: Vera 'Pete' Puckett." *Flannery O'Connor Review*, vol. 18, 2020, pp. 145–49.

Puckett, Mike. Interview. Conducted by Charles Puckett and Marshall Bruce Gentry, 14 Jan. 2017.

Robillard, Douglas, Jr. "*Rashomon* in Milledgeville: Flannery O'Connor and Pete Dexter on the Stembridge Murders." *Flannery O'Connor Review*, vol. 9, 2011, pp. 69–78.

Stembridge, Marion Wesley. Handwritten will. 8 Jan. 1951. Flannery O'Connor Collection, Special Collections, Georgia College Library and Instructional Technology Center, Milledgeville, Marion Wesley Stembridge Vertical File, Box 1, Folder 1 of 2. An official version of the will is available at Baldwin County Courthouse Probate Court in *Baldwin County Record of Wills 1933–59.* Vol. C, pp. 414–15.

A Source for E. A. T. in "A Good Man Is Hard to Find"

with Robert J. Wilson III

If only the grandmother had married Mr. Edgar Atkins Teagarden, because, as she explains to the children in "A Good Man Is Hard to Find," he "was a gentleman and had bought Coca-Cola stock when it first came out and...had died only a few years ago, a very wealthy man" (*CW* 140). Is Mr. Teagarden the lost opportunity, the great hope, much better than the man the grandmother *did* marry? Mr. E. A. T. is reduced to the basis for a joke in the grandmother's anecdote about him—one of his gift watermelons was eaten by a Black boy who interpreted the initials carved on the melon, E. A. T., as an invitation—and grandchild June Star refuses to see humor in the story, because she has little use for a man who courted the grandmother by bringing her merely a weekly watermelon. Is E. A. T. a sign of the emptiness generally of the grandmother's memories, the shallowness of her desires?

Near the center of the campus of Georgia State College for Women as Flannery O'Connor knew it in the 1940s was Arts Hall, where the English Department was located. This building, the name of which was changed to Lanier Hall (its present name) in the late 1950s, has a cornerstone (one O'Connor would surely have seen) listing the members of the Building Committee for the structure and the college's Board of Directors. A member of both these groups was a man named E. A. Tigner.[1]

Dr. Tigner lived directly across from the Cline House where Flannery lived while she attended high school and college. He was a genial,

---

[1] The authors thank Jacqueline A. Zubeck of the College of Mount Saint Vincent for pointing out the initials of E. A. Tigner on Georgia College's Lanier Hall.

generally well-liked town booster. Tigner worked as a dentist, but he also found time to be a leader in local Democratic Party politics, a participant in local musical concerts, an active member of Sons of Confederate Veterans and the Elks, and an avid local historian who wrote frequently for the Milledgeville paper, the *Union Recorder*, from the early twentieth century on. Based on written records, he even prepared a map of the penitentiary that used to be on the site of what is now Georgia College, a map that has turned out to be quite accurate. He died at the age of 79, in 1948, about five years before O'Connor wrote "A Good Man Is Hard to Find."

Most significantly, Dr. Tigner, in addition to serving for a time as Superintendent of the Baldwin County Schools, was a member of the college's Board of Directors back when it was called Georgia Normal and Industrial College. (The school's name was changed to Georgia State College for Women in 1922.) Tigner was part of a small group who would regularly travel to Atlanta to lobby the state government to improve the school's financial state, and these lobbying trips would be recorded in the local paper (Hair et al. 137; see 137–45 for additional details about Tigner). In the years just prior to the renaming of the college, this group of lobbyists succeeded in winning from the state government more financial support for the college, as well as the right to award four-year degrees.

It would seem to follow that if Flannery O'Connor was thinking of her one-time neighbor Dr. E. A. Tigner when she created E. A. T., she was thinking of a man deeply devoted to the education of women in Georgia. The grandmother appreciated him for the wrong reasons.

WORKS CITED

Hair, William Ivy, et al. *A Centennial History of Georgia College*. Milledgeville, Georgia College, [1990].

O'Connor, Flannery. "A Good Man Is Hard to Find." *Flannery O'Connor: Collected Works*, edited by Sally Fitzgerald. New York, Library of America, 1988, pp. 137–53.

E. A. T. Cornerstone of Arts Hall, now Lanier Hall, Georgia College, Milledgeville.
Courtesy Tim Vacula

What Kind of Novel Can Be Made of Flannery O'Connor's *Heathen* Manuscripts?

In July 1963, Flannery O'Connor published in *Esquire* a short section of a supposedly forthcoming novel. The section, published as a story called "Why Do the Heathen Rage?," takes up only four pages in *Flannery O'Connor: Collected Works*. For years, I did not assign this story in my O'Connor course, because the section ends just as it begins to become interesting. The plot in *Esquire* is one of almost total paralysis and inaction. As the family of the story welcomes home the father, Tilman, who is starting to recover from a stroke, the only person who seems to be deeply concerned is his Black servant Roosevelt, and Tilman returns the concern, preferring his servant over Tilman's biological son, Walter. Tilman's wife hopes that the father's stroke will force her son to finally grow up, to be a man, to take over the family farm and dominate Roosevelt and the other Black workers. But Walter seems stuck in seemingly useless pastimes.

Until one reaches the last three paragraphs of the published section, there is little sign of the rage that the title promises. "Why Do the Heathen Rage?" is a quotation from Psalm 2, but the story may also borrow its title from a popular fundamentalist newspaper column (one I noticed regularly in a Little Rock paper of my childhood). I think the answer to the question raised in the title is that it is nearly impossible to reconcile the demands of this world with the demands of the divine world. As the published section concludes, the promised rage starts to appear. And it's not just the heathen who rage; religious people in O'Connor stories rage too. Walter the useless son has fallen under the spell of a medieval call to action, in which Jesus in considered a warrior. Walter has somehow been attracted to this religious command—one that *will* change him—and his mother feels rage when she recognizes that Walter has experienced a recognition that does not suit her plans. The end.

In order to appreciate what O'Connor was up to with *Why Do the Heathen Rage?* in her years of working on it, we need to think about its connections to other works. Let me review: Back in 1957–58, she had written "The Enduring Chill." In early 1960, she completed "The Comforts of Home" and "The Partridge Festival." While she worked on *Heathen*, she completed, in 1961, "Everything That Rises Must Converge" and "The Lame Shall Enter First." After she gave up on *Heathen* as a novel, she completed, in 1964, the stories "Revelation," "Judgment Day," and "Parker's Back." My take on the manuscripts of *Heathen* at Georgia College is that those manuscripts give us insights into just about everything O'Connor was writing late in life.

A few years ago, the O'Connor Society newsletter, *Cheers!*, announced that the manuscripts of O'Connor's abandoned novel would be edited by Jessica Hooten Wilson and published as a text for "the broader public," not just a "scholarly" audience, to enjoy (Wilson and Warren 5). This won't be easy: Wilson is required by the O'Connor Estate to avoid adding anything to what O'Connor wrote. Like most people who study O'Connor, I had never taken what I call the *Heathen* manuscripts all that seriously, because I had heard that the 378 pages of manuscripts do not really constitute a novel, that there is too much repetition, too much struggling on O'Connor's part to find her way. But once the possibly forthcoming publication was announced, I thought I had better pay more attention.

Stephen G. Driggers and Robert J. Dunn provide a chart of the "Development of O'Connor's Fiction," in which they indicate that O'Connor worked on *Heathen* for over three prime years, from near the end of 1960 until the end of 1963—and the critic Marian Burns says that O'Connor's work took place *primarily* in 1963 ("Chronology" 58). In a fascinating letter (dated 4 May 1963) to Sister Mariella Gable, O'Connor says she was ready to publish a book of stories, but also that she wanted "to wait and see what this turns out to be that I am writing on now. Then if it turns out to be a long story, I'll put them all together in a collection…" (*HB* 517). O'Connor is talking about *Heathen*, and in the next paragraph of that letter, she shows remarkable self-doubt: "I've been writing eighteen years and I've reached the point where I can't do again what I know I can do well, and the larger things that I need to do now, I doubt my capacity for doing" (518).[1] So what might have been "the larger things" O'Connor felt she needed to address in fiction while trying to draft *Heathen*? What had she never solved in fiction to her satisfaction? Assuming you will forgive my attempt to read O'Connor's mind, I'll suggest that some of her goals in composing the *Heathen* manuscripts can be put into the following four categories:

1. She wanted to write realistically about what life is like after grace is suffered and accepted—producing what Jessica Hooten Wilson calls "a postconversion narrative" (192)—by placing a moment of grace early in a novel and then showing what sort of contemplative life, and what sort of action in the world, would follow. And by the way, the short section of *Heathen* published in *Esquire* makes little progress on this score; as John R. May points out, "The story as it stands is the mother's..." (57), and the mother (an interesting but minor character in the novel) finds the implied moment of grace experienced by her son, the main character of the novel, merely irritating and enraging. I should also mention here that Farrell O'Gorman compares the *Heathen* manuscripts to Walker Percy's *The Moviegoer*, and O'Gorman is willing to suggest O'Connor was influenced by Percy (153–54) to try to write the religious life of a "normal" man.

2. O'Connor wanted to write a believable love story. She had tried to make "The Comforts of Home" and "The Partridge Festival" into love stories, with mixed results. This topic receives emphasis in the work on *Heathen* by Colleen Warren. And while O'Connor was at it, she wanted to figure out what her own life of letter-writing—in which O'Connor adapted her tone to suit each of her very different correspondents—had to do with romance. As Virginia Wray has suggested, O'Connor was thinking about her relationship with Maryat Lee, who once declared her love for O'Connor and whose self-portrait O'Connor kept over her fire-

---

[1] The seven stories O'Connor had ready to go were probably the following: "Greenleaf," "A View of the Woods," "The Enduring Chill," "The Comforts of Home," "Everything That Rises Must Converge," "The Partridge Festival," and "The Lame Shall Enter First." Perhaps "An Exile in the East" or a later version of that story, "Getting Home," was also a possibility. As much as I'm inclined to emphasize the extent to which the *Heathen* manuscripts prepared for O'Connor's last three stories, it is also fairly easy to link the material in all of these seven stories to the material in the *Heathen* manuscripts.

place for a time while working on *Heathen* (unpublished letter to Maryat Lee, 2 Feb. 1962).

3. O'Connor wanted to reach some sort of conclusion about family life, perhaps to develop some sort of idea of how a mother and a father could exist peacefully in the long term with a son and daughter. The critic Ann E. Reuman treats the *Heathen* material as O'Connor's ongoing contemplation of her need to improve her relationship with her mother. We could put it this way: perhaps she wanted to revisit some of her early masterpiece "A Good Man Is Hard to Find" without murdering an entire family. Or, perhaps, O'Connor's goal was to justify the rage that could be felt by a child, to show that family peace is not the real goal. There is a reference to St. Jerome in *Heathen*, and one of Jerome's ideas is that a child *must* be cruel to a parent in order to be truly loving toward that parent (4). This is the sort of idea that would surely intrigue O'Connor, and I can imagine her referencing Jerome to hint at her novel's relevance for her relationship with her mother.

4. O'Connor wanted to make herself reach some useful conclusions about the Civil Rights Movement and how to solve the country's race problems. This issue is a major concern in Virginia Wray's important article about the *Heathen* manuscripts; Wray concludes that a major reason O'Connor did not finish *Heathen* was that she realized her initial intention to write a satire about race was wrong-headed. O'Connor's letters to Maryat Lee regularly ridicule Lee's liberalism about civil rights, and their friendship conflicted with the satire. The manuscripts' talk of openness on race eventually, if tentatively, became persuasive to O'Connor, as it becomes persuasive to the protagonist in the manuscripts.

If we ever see published a fuller version of *Why Do the Heathen Rage?*, I think we will agree that O'Connor was challenging herself on all these fronts. It is a totally honorable effort on O'Connor's part, but of course it is also understandable that O'Connor did not manage magically to pull a whole bunch of rabbits out of a hat all at once. She did not produce what we would typically call a novel, but if the bits of *Heathen* are assembled a certain way, I think we do have a fascinating draft of a long story that leaves one speculating, as O'Connor probably did, about what will happen after the story ends. Jessica Hooten Wilson's task, though difficult, is worthwhile.

Part of what O'Connor did in working on *Heathen* was to expand on "The Enduring Chill," the rather autobiographical story from 1958 about a troubled writer who retreats to a mother's southern dairy farm to discover that death is not all that imminent. In one draft of "The Enduring Chill," the water-stain that the main character sees descending toward the sickbed at the story's climax resembles not a bird suggestive of the Holy Ghost (as in the published version), but that rather challenging and insulting priest, Father Finn (file 194b, p. 28). No wonder there's another draft in which the main character flees the room rather than be overwhelmed, like the mythic figure Leda, by a descending figure of divine power (file 234). One way to read *Heathen*, then, is to see it as a continuation of the plot about the weakened but still living main character of "The Enduring Chill." Various names are applied to the main character of *Heathen*, but I will stick to the one that appears most often, Walter. Like the main character in "The Enduring Chill," Walter is shocked to think that he is a Christian and to indict himself as a bad one (files 222, 226a), and he is unsure of what to do with his belief. In draft after draft of the planned novel, Walter also does not know what to do with his family, all of whom are alive—his father, mother, and sister. A major challenge would be for Walter to figure out how to manage the Black workers on the farm. Instead of taking direct action concerning his family or the farm, Walter reads (esp. books about medieval theology) and writes bizarre letters to newspapers, and more significantly, letters to complete strangers, letters intended primarily to satirize the recipients. It is no surprise that critic Marian Burns describes the *Heathen* manuscripts as uncannily and coincidentally comparable to John Kennedy Toole's *A Confederacy of Dunces* ("O'Connor's Unfinished" 90–92). Walter's devotion to what his parents see as a life of inaction is made more complicated by his father's choice to prefer one of the Black workers to his son. The father would order Walter to work in the yard while Roosevelt rests (file 217a).[2]

---

[2] Tilman's preference for Roosevelt over Walter might make this story yet another example of O'Connor's exploration of what I call the substitute child theme. Although Chandler M. Tagliabue, a Milledgeville resident, recalls that there was a real person named Roosevelt, well known in Milledgeville as a dignified caretaker for a professor in a wheelchair, and that he was probably in his 50s or 60s when O'Connor was most serious about writing *Why Do the Heathen Rage?*, I believe O'Connor's characters, and O'Connor herself, are willing to ignore or misapprehend age in such situations.

Walter's letter-writing takes a crucial turn when he starts sending letters to a woman, a northerner usually named Oona Gibbs, to make fun of her supportive interest in an interracial, communal settlement in the South. (The settlement is clearly based on a real interracial community in South Georgia in O'Connor's time, called Koinonia.³) Oona is so interested in Black people and so interested in Walter that Walter finds himself pretending in his letters to be Black (file 218e). He even sends Oona a picture of the Black worker Roosevelt, and Walter tells Oona that the photo is of himself (file 228a).⁴ Somewhere along the way, Walter starts falling in love, more or less believably, with Oona. Generally, Walter could easily cut off one of his streams of correspondence by writing on an envelope that he had died and returning that letter to the sender. But as Walter's horrified love for Oona grows, his correspondence endures. Walter even finds himself defending the interracial community that interests Oona, albeit in a highly emotional moment, as part of an argument with his father (file 222).

The plot is cut short just as the fuse is lit for an explosion. We are told that Oona has driven down from the North to the South in her red convertible and has arrived at Walter's farm (file 220d). What we have here is potentially an ending to *Heathen*, even if it is even more abrupt than the ending of "The Life You Save May Be Your Own," which also ends without our knowing for sure what will become of any of the main characters. As I contemplate the end of *Heathen*, I wonder: Can flesh maintain the connections established between two souls created only in letters? What will happen when Oona and Walter see each other? Can love survive when it is actually between two dangerously intelligent people? (Intelligence is always dangerous in O'Connor.) Will Walter grow

---

³ Anyone needing an introduction to the history of Clarence Jordan's Koinonia Farm should see the 57-minute documentary film *Briars in the Cotton Patch*, a good source for getting a sense of Jordan's ideas is his *Cotton Patch Gospel*.

⁴ Walter's complex manipulations of photographs provided inspiration for Ruth Reiniche to write her book *Sign Language* (x). Part of what Chandler M. Tagliabue and others recall about the real Roosevelt is that he had buckteeth, and that he found it hard to cover his buckteeth with his lips. I suppose that this effort might have indirectly given Roosevelt some of his aura of dignity. One wonders, however, why O'Connor would have been inspired to make a man with buckteeth the model for a character whom Walter would pretend to be.

toward more genuine concern for racial issues, converted to take up some sort of life of action? Or will he adopt a more contemplative course, or some sort of ideal combination of action and contemplation? Can Walter remain on his parents' farm comfortably once his parents and Roosevelt discover that Walter has been pretending to be Roosevelt?

Heathen leaves me with the impression that O'Connor saw her South as a hot mess of puzzles she could not solve. I do not think that she ever persuaded herself that a life of religious and artistic contemplation could ever be considered compatible with a life of action. I do not think she ever persuaded herself that her own correspondence with a variety of close friends was ever entirely free of fakery. And I don't think she ever solved the problems of family life. O'Connor worked to make her main character defensible as a son, but critic Louise Westling is probably not alone in considering Walter a "failure" (146). While O'Connor completed only two stories during the three years she worked on *Heathen* ("Everything That Rises Must Converge" and "The Lame Shall Enter First," a shortened revision of her second novel), her spirited failure to produce a novel did set her up to make progress on the various fronts that concerned her as she started drafting *Heathen*. One way to look at *Heathen* is to see it as the primordial stew that was eventually served up as the posthumous story collection *Everything That Rises Must Converge*. *Heathen* addresses all of the shortcomings I suspect O'Connor saw when she considered most critically the seven stories she had ready for a collection by early 1963, and I think that as O'Connor abandoned *Heathen*, she was artistically prepared to compose her final three strong stories—"Revelation," "Judgment Day," and "Parker's Back"—and in those stories she made distinct progress on what she considered "the larger things." I understand Wilson's comparing *Heathen* to William Faulkner's collection of linked stories *Go Down, Moses* (Wilson 192). Perhaps O'Connor's final stories seem more powerful when we appreciate how they grew out of the problems of *Heathen*.

First, O'Connor completed "Revelation," a story that I think fulfills O'Connor's desire to write about what happens after a moment of grace. One way this story grows out of *Heathen* material is in its attention to pigs. In file 194a of *Heathen*, O'Connor's main character is envious of someone else's pig farming, and in file 225e, Walter is responsible for the death of a sow about to give birth. And Mrs. Ruby Turpin of "Revelation," like Walter of *Heathen*, takes pigs very seriously and very personally. But the prolonged treatment of grace is what is crucial here. Once the college student named Mary Grace hits our main character, Ruby, on the head with a textbook named *Human Development*, Ruby's contemplative life expands and blossoms. I think "Revelation" shows that after a moment of grace, one needs another moment of grace, which Ruby receives in the story's final paragraphs. The story leaves one with the impression that Ruby's continuing struggles and its ongoing successes are sufficiently implied—in a way that I cannot quite claim for Walter in *Heathen*. As for the other challenges O'Connor was giving herself, I would say that "Revelation" persuades me that Ruby and her husband do love each other, though how that love came about is not the story's focus. O'Connor is thinking about family life, but she reaches conclusions only subtly and tentatively, as Ruby imagines herself as a sow-mother to a gang of piglets. On the topic of race, I think "Revelation" is quite grand on showing how Ruby imagines herself Black and then joins in on chastising herself for her racism, but I have always struggled to imagine how Ruby will find a way to carry on a conversation with the African-American workers on her farm after the story ends. More grace is always required, it seems.

"Judgment Day" can be read as making more progress on the topic of race. In some drafts, one can clearly see *Heathen* material feeding into this story, as Walter's parents are transformed into the father and daughter in "Judgment Day." O'Connor once talked about "Everything That Rises Must Converge" as a new sort of story for her, the sort of thing she wished she could do more of (4 Mar. 1962, *HB* 468). As O'Connor worked on *Heathen*, with Walter imagining himself Black and defending an interracial commune, O'Connor set herself up for the sophisticated treatment of race in "Judgment Day." O'Connor simultaneously condemns the racism of her main character, the old White man Tanner; persuades us that her racist character could imagine in detail that he loves a Black man, Coleman; and also suggests that Coleman does not love Tanner back. Compare this complex relationship to the brief passage in "Everything That Rises Must Converge" in which Julian's mother remembers her mammy, Caroline (*CW* 499–500), and I think we can see O'Connor making progress on the subject of the complicated future of race relations. For more evidence of O'Connor's focus on the future in "Judgment Day," notice also the inclusion and acceptance directed toward the multiracial character called Doctor Foley, for whom White people will someday wish to work (680–81).[5]

In "Parker's Back," O'Connor writes her most effective story about a romantic relationship, and once again, I think we can conclude that the work on *Heathen* prepared for O'Connor's success, this time with an unsentimental and believable treatment of romantic love. O'Connor had tried many times to suggest romantic connections—from Mrs. Flood's final interest in Hazel Motes, to Hulga's repeated "Yes" in response to Manley Pointer's need for a profession of her love (*CW* 280), to Thomas's obsession over Sarah Ham in "The Comforts of Home," to the manuscripts of "The Partridge Festival," one full draft of which makes quite explicit that Calhoun is falling in love with Mary Elizabeth (file 200). "The Partridge Festival" is the last story O'Connor completed before starting on *Heathen*, and when one compares the drafts of "Partridge" to the finished story, one sees O'Connor pulling back, making safer points about similarities between Calhoun and Mary Elizabeth, and not claiming that their emotional war would lead to love.

In the *Heathen* manuscripts, Walter and Oona are another couple O'Connor tries to make fall in love, but perhaps they are only in love with fantasies about each other. When Oona walks into Walter's house, chaos will surely result, and one wonders how O'Connor might have tried to finesse the survival of love. When O'Connor started in on "Parker's Back," she went further than she had before in making sure that both O. E. Parker and Sarah Ruth Cates are clearly seen by each other. Sarah Ruth has eyes like "icepicks" (*CW* 655), so we know she is fully aware of what she is getting into when she marries Parker and becomes pregnant by him. And what better way to draw attention to the full physical reality of Parker than to cover him with tattoos? Both Sarah Ruth and Parker outspokenly reject the looks of the other, but I think O'Connor's strategy is to make dislike a reinforcement of love. A bit from *Heathen* that made it into the excerpt published in *Esquire* is instructive here. Walter repeats a passage from *The Satirical Letters of St. Jerome* that insists, "Love should be full of anger" (*CW* 800; Jerome 3).

---

[5] O'Connor never stopped needing more grace on the subject of race. Her letters to Maryat Lee in 1964, when she was composing "Judgment Day," generally continue the ridicule for Lee's liberalism. And O'Connor was quite capable of making racist statements even in the final year of her life.

This quotation makes it somewhat more believable that Walter loves Oona. In "Parker's Back," O'Connor pushes the idea even further and to more successful effect, persuading us that all the expressions of anger that Sarah Ruth and Parker throw at each other are also evidence of a deep affection. When Parker finally admits "that, all along, that was what he wanted, to please" Sarah Ruth (*CW* 672), I think O'Connor has made her best case that two of her characters love each other, precisely because anger leads to and intensifies love.

I once asked Colleen Warren, who has done some of the most important work on the *Heathen* manuscripts, whether she agrees with me that O'Connor made Walter and Oona into O. E. Parker and Sarah Ruth Cates. Colleen Warren politely declined to endorse my theory, but I'm sticking to my guns here. Of course Oona is quite different from Sarah Ruth, but I find particularly persuasive the drafts of *Heathen* featuring a character I have yet to mention, called Gunnels. Gunnels works on Walter's farm, and he has a tattoo of the face of Christ on his back. The face comes from the *Crucifixion* by Matthias Grünewald, and the misery on that face, and its signs of skin disease, are so shocking that Gunnels says he had nothing to do with selecting the image. The person who is truly impressed by the Christ tattoo, indeed overwhelmed by it, is Walter (file 228a, p. 35). So my speculative theory is that O'Connor combined parts of Gunnels (his tattoo, as well as his lack of intellect), along with the profound reaction to the face of Christ on Walter's part, to create the character O. E. Parker. And then O'Connor created Sarah Ruth as the partner who could fully see, and be angry with, and then love the tattooed man.

When I think of all the connections between the *Heathen* manuscripts and all the stories in the collection *Everything That Rises Must Converge*, I find myself endorsing something like Jessica Hooten Wilson's idea that *Heathen* could be presented as a collection of loosely linked stories that also approaches being a novel. The critic Stuart Burns once insisted that all the good material in *Heathen* found its way into the stories of *Everything That Rises Must Converge*, and he too has a point. Whereas O'Connor worried that she needed to work to make sure that her final collection of stories demonstrated variety, that she needed to work to disguise the overlaps among stories, I think that recasting *Heathen* as a story within the final collection would give us a more consistent working out of O'Connor's progress on the themes of race, religion, and romance. It might not make a popular success—I can already imagine the complaining book reviews about a new book that looks too much like an already published story collection—but there are many people—in the scholarly community, at least—who would enjoy reconsidering the products of O'Connor's final years. Perhaps the best course (the course of action I imagine I would take, if it were up to me) is to admit a version of "Why Do the Heathen Rage?" as a long story—along with "The Partridge Festival," which O'Connor once intended to include—into an expanded version of O'Connor's final collection. It would be nice to admit also some of the fascinating variants in the drafts of other stories. That way, the title of that final collection might take on some more meaning, as it would be much easier to appreciate how everything in O'Connor's late work does indeed converge.

WORKS CITED AND CONSULTED

Briars in the Cotton Patch. Directed by Faith Fuller, Cotton Patch Productions, 2003. DVD.

Burns, Marian. "The Chronology of Flannery O'Connor's 'Why Do the Heathen Rage?'" *The Flannery O'Connor Bulletin*, vol. 11, 1982, pp. 58–75.

_____. "O'Connor's Unfinished Novel." *The Flannery O'Connor Bulletin*, vol. 11, 1982, pp. 76–93.

Burns, Stuart. "How Wide Did 'The Heathen" Range? *The Flannery O'Connor Bulletin*, vol. 4, 1975, pp. 25–41.

Driggers, Stephen G., and Robert J. Dunn, with Sarah Gordon. "Development of O'Connor's Fiction." *The Manuscripts of Flannery O'Connor at Georgia College*. Athens, University of Georgia Press, 1989, pp. xx–xxi.

Faulkner, William. *Go Down, Moses*. 1942. New York, Vintage International-Random House, 2011.

Jerome, Saint. *The Satirical Letters of St. Jerome*, translated by Paul Carroll. Chicago, Gateway, 1956.

Jordan, Clarence. *Clarence Jordan's The Cotton Patch Gospel: The Complete Collection*. Macon, Smyth & Helwys, 2012.

May, John R. *The Pruning Word: The Parables of Flannery O'Connor*. Notre Dame, IN, University of Notre Dame Press, 1976.

O'Connor, Flannery. *Flannery O'Connor: Collected Works*, edited by Sally Fitzgerald. New York, Library of America, 1988.

_____. *The Habit of Being: Letters*, edited by Sally Fitzgerald. New York, Farrar, 1979.

_____. Unpublished manuscripts. Flannery O'Connor Collection, Special Collections, Georgia College Library and Instructional Technology Center, Milledgeville.

O'Gorman, Farrell. *Peculiar Crossroads: Flannery O'Connor, Walker Percy, and Catholic Vision in Postwar Southern Fiction*. Baton Rouge, Louisiana State University Press, 2004.

Percy, Walker. *The Moviegoer*. 1961. New York, Farrar, 2019.

Reiniche, Ruth. "Preface." *Sign Language: Reading Flannery O'Connor's Graphic Narrative*. Macon, Mercer University Press, 2020, pp. ix–x.

Reuman, Ann E. "Revolting Fictions: Flannery O'Connor's Letter to Her Mother." *Papers on Language and Literature*, vol. 29, no. 2, 1993, pp. 197–214.

Tagliabue, Chandler M. Interview. Conducted by Irene Burgess and Marshall Bruce Gentry, 22 June 2020.

Toole, John Kennedy. *A Confederacy of Dunces*. 1980. New York, Grove Press, 2002.

Warren, Colleen. "Black Doubling in Flannery O'Connor's 'Why Do the Heathen Rage?'" *Critical Insights: Short Fiction of Flannery O'Connor*, edited by Robert C. Evans. Ipswich, MA, Grey House-Salem Press, 2016, pp. 190–206.

———. "Seeing Potential in the Heathen: Flannery O'Connor's Unfinished Novel." *Flannery O'Connor Review*, vol. 13, 2015, pp. 105–22.

Westling, Louise. *Sacred Groves and Ravaged Gardens: The Fiction of Eudora Welty, Carson McCullers, and Flannery O'Connor*. Athens, University of Georgia Press, 1985.

Wilson, Jessica [Lynice] Hooten. "O'Connor's Unfinished Novel: The Beginning of a Modern Saint's Life." *Revelation and Convergence: Flannery O'Connor and the Catholic Intellectual Tradition*, edited by Mark Bosco, S.J., and Brent Little. Washington, DC, The Catholic University of America Press, 2017, pp. 191–214.

Wilson, Jessica [Lynice] Hooten, and Colleen Warren. "'Why Do the Heathen Rage?' Manuscripts to Be Published." *Cheers!*, vol. 20, no. 3–4, Fall 2017, p. 5.

Wray, Virginia. "Flannery O'Connor's *Why Do the Heathen Rage?* and the Quotidian 'larger things.'" *The Flannery O'Connor Bulletin*, vol. 23, 1994–1995, pp. 1–29.

Flannery O'Connor's Letters and the Editing of Authorial Intent

Review-essay on Good Things out of Nazareth: The Uncollected Letters of Flannery O'Connor and Friends *by Flannery O'Connor et al. Edited by Benjamin B. Alexander. New York, Convergent Books-Random House, 2019. xxi + 389 pp. $26 cloth. Available as e-book and audiobook.*

Flannery O'Connor typically spent her mornings writing her fiction. In her afternoons, as her energy would start to decrease because for much of her writing life she was ill with lupus, she carefully composed—after taking care each day of her large collection of birds, of course—some of the most interesting letters of the twentieth century. People who study O'Connor are justified in taking her letters very seriously, as a guide to her friendships, as a guide to her philosophical and religious thoughts, as a source of hints to O'Connor's opinions on the social issues of her time, and even as a guide to how to read her fiction. In her letters and her essays, whatever the original intentions behind them, O'Connor was quite successful—too successful, perhaps—in guiding how her works are interpreted. Surely, to a significant extent, O'Connor realized what she was setting up: she wrote a great many letters, and she kept carbon copies.

So it matters how O'Connor is edited and how much of her writing is available to scholars and students. An editor can have significant influence on what will be seen as O'Connor's authorial intentions. Sally Fitzgerald is famous for having done the major work of negotiating and editing to produce two books that significantly advanced O'Connor's reputation as the great Catholic writer of her era: *Mystery and Manners: Occasional Prose* and *The Habit of Being: Letters*. And these two books remain among the most important sources for anyone studying O'Connor. With *Mystery and Manners*, Fitzgerald made choices that could easily be second-guessed, as Fitzgerald herself did when she re-edited O'Connor's essays for the "Occasional Prose" section of the Library of America volume *Flannery O'Connor: Collected Works*. It can be rather shocking to notice how much the contents of a given essay differ between the two editions. And there is plenty in the manuscripts of O'Connor's essays that has never been published. Surely someday we will have access to much fuller versions of O'Connor's essays.

With the letters, the situation is even more complicated. Fitzgerald worked hard and with admirable patience to persuade Flannery O'Connor's mother, Regina Cline O'Connor, to give permission for the publication of nearly 600 pages of personal letters, even though Regina might suspect that someone mentioned in a letter would likely be offended, and even though O'Connor's opinions might not make her look good. (See Daniel Moran for a thorough treatment of the negotiations involved in the compiling of *The Habit of Being*.) Fitzgerald left out, for example, some of O'Connor's critical comments about W. A. Sessions—who had worked for years to write an authorized biography of O'Connor before he realized how often O'Connor mocked him—and Fitzgerald also left out some of O'Connor's racist comments, esp. those in her letters to Maryat Lee. *The Habit of Being* is a wonderful, award-winning book, but it is also a version and a vision of O'Connor that Fitzgerald wanted to promote. To teach O'Connor's letters and relate them to her fiction productively, one needs to be prepared to take a critical attitude toward them, as Will Brantley has recently suggested. When Fitzgerald re-edited the letters for the Library of America volume, she was more selective, publishing fewer letters than appear in *The Habit of Being*, but also including twenty-one new letters.

One must note Fitzgerald's ellipses in her published editions and wonder what else, what more, is left out. Robert C. Evans published a twenty-five-page article summarizing the high points of what Fitzgerald did not print from the letters to one correspondent, Elizabeth "Betty" Hester, who seems to have been particularly good at getting O'Connor to write revealingly about herself. Of course, much of what Fitzgerald did not print was material to which she did not have access. In 2002, R. Neil Scott and Valerie Nye published *Postmarked Milledgeville*, which lists a great many collections of O'Connor's letters in libraries throughout the US, and some of these collections are of letters that are still not available to scholars.

When one sees some of what Fitzgerald did not publish, one may also wonder how these additional glimpses are made possible. Angela Alaimo O'Donnell, who helps produce a book series for Fordham University Press called Studies in the Catholic Imagination: The Flannery O'Connor Trust Series (a series that receives financial support from the Mary Flannery O'Connor Charitable Trust), gives us, in her book *Radical Ambivalence*, a few excerpts that Fitzgerald could not or would not publish on the subject of race. O'Donnell quotes a short passage, for example, from a still-not-published-in-its-entirety letter, to Maryat Lee on 3 May 1964: "You know, I'm an integrationist by principle & a segregationist by taste anyway. I don't *like* negroes. They all give me a pain & the more of them I see, the less & less I like them. Particularly the new kind" (qtd. in O'Donnell 19). Where can one go for the rest of this letter? For now, one must visit Special Collections at Georgia College. Or consider this quotation from a letter housed at Emory University, from a letter dated 27 Jun. 1964 to Betty Hester: "I sho am sick of niggers" (qtd. in O'Donnell 65). Most of this letter appears in *The Habit of Being* (587–88), but readers have only ellipsis points to indicate that Fitzgerald could not or would not publish the complete letter. When Fitzgerald selected the letters for the Library of America edition of O'Connor's works, she left out altogether this one to Hester. The suppression of such racist material from O'Connor's final months of life makes us realize the extent to which the people favored with permissions are able to influence what most readers are going to know about how complex O'Connor was.

One wise choice Fitzgerald made is presenting O'Connor's letters in chronological order. I have sometimes heard that *The Habit of Being* could and should be read as O'Connor's autobiography. What is lost in such an arrangement, of course, is that it is difficult to follow straightforwardly the sequence of events in the correspondence between O'Connor and any particular correspondent. One wants to be able to do such reading, because O'Connor was willing and able to take on a different persona with each correspondent—in order, one might conclude, to be the person her correspondent needed her to be. It is probably for something like this reason that Connie Kirk went to the trouble—for well over a hundred pages in her *Critical Companion to Flannery O'Connor*—of summarizing each of the letters sent to a given recipient in *The Habit of Being*.

There have been three major collections of O'Connor letters by editors other than Sally Fitzgerald, and all of them give the reader the ability to read some of the back-and-forth between O'Connor and her correspondents: C. Ralph Stephens edited *The Correspondence of Flannery O'Connor and the Brainard Cheneys* in 1986. Christine Flanagan edited

The Letters of Flannery O'Connor and Caroline Gordon in 2018. And now, Benjamin B. Alexander presents *Good Things out of Nazareth*. In all of these collections, one gets to examine some of the letters O'Connor received, and this helps make sense of O'Connor's replies.

O'Connor scholars will want to examine most closely the previously unpublished letters by O'Connor in Alexander's volume, and by my count, there are over 140 of these. One begins to be amazed by how many letters O'Connor could write to different people on the same day. There are a significant number of letters from O'Connor to a number of people who appear only slightly or not at all in previous collections of letters: Roslyn Barnes, Maurice-Edgar Coindreau, Ward Allison Dorrance, Thomas and Louise Gossett, James McCown, Janet McKane, Scott Watson. Perhaps even more interesting and/or surprising are the letters to Katherine Anne Porter (one of which reveals O'Connor's "favorite Bible verse" [271]), letters to Betty Hester, and even letters to the Fitzgeralds. And of course there are some great lines by O'Connor about what she read and what she did not read, whom she liked and disliked, and what she thinks about politics and theology. (I find that I need to make significant adjustments to some of my published articles, and I have told several people already that they need to use for their current projects what is found in Alexander's collection.) Here are a few of my favorite bits: to Ethel Daniell on 6 Feb. 1956, O'Connor said about her own characters, "…they're all, even the worst of them, me, so my tolerance of them is supreme" (55). To Betty Hester on 5 Sept. 1959, O'Connor wrote, "All good Catholics become anti-clerical sooner or later" (187). To Janet McKane on 31 Mar. 1963, concerning O'Connor's "Catholic friends who are interested in reading," O'Connor exaggerated: "The ones who are have left the church, the ones who don't read, manage to stay in" (280). This bit comes from a letter that Sally Fitzgerald did publish (*HB* 512), but Fitzgerald left out the passage from which I am quoting. To Ward Allison Dorrance on 3 Nov. 1963, O'Connor says that Regina "listens…very seriously" to her Black workers, and that "…they lie like artists" (287).

Then there is the correspondence between Flannery O'Connor and Caroline Gordon. Alexander proceeds as if Christine Flanagan had not published her 2018 study of those letters. While Alexander includes a few letters that Flanagan did not include in her volume, Alexander's collection skips quite a few letters that Flanagan includes, and some of the letters he excerpts are included in Flanagan's volume in their entirety.

His annotations and bracketed explanations are different from Flanagan's. What is a student, or a scholar, to do? I suggest that one take copious notes about Alexander's collection (recording dates and page numbers carefully) and then read Flanagan's collection for a fuller rendition with different explanations. While Flanagan follows chronological order, Alexander often does not, so when one finds something especially interesting in Flanagan and then tries to locate that same letter in Alexander, there will be difficulty. Which collection to use for a citation of a given letter sent between O'Connor and Gordon will have to be decided on a case-by-case basis.

Alexander's subtitle says that the volume contains "Uncollected" letters, but some of the letters here have appeared in *The Habit of Being* and some have appeared in *Flannery O'Connor: Collected Works*. Alexander occasionally provides fuller versions of letters than Sally Fitzgerald provides, so I think we should tolerate the repetitions. There is also some repetition of a few of O'Connor's letters to and from Brainard and Frances Neel Cheney, and I have a hard time figuring out what Alexander adds to the work of editor C. Ralph Stephens. Perhaps Alexander's volume will inspire scholars to revisit Stephens's.

Then there are the letters between people who knew O'Connor. To anyone puzzling—and aren't we all?—over O'Connor's claim that "When tenderness is detached from the source of tenderness [Christ], its logical outcome is terror" (*MM* 227), I recommend thinking about a letter by Roslyn Barnes, who was mentored by O'Connor, to James McCown. Writing in Aug. 1964 after she has learned of O'Connor's death, Barnes, wondering why she and O'Connor were never closer, writes the following: "I hope she really cared for me and was not just 'doing her Christian duty.'...To be loved 'for God's sake' is so often not to be loved at all" (337).

I also find particularly interesting the communication between Caroline Gordon and Walker Percy, in which Gordon expresses some interesting thoughts on O'Connor and her works, thoughts she probably would not have shared with O'Connor, such as her opinion early in 1952 about a draft of *Wise Blood*: "...practically everything in it is damned" (41). Percy fans will also want to take a careful look at Alexander's volume to see such documents as a syllabus for a course Percy was preparing to teach and a fascinating letter from Stanley Kauffmann rejecting an early version of what would become Percy's prize-winning *The Moviegoer*. The connection to O'Connor may become tenuous at times, but many people interested in the writers of O'Connor's era will still feel grateful that Alexander was able to get all the many permissions, from a variety of authors' estates, in order to print these documents.

Perhaps in an attempt to draw together all of the documents he includes, Alexander does a great deal of editorializing. He knows a number of people who knew O'Connor, and that may have emboldened him to express his opinions about the correspondents' politics, the teaching of southern literature, and for that matter, most of American history (all the way from the Founding Fathers to Alexander's [incorrect] prediction for the 2020 presidential election results). Sometimes Alexander's commentaries are longer than the letters to which he connects them. The value here, I suppose, is that Alexander may provoke an imaginative response in a reader, but one rarely encounters a situation in which it is necessary to make O'Connor seem even more provocative than she already clearly is. Consequently, I am of two minds about Alexander's collection. On the one hand, there is so much commentary on the significance of O'Connor's letters that one can feel as if one is being bullied by an editor who has very strong views on how we should regard O'Connor. On the other hand, since the book at times appears to be something of a grab bag, one is able to trust that Alexander was trying to present as many jewels as possible, that he probably avoided deleting materials about O'Connor simply because they might not make O'Connor look less saintly.

Alexander's *Good Things out of Nazareth* provides plenty of material that students and scholars will want and need to use. While it is clear that this will not be the final collection of O'Connor-related letters—when can we hope to learn the full story about Flannery O'Connor and Betty Hester, or the full story about O'Connor's many letters to her mother?—anyone doing serious research on O'Connor will need to examine this volume carefully before returning to the previous collections of O'Connor letters.

WORKS CITED

Brantley, Will. "O'Connor Through Her Letters." *Approaches to Teaching the Works of Flannery O'Connor*, edited by Robert Donahoo and Marshall Bruce Gentry. New York, Modern Language Association, 2019, pp. 40–47.

Evans, Robert C. "Flannery O'Connor's Letters to Betty Hester: Passages Omitted from *The Habit of Being*." *Critical Insights: Short Fiction of Flannery O'Connor*, edited by Robert C. Evans. Ipswich, MA, Salem-Grey House, 2016, pp. 220–44.

Kirk, Connie Ann. "*The Habit of Being*: Letters." *Critical Companion to Flannery O'Connor: A Literary Reference to Her Life and Work*. New York, Facts on File, 2008, pp. 183–310.

Moran, Daniel. "Robert Giroux, Sally Fitzgerald, and *The Habit of Being*." *Creating Flannery O'Connor: Her Critics, Her Publishers, Her Readers*. Athens, University of Georgia Press, 2016, pp. 91–131.

O'Connor, Flannery. *The Habit of Being: Letters*, edited by Sally Fitzgerald. New York, Farrar, 1979.

———. "Letters." *Flannery O'Connor: Collected Works*, edited by Sally Fitzgerald. New York, Library of America, 1988, pp. 865–1234.

———. *Mystery and Manners: Occasional Prose*, edited by Sally Fitzgerald and Robert Fitzgerald. New York, Farrar, 1969.

———. "Occasional Prose." *Flannery O'Connor: Collected Works*, edited by Sally Fitzgerald. New York, Library of America, 1988, pp. 801–64.

O'Connor, Flannery, et al. *The Correspondence of Flannery O'Connor and the Brainard Cheneys*, edited by C. Ralph Stephens. Jackson, University Press of Mississippi, 1986.

O'Connor, Flannery, and Caroline Gordon. *The Letters of Flannery O'Connor and Caroline Gordon*, edited by Christine Flanagan. Athens, University of Georgia Press, 2018.

O'Donnell, Angela Alaimo. *Radical Ambivalence: Race in Flannery O'Connor*. New York, Fordham University Press, 2020. Studies in the Catholic Imagination, The Flannery O'Connor Trust Series.

Percy, Walker. *The Moviegoer*. 1961. New York, Farrar, 2019.

Scott, R. Neil, and Valerie Nye, compilers. *Postmarked Milledgeville: A Guide to Flannery O'Connor's Correspondence in Libraries and Archives*, edited by Sarah Gordon and Irwin Streight. Milledgeville, Georgia College, 2002.

The History, and the Future, of Flannery O'Connor Studies

Review-essay on *The Critical Reception of Flannery O'Connor, 1952–2017: "Searchers and Discoverers"* by Robert C. Evans. Studies in American Literature and Culture: Literary Criticism in Perspective. Rochester, NY, Camden, 2018. ix + 270 pp. $85 cloth.

When I teach my annual course on the works of Flannery O'Connor, I am in the habit of putting on library reserve about fifty books of O'Connor criticism. While this list of reserves may make my syllabus rather scary, it serves the purpose of directing students toward major critical sources. There are about twenty shelves of O'Connor books in the circulating collection of our library at Georgia College, O'Connor's alma mater, and when in class I wave about R. Neil Scott's bibliography of over one thousand pages (*Flannery O'Connor: An Annotated Reference Guide to Criticism*), I do fear that my students might become even more intimidated. Where can one begin? Part of the rationale for Robert C. Evans's impressive study of O'Connor criticism is to help teachers and students find their way through the many, many studies of O'Connor to locate the best things to read and the best strategies for conducting research. Evans is very consciously trying to supplement previous attempts to report the history of O'Connor criticism. In addition to Scott's bibliography, there is Robert E. Golden's early bibliographic compilation (Golden and Sullivan, 1977); a book collecting nearly all the major reviews of O'Connor's books, co-edited by R. Neil Scott and Irwin H. Streight (2009); Daniel Moran's 2016 study of how O'Connor has been received by critics (as well as by the publishing establishment and by casual readers); a number of volumes that reprint what have been judged to be superior works of criticism; and various article-length overviews of the history of O'Connor criticism. In order to evaluate fully the results of the tremendous amount of work that surely went into producing Evans's study, one has to consider how it can and will be used.

The good news is that Evans's book will be useful to many students and to the teachers who help them. Scholars, too, will find the book quite helpful in terms of suggesting important articles they have missed. It is fairly easy to imagine that a student will be able to figure out which portion of Evans's book can help with a research assignment, and students will be pleased to realize that they do not have to read the whole book. Note that Evans's index does direct the reader to those pages where a specific work by O'Connor is mentioned. Teachers might, of course, worry that students will confuse Evans's opinions with the opinions of the critics about whom Evans reports. But there are more important challenges involved in using Evans's book, and some of the challenges of working professionally on O'Connor can be best explained if the sections of the book are discussed from back to front.

The final section ("Conclusion: O'Connor Criticism: What Now? What Next?") is focused on the future. Here Evans suggests that religious readings of O'Connor are not going to appeal to students in the years to come. And the problem, Evans says, is broader: "O'Connor's politics, theology, and social attitudes, not to mention her frequent use of the N-word, are likely to make her less and less appealing to a wider and wider range of readers" (234). Evans may be correct here, however sad it is to admit that O'Connor's religiosity and her opinions could make her unfashionable. So, what is Evans's solution? We should emphasize "O'Connor *as an artist*, as a gifted *writer*, rather than (or in addition to) as a thinker or theologian" (234–35; emphasis in original). Evans also recommends that critics and teachers use what Evans calls "'archetypal' approaches to literature" in order "to reach out to readers who will inevitably inhabit a more diverse, more multicultural, more secular world than the one most of us knew growing up" (235). O'Connor is very good on the topics of death and of family, so Evans also believes those subjects need more attention.

Given this concluding advice, one might reasonably ask how well Evans's book does the job of helping us to start investigating O'Connor in these fresh ways. My general sense that Evans's book can solidify O'Connor's place in the canon has to be qualified. Where are the sections about critical responses to O'Connor on death, about O'Connor and family? What about technology, disability, ecology? I realize I am not being entirely fair here; someone will write these critical overviews, someday, and Evans does mention critical studies that touch on all these topics. Still, one might also wonder why it is so important to survey so much of the O'Connor criticism of the past if the criticism of the future needs to change course, to be quite different.

In my opinion, Evans's best chapters are near the end. Just before the conclusion, in chapter 6, Evans addresses gender, a topic that Evans notes was unpopular in O'Connor studies until the 1990s. I agree that gender is a topic on which O'Connor is conflicted and fascinating, and Evans surveys the criticism well. Anyone researching questions about O'Connor and feminism, and anyone teaching or taking a women's studies course in which O'Connor figures, would be well advised to read this chapter. Chapter 5 is on race, a topic that Evans sees as a threat to O'Connor's reputation. Even so, the controversies here can be interesting and instructive; Evans surveys the critical history well, and he is fair to all points of view. Chapter 4, on the South, seems equally valuable, and it is easy to see that critics will be able to continue to sort out O'Connor's mixed feelings about southern social customs, about other southern writers, about how the South was radically changing during the era when she was writing.

Chapter 3 is about history, and to a large extent, the subtopics within this section overlap with the concerns of other chapters. Clearly, Evans respects the work of historical critics—Jon Lance Bacon, for example, receives a large amount of well-deserved praise. Much of the time, however, it seems that history could have been dealt with under the heading of the South and that a great deal of what Evans has to say on the subject of history has already been said in the preceding chapter. That preceding chapter (chapter 2) is on religion, a topic that for some scholars is the key topic, the all-encompassing topic, the only O'Connor angle worth pursuing. Evans shows his tendency to put religion at the forefront when he says, at the beginning of chapter 3 (on history), that of course O'Connor's view of history must be a Christian view of history. It is something of a wonder that the religion chapter is no longer than it is. The majority of O'Connor critics discussed at length in this book are inclined to emphasize a religious approach. Evans surveys the issues and tries to be fair to minority opinions, and he leaves out a lot of religious commentary, but if he truly believes that religious readings are not what O'Connor studies most needs, perhaps he could have made this section even shorter. On several occasions, Evans refers to religious readings as the sort of interpretive work that O'Connor herself would approve. To some extent, this is clearly correct, but what Evans says at the end of his conclusion may be even more correct:

as long as people care about literature *as literature,* O'Connor will have a high place in the canon and in our culture. A tremendously skillful writer: this is perhaps the chief way she herself would have wanted to be read, remembered, and valued. Perhaps we should focus more attention on this aspect of her quite impressive achievement. (235; emphasis in original)

O'Connor would willingly bend or break dogma in order to tell a good story, or perhaps it is better to say that, once O'Connor got caught up in her writing process, she could comfortably relax her dogmatic principles. If O'Connor herself were surveying the criticism written about her through 2017, she might be quite pleased overall to see that her religious sophistication has come to be appreciated, but she might also agree that some critical assertions do not need additional repeating.

So, what is in chapter 1, the section placed in front of the discussion of religion? Here Evans works hard to act on his commitment to the idea that O'Connor is, first of all, an artist. But the results are mixed. Chapter 1, by far the longest in the book, concerns "Aesthetics," with sections on style, form, themes, and characterization. Few works of criticism explicitly set out to explore any single one of these subtopics, so there is a large amount of repeatedly revisiting given secondary sources, and there is also a tendency to report on critics' offhand comments. Evans surely sees this chapter as the most important one, and it does give the reader a sense of the overall course of critical reception. And I admire that Evans is fair to the naysayers and even to the cranks and oddballs. But at the same time, this is the chapter that I suspect I will be least likely to recommend as a starting point for reading this book.

I have already had occasion to recommend Evans's book to a graduate student who knew simply that he is quite interested in O'Connor but did not know how to locate a topic for a master's thesis. Even though the Scott bibliography has a very, very long index, Evans's book does a service by grouping discussions of critical works by approach and by topic. I can also imagine that this book will be quite valuable to anyone wanting to expand and deepen an already written paper. Dipping into Evans's book, one can get a sense of the professional significance of the critical sources that one has already read, and one can figure out what else is significant and relevant to one's project. Perhaps Evans pays a bit too much attention to criticism from decades ago. Perhaps there is too little attention to the articles and chapters about O'Connor in collections and books that move well beyond O'Connor in their concerns; missing from Evans's book, for example, is Gary M. Ciuba's long chapter on violence in *The Violent Bear It Away* in his study of four southern authors. On the whole, and in less than three hundred pages, Evans has done a very good job of surveying the major issues in O'Connor studies and of suggesting what is now worth researching.

WORKS CITED

Ciuba, Gary M. *Desire, Violence, and Divinity in Modern Southern Fiction: Katherine Anne Porter, Flannery O'Connor, Cormac McCarthy, Walker Percy*. Baton Rouge, Louisiana State University Press, 2007. Southern Literary Studies.

Golden, Robert E., and Mary C. Sullivan. *Flannery O'Connor and Caroline Gordon: A Reference Guide*. Boston, G. K. Hall, 1977.

Moran, Daniel. *Creating Flannery O'Connor: Her Critics, Her Publishers, Her Readers*. Athens, University of Georgia Press, 2016.

Scott, R. Neil. *Flannery O'Connor: An Annotated Reference Guide to Criticism*. Milledgeville, Timberlane, 2002.

Scott, R. Neil, and Irwin H. Streight. *Flannery O'Connor: The Contemporary Reviews*. Cambridge, UK, Cambridge University Press, 2009.

Biographies of Some Contributors

Marshall Bruce Gentry is Professor of English at Georgia College and Editor of the *Flannery O'Connor Review*. He is the author of the book *Flannery O'Connor's Religion of the Grotesque* (University Press of Mississippi), editor of the volume *The Cartoons of Flannery O'Connor at Georgia College*, co-editor with Robert Donahoo of *Approaches to Teaching the Works of Flannery O'Connor* (Modern Language Association), and co-editor with Craig Amason of *At Home with Flannery O'Connor: An Oral History*. Gentry twice co-directed "Reconsidering Flannery O'Connor," an NEH Summer Institute, at Georgia College, and he has directed several academic conferences on the works of O'Connor. Other American fiction writers that Gentry has published on are E. L. Doctorow, Raymond Carver, Philip Roth, and David Bottoms. Gentry is married to Alice Friman.

Michael Faulknor attended Georgia College from 2013 to 2019, earning both his BA and his MA in English. Faulknor has been an English Instructor at Oconee Fall Line Technical College in Dublin, Georgia, since 2019.

Alice Friman's seventh full-length collection of poetry is *Blood Weather* from Louisiana State University Press. Her previous books, also from LSU, are *The View from Saturn* and *Vinculum*, for which she won the Georgia Author of the Year Award in Poetry. She is a recipient of two Pushcart Prizes and is included in *The Best American Poetry* Series. Professor Emerita of English and Creative Writing at University of Indianapolis, Friman served for years as Poet-in-Residence at Georgia College. alicefrimanpoet.com.

Patricia A. Martell was born, raised, and educated in Wisconsin. She and her family enjoyed thirty years of southern living in Wilmington, NC, and Lilburn, GA. In 2013 she retired from over twenty years as a real estate professional and turned to artistic pursuits. Her creative moniker, G Patti, is a tribute to her three beloved grandsons.

Charles Puckett graduated from Georgia College with Bachelor's, Master's, and Specialist's degrees in secondary education. He taught public school for over thirty years, including years at Georgia College Early College. He now serves as an adjunct professor in the teacher education program at Georgia College.

Elaine E. Whitaker (1942–2020) was Professor of English and Chair of the English Department at Georgia College. She earned her PhD in English and American Literature at New York University, and she co-edited *The Mirroure of the Worlde: A Middle English Translation of* Le Miroir du Monde (University of Toronto Press). Her article on O'Connor's "Parker's Back" appears in the *Flannery O'Connor Review*.

Robert J. Wilson III serves as University Historian at Georgia College after retiring from the Georgia College History Department. He is the author of *The Benevolent Deity: Ebenezer Gay and the Rise of Rational Religion in New England, 1696–1787* (University of Pennsylvania Press). His PhD in Early American History is from the University of Massachusetts. His updated book-length history of Georgia College is forthcoming.

Index of the Works of Flannery O'Connor

Note: This index covers the contents of the articles except for Works Cited lists. A reference to an O'Connor work that appears in a footnote is indexed here only if that work is not discussed elsewhere on that page.

"An Afternoon in the Woods," 77, 81, 93, 127
"The Artificial Nigger," 7, 62, 70, 93, 120-21, 125n6, 157
The Cartoons of Flannery O'Connor at Georgia College, 146-47
"A Circle in the Fire," 8, 31-32, 37, 68-69, 87, 89, 95n6, 121, 146
"The Coat," 24
"The Comforts of Home," 7, 38, 69, 86, 92, 129-40, 151, 157, 182, 206, 238, 239, 245
The Complete Stories (see also individual story titles), 62
Conversations with Flannery O'Connor, 57, 144
The Correspondence of Flannery O'Connor and the Brainard Cheneys, 251
"The Crop," 5, 24n2, 62, 85, 86, 129, 149, 152-53
"The Displaced Person," 2, 8, 23, 39-45, 51-59, 62, 65, 66-67, 78, 80, 85, 89, 90, 93, 135, 157
"Elegance Is Its Own Reward," 24
"The Enduring Chill," 19, 34n9, 70, 72, 75-76, 77, 81, 86, 91-92, 129, 182, 238, 239n1, 240-41
"Everything That Rises Must Converge" (story), 5, 33, 37, 62-63, 65-66, 69, 72, 85-86, 92, 129, 190, 238, 239n1, 243, 244
Everything That Rises Must Converge (collection), 91, 151, 243, 246-47
"An Exile in the East," 239n1
"The Fiction Writer and His Country," 23, 125
Flannery O'Connor: Collected Works (see also essay and story titles—most page numbers here refer to letters), 3, 24n3, 75, 76-77, 79-80, 84, 88, 89, 117n2, 144, 222, 237, 249-50, 251, 253
"The Geranium" (story), 30, 145, 148-49, 151
The Geranium: A Collection of Short Stories (MFA thesis), 24, 127, 148
"Getting Home," 239n1
"Good Country People," 33-34, 37, 38n11, 62, 80, 81, 87, 90, 91, 93, 95, 153, 183-85, 186, 187n2, 194, 195n1, 227-29, 231-32 (and photos), 245
"A Good Man Is Hard to Find" (story), 2, 35-37, 62, 93, 119, 135, 193, 194-98, 200, 202-03, 207, 212, 214, 215, 216, 217, 221, 222-23, 235-36 (and photo), 240
A Good Man Is Hard to Find and Other Stories (collection), 77, 93, 118, 119, 120, 121, 127
Good Things out of Nazareth: The Uncollected Letters of Flannery O'Connor and Friends, 43n15, 57, 158, 249-54
"Greenleaf," 8, 30-31, 37, 62, 67, 80, 89, 90, 155, 194, 239n1

The Habit of Being: Letters, 3, 6, 14, 16, 19, 26, 27, 35, 36, 37, 84, 88, 136, 143, 145, 152, 194, 222, 228, 231, 238-39, 244, 249, 250, 251, 252, 253
"The Heart of the Park," 62
"Introduction to *A Memoir of Mary Ann*," 126
"Judgment Day," 24n2, 29-30, 37, 62, 70-71, 151, 238, 243, 244-45
"The Lame Shall Enter First," 6, 7, 26-27, 92, 93, 126, 206-07, 238, 239n1, 243
"A Late Encounter with the Enemy," 6, 93, 207
The Letters of Flannery O'Connor and Caroline Gordon, 43n15, 251-52
"The Life You Save May Be Your Own," 52, 90, 120, 145n2, 155, 156-58, 183, 185-86, 187, 212, 213, 242
Mystery and Manners: Occasional Prose (see also individual essay titles), 249
"The Nature and Aim of Fiction," 129
"On Her Own Work," 23, 35, 203-04, 207
"Parker's Back," 2, 5, 71, 85, 90, 94, 106n6, 151, 156, 238, 243, 245, 246
"The Partridge Festival," 86, 129, 229, 230-31, 232, 238, 239, 245, 247
"The Peeler," 107
"A Place of Action," 24
"Revelation," 4, 7, 32-33, 37, 62, 66, 67-68, 89, 90, 95, 126, 238, 243-44
"The River," 6, 7, 34-35, 37, 62, 94, 119, 193, 194, 200-02, 206
"Some Aspects of the Grotesque in Southern Fiction," 159
"A Stroke of Good Fortune," 62, 91, 120, 150
"A Temple of the Holy Ghost," 41n13, 62, 71, 80, 87, 89, 90, 96, 120, 145-46, 207
Three by Flannery O'Connor, 75
"The Train," 62
"The Turkey," 24n2, 77, 78, 93, 127
"A View of the Woods," 6, 7, 13-21, 27, 38, 90, 92, 126, 157, 239n1
The Violent Bear It Away, 6, 19, 25, 27n5, 38-39, 52, 53, 70, 81, 86, 90, 92, 93, 106n6, 118n3, 119, 121-26, 129, 151, 154, 155-56, 206, 212, 243, 261
"Why Do the Heathen Rage?" / *Why Do the Heathen Rage?* (manuscript of story/novel), 9, 30, 237-47
"Wildcat," 24n3, 93
Wise Blood, 6, 19, 24, 25, 38-39, 41, 66, 71, 75, 80, 89-90, 94-95, 99-115, 118-19, 125, 149-51, 153-54, 155, 200, 206, 212, 213, 214, 221, 245, 253
"Writing Short Stories," 231-32
"You Can't Be Any Poorer Than Dead," 62

Index of Names

Note: This index covers real people, not characters, in the contents of the articles except for Works Cited lists. A reference to a person who is mentioned in a footnote is indexed here only if that person is not discussed elsewhere on that page.

Alexander, Benjamin B., 43n15, 158, 249-54
Andrews, Carol M., 187n2
Andrews, Lowell Lee, 197n4
Anthony, Saint, 131-32
Aquinas. *See* Thomas Aquinas, Saint.
Armstrong, Julie, 61
Arnold, Edwin T., 158
Asals, Frederick, 130, 134n5, 135, 139n11, 206
Ashley, Jack Dillard, 76
Babinec, Lisa, 32, 34
Bacon, Jon Lance, 13, 39, 45, 259
Bakhtin, Mikhail Mikhailovich, 3, 5, 7, 8, 83, 92n3, 95, 96, 121
Baldwin, James, 3
Barnes, Roslyn, 252, 253
Barounis, Cynthia, 100n1
Bauer, Dale M., 83n1, 86, 95
Bellow, Saul, 151
Beringer, Cindy, 34, 44
Bernick, Susan E., 187
Bloom, Harold, 158, 211
Bonner, Anthony, 198
Booth, Wayne C., 83
Bosco, Mark, 10, 184, 228
Bowlin, Catherine L., 104
Boyer, Clif, 62
Bragg, Beauty, 72n5
Brantley, Will, 250
Bray, Nancy Davis, 10
Breit, Harvey, 144
Brinkmeyer, Robert H., Jr., 4-5, 85-86, 93, 155

Brooks, Cleanth, Jr., 40
Brown, Ashley, 163-67
Brown, Hugh, 80
Bruner, Michael Mears, 5
Brunson, Beverly, 89
Burgess, Irene, 10
Burke, Kenneth, 153
Burkle, Howard, 20
Burns, Marian, 132n4, 238, 241
Burns, Michael, 167
Burns, Stuart L., 246
Burt, John, 78
Butler, Jack, 219
Caldwell, Erskine, 106n6, 143-44, 147, 151-59
Caldwell, Mark, 76
Capote, Truman, 23n1, 193-207
Caron, Timothy P., 61, 71
Carr, Virginia Spencer, 143
Carson, Johnny, 188
Cartridge, David R., 137n9
Cash, Jean W., 13, 92, 143, 147, 205n9, 228
Chambers, E. K., 118n3
Chaucer, Geoffrey, 138
Chen, Connie, 123n4
Cheney, Brainard, 163, 164, 253
Cheney, Frances Neel, 163, 164, 253
Cherry, Caroline L., 138
Chew, Martha, 90-91
Christensen, Peter G., 194
Ciardi, John, 177
Ciuba, Gary M., 25n4, 124, 261
Clarke, Gerald, 200

Clinton, Bill, 169
Clutter, Bonnie, 193, 195, 199
Clutter, Nancy, 193, 199
Coffman, Elizabeth, 10
Coindreau, Maurice-Edgar, 158, 252
Coles, Robert, 44, 52-53, 54, 157n5
Cook, Sylvia Jenkins, 158
Coulthard, A. R., 217
Cox, John D., 10
Crafton, John Michael, 216
Creeger, George R., 199
Crews, Frederick, 84, 139-40, 182
Croly, David Goodman, 61n1
Cunningham, Frank R., 218
Daniel, Scott, 100n1, 182
Daniell, Ethel, 252
Davies, Stevan L., 137n9
De Bellis, Jack, 200
Dessommes, Nancy Bishop, 218
Dewey, Alvin, 198, 200
Dexter, Pete, 227-28, 230
Di Renzo, Anthony, 5, 117
Donahoo, Robert, 10, 25n4, 45n16, 53, 104, 115, 122, 190
Dorrance, Ward Allison, 252
Dos Passos, John, 151
Dostoevsky, Fyodor, 124
Driggers, Stephen G., 150, 229, 238
Dunleavy, Janet Egleson, 52
Dunn, Robert J., 150, 229, 238
Duvall, John N., 7
Dylan, Bob, 216
Dyson, J. Peter, 206
Easterley, Joan, 216
Edmondson, Henry T., III, 20
Eggenschwiler, David, 130, 136
Elie, Paul, 72
Eliot, T. S., 75, 103
Emery, Elizabeth, 117n1
Engle, Paul, 147-48
Erasmus, Desiderius, 118n3
Evans, Robert C., 7, 250, 257-61
Farrell, Susan, 187n2
Faulkner, William, 75, 106n6, 137, 151, 159, 243
Faulknor, Michael, 2, 43, 51-59
Feeley, Kathleen, 130n3, 135

Fennick, Ruth, 85, 86
Fickett, Harold, 80
Fitts, Karen, 91
Fitzgerald, Robert, 84, 252
Fitzgerald, Sally, 20, 24n3, 33-34, 46, 75, 79, 84, 249-50, 251, 252, 253
Flanagan, Christine, 43n15, 251-53
Flaubert, Gustave, 75
Flynn, Errol, 41
Ford, Ford Madox, 166-67
Foster, Shirley, 77
Fowler, Doreen, 25n4, 31
Fox, Joe, 198
Freud, Sigmund, 131
Friedan, Betty, 104
Friedman, Ellen G., 216
Friedman, Melvin J., 195n1
Friman, Alice, 2, 5, 64-65, 169-79, 186
Frost, Robert, 177
Fugelso, Karl, 117n1
Gable, Mariella, 238
Galloway, David, 199
Garson, Helen S., 36n10, 38, 137, 194, 201
Giannone, Richard, 17, 19, 20, 39, 42
Gide, Andre, 186
Gilbert, Douglas R., 80
Gilbert, Sandra M., 81
Gilbert, Susanna, 46
Gilbert, W. S., 206
Glazener, Nancy, 88n2
Gogol, Nikolai, 165
Golden, Robert E., 257
Gooch, Brad, 56, 117, 146, 147-48, 228
Gordon, Caroline, 6, 43n15, 79, 164, 166-67, 194-95, 252-53
Gordon, Ira J., 32n7
Gordon, Mary, 190
Gordon, Sarah, 5, 10, 40, 57, 103, 104-05, 146-47, 153, 183, 190
Gossett, Louise Y., 25, 252
Gossett, Thomas, 252
Graham, Billy, 78
Gratz, David K., 216, 218
Gray, Thomas, 197n4
Greer, Seth Ellis, 123

Index of Names

Gretlund, Jan Nordby, 54
Grobel, Lawrence, 194, 196n3
Grünewald, Matthais, 246
Gubar, Susan, 81
Guerin, Wilfred L., 187
Guest, David, 200
Hair, William Ivy, 236
Harris, Carole K., 102n2
Harrison, Mary Virginia, 46
Hawkes, John, 26, 117n2, 204
Hemingway, Ernest, 151
Henderson, Bruce, 8
Hendin, Josephine, 46, 93, 137, 204-05, 217
Henry (worker at Andalusia), 56
Hersey, John, 201n6
Hester, Elizabeth (Betty), 14, 16, 19, 27, 46, 79, 84, 88, 194, 203, 220, 228, 231, 250, 251, 252, 254
Hewitt, Avis, 25n4
Hickock, Richard, 193, 195, 196-97, 198, 200, 207
Hicks, Jack, 202
Hill, Louise, 59
Hill, Pati, 194
Hill, Robert "Jack," 59
Hirsch, Marianne, 189
Hitler, Adolf, 14, 15, 45
Holman, C. Hugh, 153
Holquist, Michael, 95
hooks, bell, 71-72
Hooper, Johnson Jones, 153
HopKins, Mary Frances, 95n7
Humphries, Jefferson, 77
Hurley, D. F., 217
Ingram, Harry, 64
Jerome, Saint, 240, 245-46
Jesus Christ, 29, 38, 39, 42, 54, 58, 65, 67, 71, 90, 94, 103, 110, 125, 136, 137, 196, 215, 217, 253
Jezebel, 17, 28
Johnson, Greg, 216, 218
Johnson, Samuel, 6, 79
Jones, Madison, 164, 217
Jordan, Clarence, 242n3

Joyce, James, 40-41, 75, 164-65
Kafka, Franz, 31, 75
Kahane, Claire [Katz], 42, 89, 91, 95n6, 96
Kauffmann, Stanley, 253
Kazin, Alfred, 20
Keetley, Dawn, 37
Kessler, Edward, 75
Kilcourse, George A., Jr., 55
Kinney, Arthur F., 41, 152
Kirk, Connie Ann, 251
Klevar, Harvey Lee, 154
Knapp, Bettina L., 33
Korges, James, 154
Lake, Christina Bieber, 45
Langkjaer, Erik, 80, 184, 228-29
Lasseter, Victor, 217
Latham, James, 196
Lebeck, Sherry Lynn, 34n9
Lee, Maryat, 3, 239-40, 245n5, 250, 251
Lesgoirres, Daniel, 52
Lincoln, Abraham, 61n1
Long, Mary Ann, 126
Longstreet, Augustus Baldwin, 153
Luft, Joseph, 64
Lytle, Andrew, 164, 204
MacKenzie, Niel, 118, 119, 120
Magistrale, Anthony, 135
Maier, Kristy, 10
Mani, 130, 136-37
Maritain, Jacques, 231
Martin, Carter W., 52
Martin, Karl E., 123
Martin, Marcelina, 110n9
Mary, Virgin, 89, 90, 111, 115, 137
Matysiak, Mr. (worker at Andalusia), 43n15
Maxwell, Allen, 24n3
May, John R., 130n2, 134, 239
McCown, James, 252, 253
McCullers, Carson, 89, 143-51, 152, 159
McDonald, Marci, 80
McKane, Janet, 252
McMullen, Joanne Halleran, 21
Meyer, R. T., 132

Meyer, William, Jr., 68n4
Meyers, Bertrande, 130n1
Miller, Alice, 14-15, 17
Millichap, Joseph R., 138
Moran, Daniel, 143, 250, 257
Moser, Don, 217
Muller, Gilbert H., 135, 138
Munk, Linda, 52
Murphy, George D., 138
Nabokov, Vladimir, 165
Nance, William L., 199
Nemerov, Howard, 177
Noon, Mark A., 8
Nordan, Lewis, 151
Nye, Harold, 198
Nye, Valerie, 250
O., Mr. (resident of Milledgeville), 84
O., Mrs. (resident of Milledgeville), 84
Oates, Joyce Carol, 211-13, 214, 215-19, 220, 223
O'Connor, Regina Cline, 6, 9, 43n15, 46, 88, 152, 164, 174, 175, 183, 228, 230, 250, 252, 254
O'Donnell, Angela Alaimo, 61, 250-51
O'Gorman, Farrell, 45, 63, 239
Orvell, Miles, 135n6, 137
Owens, James, 233
P., Mrs. (resident of Milledgeville), 84, 85
Paul, Saint, 202n7
Paulson, Suzanne Morrow, 52, 76, 217
Pearson, Michael, 153
Pennington, Deborah Puckett, 227
Percy, Walker, 166, 239, 253
Peter, Saint, 137
Plimpton, George, 198, 204n8
Poe, Edgar Allan, 24, 75, 144, 159
Porter, Katherine Anne, 152, 164, 166, 252
Presley, Susan F., 24n2
Prown, Katherine Hemple, 17, 20, 24n3, 104-05, 106-07, 152
Puckett, Charles, 2, 227-33 (and photos)
Puckett, Linus A. (Vera/Pete Puckett's father), 231n2, 233
Puckett, Mike, 227

Puckett, Odessa M. (Vera/Pete Puckett's mother), 229
Puckett, Vera/Pete, 2, 227-33 (and photos)
Quinn, M. Bernetta, 136n7
Quirk, Tom, 216
Quispel, G., 136
Rabelais, François, 83n1
Ramos, Rufel F., 117
Ransom, John Crowe, 164
Raymond, Claire, 29
Reiniche, Ruth, 242n4
Reuman, Ann E., 46, 240
Rheims, Maurice, 80
Robillard, Douglas, Jr., 108n8, 230
Robinson, Gabrielle Scott, 41n13
Rockwood, R. J. R., 216
Rodriguez, Richard, 63
Roos, John, 16, 20, 53, 54, 55, 56, 57
Roosevelt (resident of Milledgeville), 241n2, 242n4
Rorem, Ned, 198
Roth, Philip, 217
Rowland, Beryl, 138
Rubin, Larry, 216, 218
Rubin, Louis D., Jr., 147n3, 148, 152, 164
Salter, Mary Jo, 76
Schaub, Thomas Hill, 223
Schmid, Charles, 216-17
Schneiderman, Leo, 40
Schulz, Gretchen, 216
Scott, R. Neil, 250, 257, 260
Seel, Cynthia L., 112
Seidel, Kathryn Lee, 90
Sessions, W. A., 250
Sexton, Mark S., 158
Sharp, Paula, 211-15, 219-22, 223
Shaw, Mary Neff, 5
Shinn, Thelma J., 88
"Shot" (William P. Mason, worker at Andalusia), 43n15, 59
Siegle, Robert, 201, 203
Sloane, Thomas O., 76
Smith, Fern/Joy, 195n1
Smith, Leanne E., 69

Index of Names

Smith, Perry, 193, 195, 196, 197, 198, 199, 200, 202
Spivey, Ted R., 147, 194
Srigley, Susan, 25n4, 100
Stallybrass, Peter, 96
Stembridge, Marion Wesley, 227, 228-29, 230-31, 232, 233
Stephens, C. Ralph, 251, 253
Stephens, Elizabeth, 46n17
Streight, Irwin H., 32n7, 257
Sullivan, Arthur, 206
Sullivan, John, 80
Sullivan, Mary C., 257
Sykes, John D., Jr., 45, 71
Tagliabue, Chandler M., 241n2, 242n4
Tate, Allen, 163, 164, 166, 194-95
Tate, J. O., 35, 94n5, 190, 217
Tate, Mary Barbara, 10
Taylor, Jacqueline, 78
Thimme, Jane, 110n9
Thomas, Saint, 135-36
Thomas Aquinas, Saint, 117
Thomson, Rosemary Garland, 145n2
Tierce, Mike, 216
Tigner, E. A., 235-36 (and photo)
Toole, John Kennedy, 241
Truman, Harry S., 197
Tuttle, Jon, 195-96
Twain, Mark, 153
Tynan, Kathleen, 198
Tynan, Kenneth, 198
Utz, Richard, 117n1
Villon, François, 198-99
Wakeman, George, 61n1
Waldmeir, John C., 202n7
Walker, Alice, 99-100, 181-83, 186-90
Walker, Barbara G., 112
Waller, G. F., 215
Walters, Dorothy, 138
Warren, Colleen, 238, 239, 246
Warren, Nagueyalti, 187n2, 190
Warren, Robert Penn, 40
Watson, Scott, 252
Waugh, Evelyn, 165
Wegs, Joyce M., 216
Weil, Simone, 228
Weinberger, G. J., 216

Welty, Eudora, 92n3
Wesley, Marilyn C., 218
Westling, Louise, 20, 38n11, 79, 80, 84, 88, 89, 91, 96, 112, 146, 189, 243
Whitaker, Elaine E., 2, 117-27
White, Allon, 96
White, Terry, 216
Whitt, Margaret Earley, 4, 17, 19, 61, 152
Williams, Hank, 173
Williams, Jordan, 173
Williams, Lucinda, 170-71, 173
Williams, Miller, 2, 169-79
Williamson, Samuel H., 42n14
Wilson, Jessica Lynice Hooten, 124n5, 238, 239, 240, 243, 246
Wilson, Robert J., III, 2, 46n17, 235-36
Winnicott, D. W., 34n9
Winslow, Joan D., 216
Winters, Yvor, 166
Wood, Ralph C., 57, 61, 76-77, 109
Workman, Leslie, 117
Wray, Virginia, 24, 239-40
Wyatt, Bryan T., 20
Yaeger, Patricia S., 63-64, 67, 68, 69, 92n3, 100
Yeats, William Butler, 75, 81, 91-92, 164-65
York, George, 196
Yourcenar, Marguerite, 80
Zacharasiewicz, Waldemar, 144n1
Zaidman, Laura Mandell, 205
Zubeck, Jacqueline A., 235n1